CW01017925

Preface

In 2010, Rugby U3A created a new general interest group to be called Living History. At the inaugural meeting the question was asked "What is Living History?" A discussion about this decided that, for us, it was *Our History;* what life was like for us during our lives and not a history written by intellectuals sometimes centuries later.

So, the format was decided, each month we would meet having written our experiences on a particular subject. The result was a number of short pieces often giving a different aspect of the subject. Several members said "What do you mean by that subject?" to which the answer was, "It's whatever you choose it to mean." That led to a diverse set of views.

Although the members of the group are all members of <u>Rugby</u> U3A it became clear that only a few were brought up in Rugby so the *Histories* define cultures and occurrences from a wide area.

But why did we do it? Well, it was pointed out that today's younger generation are likely to be less than totally interested about the life of the older generation until one day, they will be the older generation who will say, "I wish I'd asked what it was like in those days." So we will write it down. We always enjoyed reading out our pieces for each other and our discussion generated many other thoughts when we heard of others experiences. We realised then that these pieces we had written might also be interesting to others of our own generation as well as the younger generation later.

So the next job was to consolidate all the pieces and put them into one folder. That's when we realised the huge quantity of *Histories* we had produced. So this first volume is a random selection of subjects – there will be further publications of other subjects but for now, this is it.

We ask the reader to understand that no attempt has been made to edit, correct, or re-structure these accounts. To do so, it is felt, would compromise the individuality, uniqueness and spontaneity of these stories. They have been written as they have been told preserving the colloquial wording used by the individual contributor. These are the words of those who have lived their history and not those of an editor.

The University of the Third Age (U3A) movement is a unique and exciting organisation which provides, through its U3As, life-enhancing and life-changing opportunities. Retired and semi-retired people come together and learn together, not for qualifications but for its own reward: the sheer joy of discovery!

Members share their skills and life experiences: the learners teach and the teachers learn, and there is no distinction between them.

The U3A movement is supported by its national organisation, the Third Age Trust.

Contents

RUGBY

Our Living History

That's (Was) Entertainment

Bilton House
Reminiscence Group

Lead by John and Margaret

Margaret observed that the generation of the members of the group preceded that of herself and John. The childhood and youth of members was in the 1920's -30's, that of Margaret and John the 40's and 50's. Nevertheless mutual experiences of both generations carried over from the earlier to the latter and there is was no clear demarcation, despite the coming of World War IL Rather it was a transition with much shared in common. But now everyone, being grand-parents and great-grandparents, the view was that the present day situation for children and youngsters is much changed from those of previous times.

A distinction was drawn by the term 'entertainment'. It was considered to be one of interests and enjoyment rather than 'amusement'. It lay more in what one did, rather than that was impersonally provided by others.

There was almost unanimous agreement that past times offered children greater freedom to roam and be away from the confines of the home environment. There was a greater degree of trust within communities for the safety and security of their children. Parents knew where their children were likely to be, who they would be with, and what they were doing, or getting up to! This was possibly more so in rural than urban environments. It was not unusual for children to be out of the house for hours, playing and pursuing their own activities. One example was given from 10.00 a.m. to 5.00 p.m. Often sandwiches and lunch were packed up. One member stated that the boys, and not the girls, were allowed to be away camping overnight.

The virtual absence of motorized transport in those days considerably reduced the safety risk on the roads and lanes. There was greater use of the bicycle and members recalled travelling long distances by this means. One lady used to ride a tandem with her boyfriend. From Rugby to Badby Woods and Northampton to Kettering and Wickstead Park were mentioned. One lady walked a great deal by herself and recalls exploring the cement quarry, (oblivious to the danger), in Rugby to discover fossils.

Sports activities, especially in the villages, were common and popular social gatherings, attracting keen support. Tennis, football, hockey, Rugby (rugger) clubs were mentioned. Swimming trips to the local town pools were not so common, but in the country the canals and the rivers (Avon) were used. These were also the locations for fishing expeditions, often with the most rudimentary of kit and sometimes lasting all day.

As has been mentioned in a previous theme church played a major part in the everyday life of communities, especially in predominantly non-conformist ones. Members recalled being in choirs and attending other functions centred around the local church.

The group were split equally about going to dances. This was mainly due to the approval or otherwise given by parents, or the holding of dances in the locality. Those that did go appeared to enjoy it. Considerable effort through cycling, walking or by bus was made to get to dances, (no doubt to meet members of the opposite sex).

There were also visits to the cinema. In rural areas a weekly treat would be the showing of films in the village hall or similar community gathering place. Where there was access to a cinema in a town several members remembered going to special children's Saturday Morning Pictures. They fondly remembered them as being a riot of bad behaviour. One lady remembers balls of paper being thrown over the balcony onto the people below.

There were occasional visits to the theatre. One lady recalled travelling players coming to the village where she lived.

Popular children's games were played outside in the neighbourhoods and in the playgrounds at school. Examples were rounders, marbles, conkers, skipping and hopscotch, (where adults could complain about the marking out of pitches in chalk). Often these games could be accompanied by traditional songs accompanying the specific game. The mystery was that the games and the songs 'appeared' without any specific reason, were immensely popular and then just ceased. .until they re-appeared again. The tunes and words to the song, and the movements of the game were not formally 'taught' but appeared to be learnt spontaneously. One gentleman recalls a street game where contestants threw darts into fences to see who could get around a circuit first. Winter snows and ice brought slides and snowball fights in the school playground.

Board games such as Ludo, draughts and Snakes and Ladders were played in the home, but Monopoly had not yet arrived. Little reference or interest was shown in card games. The wireless, with its accumulator batteries, was making its way into homes and was frequently listened to.

Less physically active was reading in the home. Most members had experience of this. This included the reading of comics as well as books.

The above entertainments described by the members seemed to be innocent and healthy to mind, body and spirit. We enquired if they ever delighted in anything 'naughty'. Scrumping was common. This 'crime' was extended by one member who, with his mates, went on to sell the products (walnuts) through 'tickets of credit', and pocket the proceeds.

One lady defied her parents and joined the A.T.S. at the beginning of the war.

March2011

Entertainment from 1936

My earliest memory of entertainment was my father bouncing me up and down on his knee in time to the tune of KKK Katey When The Mmm Moonshines. I'll be waiting at the kitchen door. Many Nursery Rhymes especially The Grand Old Duke of York and when they marched down again we were always dropped through his leg's on to the floor amid much laughter and screams.

When a little older, our favourite pastime was acting out people in the street along with hats scarves or any appropriate props. Mrs Smith always a bit superior or Mrs Wood next door moaning about her husband and: Mrs Reynolds a real broad brummmy, a dresser at The Theatre Royal in the City. To hear her description of taking the feathers off her cockerel and then drawing out the innards never failed to get us rolling around the sitting room in fits of laughter.

Acting always had a top priority. We made up concerts, .sang, recited, dressed up, made programmes, sent out invitations. I remember sewing three skirts from grown up dresses together with an elastic waistband. Having acquired a battery operated signal army light with a green and. red slide over the bulb to be used as spot lights for our dance routine for Anna Neagle and Michael Wilding singing Spring in Park Lane

We entertained ourselves making dens and tents out of old wood, cardboard or airing racks and old blankets, picnicking inside them. The old chicken shed under the railway was scrubbed painted and used as a play house even digging our own garden outside it. One extra curved side of the Anderson shelter was made of corrugated iron and it rocked forwards and backwards and we made many adventurous journeys driving our imaginary horses and covered wagons at speed over stony terrain.

Our games of shop would empty store cupboards and displays built up to tempt imaginary customers. Then we would be cutting and pasting in scrapbooks with paste made from boiling up flour and water in the saucepan. Old bicycle tyres were used as hoops and beaten up to speed with wooden batons. Hospitals were a great game with rows of dolls and teddies all in separate beds under the table.

Lots of games were played at Brownies which were held in a big detached house in Sherbourne Road up three flights of stairs in the attic. Camp fire songs were popular as were gatherings on Saturday night with friends and relations around the piano. You Are My Sunshine, Daisy Daisy, Lily Marlene, Run Rabbit Run, Keep the Home Fires Burning, We'll Meet Again and the White Cliffs of Dover were our favourites.

Then came youth club entertainments table tennis billiards quizzes but no dancing or games of chance like Monopoly and definitely no playing outside on a Sunday. I remember staying at a boarding house in St Ives and we had to hide upstairs for an illicit game of rummy or strip Jack naked because the landlady was a Salvationist.

We always went to the Olton Cinema in the Hollow for an early film at 5 pm on a Saturday and then had a bag of chips on the way home sitting on the huge concrete road blocks put on the canal bridge in case the Germans invaded us. Sometimes the children stayed at auntie's house whilst the adults went to the Pictures and then we would have prolonged games of Rummy. The Warwick cinema was on Shirley Road but the Tyseley Bughouse was a short bus ride away. It had pin holes in the ceiling and a cat sat on your lap when a cup of tea was brought round in the interval.

We were taken to the Theatre Royal on lots of Saturdays it cost one and sixpence to see Eddie Calvert and his trumpet.

I remember seeing Bambi and Dumbo and later In Which We Serve, The Way to The Stars, Bob Hope and Dorothy Lamour, Googie Withers in White Corridors, Mario Lanza and Jack Hawkins in the Cruel Sea.

The radio played a large part in our entertainment and complete silence was expected whilst dad listened to the news. Dick Barton and the circus programme of the Daring Dexters was a favourite evening excitement. ITMA caused lots of laughter but it was a pity I never knew what everyone was splitting their sides at. I remember the song It's That Man Again with Tommy Handlev. The German spy THIS IS FUMF SPEAKING we used to practice this using a glass held over our mouths. Mrs Tickle came later and became Mrs Mopp Can I Do You Now Sir? Mona Lott and Sir Short Supply and also Ali Oop was well known exclamation in our house (he was a saucy post card vendor) with Colonel Chinstrap I don't mind if I do, TTFN. Then there was After You Claud, No, after you Cecil and Gracie Fields with her biggest aspidistra in the world. Tony Handcock with his classic blood transfusion sketch.

Entertainment In Kettering From September 1939

Thinking that money could be spent more wisely elsewhere, all entertainment was curtailed. Our radio programme The Home Service was mostly news and boring subjects arid together with rationing air raids and general low morale. The Light Programme was introduced to help cheer people up. Tommy Handley in ITMA with Colonel Chinstrap Mrs Mopp Can I do You Now Sir? TTFN were all popular catch phrases. Workers Playtime put on for factories with Vera Lynn the Forces sweetheart singing We'll meet again, The White Cliffs of Dover and many more popular songs.

Monday night at eight o'clock was not to be missed. Paul Temple (secret agent). We were left with a cliff hanger waiting for the next episode to find out what happened next.

Radio Hamburg now arrived with William Joyce alias Lord Haw-Haw telling us all Nazi Propaganda about how well the Germans were doing beating our bombing attempts etc. The Ovaltinies was also popular with the children,

When the Americans arrived The American Forces Network came into being quite lively with Glen Miller and his orchestra playing swing music and young Frank Sinatra. What more could anyone want?

The Cinemas were now opened. The Regal Odeon and The Empire to name but a few. Prices were Stalls 9 pence and 1 and 9 pence with 2 and threepenny seats in the balcony. Millions of people queued for hours to see some really good films. Most had patriotic subjects Mrs Minever, 1942, Target for Tonight, 1941, In Which we Serve etc.

Who could ever forget Clarke Gable, Vivien Leigh in Gone with The
Wind. Lawrence Oliver in Henry V to name just two of many good
films. George Formby was also in Keep Your Seats Please. The
cinema programme was good a support film, Pathe Gazette News
showed the horrors of the war and the blitz and then the major film.

Usherettes with their ice cream trays and torches showed us to our seats
in the dark. Some cinemas had an organ that rose up onto the stage to
play for a short interval

Saturday morning cinema for the children started later and was a huge
success. Noise, Popcorn and Flash Gordon Serial making certain that
you came next week to see what had happened. Any films with love
scenes in them were removed to avoid the jeers and shouts of the
children.

Cinema was the poor man's entertainment now that theatres were being
opened as they were more expensive. The Dancing Years and other
great musicals were very cheering. Whilst the variety theatres with
Max Miller, The Crazy Gang and loads of other well-known stars
provided the laughter.

The Windmill Theatre in Soho, which boasted it NEVER closed, had
beautiful girls scantily dressed, naked. What more could the men ask
for?

The London Palladium had all the best American Stars Judy Garland
Frank Sinatra and Bob Hope were but a few.

Sunday Night at the London Palladium with Bruce Forsythe and the
Tiller Girls dancing --- Beat the Clock and all the other games he hosted
were popular for years to come.

Then there was ballroom dancing so popular it was estimated that 10 million people danced. All were very polite and orderly until the suave well uniformed gum chewing American arrived on the scene. They arrived complete with gum and chocolates and the girls loved them. No wonder our lads resented them so but they introduced the Jitterbug and we all joined in flying over the floor having a great time.

Entertainment

Before embarking out on this article I asked a few of my friends what entertainment meant to them and the main reply was that when they were children they were able to 'play out' without the worry of anything awful happening to them. This is what entertainment meant, playing hide and seek and participating in the seasonal crazes at the time. It closely resembles hobbies and pastimes as we never had the luxury of cinema or theatres where I lived.

During the seemingly long summer holidays from school is where we were very inventive, armed with some sandwiches and a drink we took the bus to "Coate Water" a large water park where we could swim, play ball games and generally let off steam, absolute heaven. No mobile phones so Mum and Dad never worried about us being far from home, the only instruction was to be home for tea, we had plenty of freedom then.

Saturday morning cinema was a great hit with us, armed with bus fare and sixpence to go downstairs or nine pence to go upstairs we were very excited in anticipation of the film treats ahead. I clearly remember there being at least 3 films, one, an advertising feature or a newsreel, the other a short adventure film and the main feature a top Children's film, always very exciting and the topic of conversation for the rest of the week.

Like most young girls I persuaded my mum to let me go for ballet and tap dancing lessons, she always knew I wouldn't make a ballerina but I had to try it and I soon realised she was right and I soon found something else to do.

Youth Clubs were always available in many locations, church halls, schools and community centres so we were always able to meet our friends and play various sports etc. The local swimming baths was also a community centre and in the winter the large pool was boarded over and was a roller skating rink on a Saturday.

There were many 'seasonal' fads that we undertook, i.e. tennis in the summer straight after Wimbledon, marbles, we made holes in the grass and played for hours, many times accumulating hundreds of different type of marbles. Playing on our skates, very basic then but great fun nevertheless. Rounders was a team game that we played much to the annoyance of the neighbours

As with most towns Swindon underwent many changes in the late 60's and into the 1970's and many local youth clubs community halls etc. closed down and large sports halls emerged. All the cinemas in the town closed and merged into a large cinema multiplex on the outskirts of Swindon with a new Theatre built in the town centre. As more and more people owned cars it wasn't difficult to find the entertainment, large dance bands and celebrities of the time would either perform at one of the Sports Centres or The Wyvern Theatre and of course there were many pubs scattered around Swindon.

As we would expect progress in an expanding town like Swindon, but I can't help feeling a little sad that the town lost a lot of its village type feel. We seemed to know everyone when we went out as we always congregated in the same venues and ended up at the same parties. It is so different now but the everywhere has changed but not always for the better.

Entertainment

The radio featured largely in my life as a child, and I loved it. It was always the Light Programme which was predominantly light music (the only music I knew) and comedy shows. The music when heard now transports me back to a time and place. The programmes which come to mind are Take it From Here, Much Binding in the Marsh, ITMA and Round the Horn both of which were full of innuendos which went straight over my head, and proved so funny in later years. Workers' Playtime and Two-Way Family Favourites which was always on at Sunday lunchtime, as was Billy Cotton's Band Show. It was only when I married that I discovered the delights of the Home Service (now Radio 4) and I have never wavered in my devotion. During the war all the news was either via the radio or the Pathe Gazette News at the cinema. I remember as yesterday, the scenes from Belsen which were shown — I am sure we all carry those with us, it is incredible that such conditions are still echoed throughout the world.

The cinema was going to the pictures. Normally just once a week, in the 1/9s. There were some wonderful British films, when the film industry was at its height. Jassy with Margaret Lockwood, also The Wicked Lady, slightly and delightfully shocking — Margaret Lockwood again plus Stewart Granger and James Mason. James Mason was always the villain, Stewart Granger a somewhat risqué romantic hero. Phyllis Calvert was the good girl, Ann Todd enigmatic, Patricia Roc the girl next door. Stanley Holloway and Alistair Sims in fantastic comedy roles. I have always loved British cinema. By complete contrast there were the Walt Disney films — which with hindsight seem more innocent and child orientated than the later ones. I cried and cried every time I saw Bambi's mother die to the tune "Love is a song that never ends". The ending has now been changed and she lives. The grief did no harm — death happens. Scenes from Cinderella were frightening — but we liked being frightened. I didn't miss a single Walt Disney film. My mother loved all the American films, even then I thought it was an alien culture to ours without being able to express the feeling in words. But we missed none. The musicals usually at some point had the chorus girls descending both sides of a white staircase. I suppose they were quite predictable but there was some fantastic music which became part of our lives. Some of these films live on in my mind. I have seen Mrs Minerva and Random Harvest on the TV several times and would watch the latter again and again given the chance. I loved Greer Garson. Then It's a Wonderful Life, Miracle on 34 Street — you all remember these — they made you feel good. And during the war that is what cinema was about, either to buck us up, or to remind the viewers what they were fighting for. A lot of films were full of propaganda, but so what? It fitted the times.

By the time I was in my mid-teens dances featured largely in my life. This was a chance to meet boys — not an easy thing to do. My best friend Mary Brock (she looked like a young version of Glynis Johns which was to my disadvantage, but I forgave her) and I went either to The Savoy or Kimbles in Southsea or The Empress in Portsmouth — where I met David when I was 15 — he was 16 and told me he was 19 next birthday and I believed him. There were a group of four boys and they all looked towards Mary— but hey ho I was noticed and here we are 56 years later. These dances were well run. No rowdiness, nor drunkenness. The boys probably made a glass of beer last a very long time and the girls had squash or lemonade. In the Southsea dance halls there were usually a fair sprinkling of sailors, which created a slightly more adult atmosphere, on the whole we preferred the local Empress. The Big Bands came to The Savoy — such as Ted Heath and Geraldo. Ted Heath was immensely popular and it was very crowded. These were good evenings, the planning of what one would wear took up a lot of time. We did not have a throw away wardrobe then and the same clothes had to be livened up. Make-up was essential on our already flawless skins — it was part of the whole ambience at that time.

I look back happily on these days, the memories are with me forever and I am so grateful to be pressured to write them down.

Sylvia Edwards/19.3.11

WARTIME MUSIC

You are my sunshine, my only sunshine

Sung my mother as she danced around the kitchen
While I carefully crayoned at the table

You make me happy when skies are grey

Unaware of the meaning of war
Or that families, like glass, could be shattered

Please don't take my sunshine away.

Sylvia Edwards

15.6.10

Memories Of Entertainment In Childhood

Growing up in Newcastle in the late 1940's brings back some wonderful memories. Some far removed from today's generation, but somehow magical in their simplicity.

I was the youngest in my family. My two elder sisters were closer in age — two years apart — I was four years younger than the middle sister, Carol. They tended to do lots of things together but sometimes I had to tag along, much to their disapproval!

One of my earliest memories was of a show/garden fete held in our next door neighbours back garden. My eldest sister Anne had organised the whole thing — she must have been about 13 years old at the time. She'd written sketches to perform, found other children to recite poetry, sing, do magic tricks etc. etc. We couldn't have the show in our own garden because of the vegetable plot, whereas Mrs. Dodd's garden was all laid to grass, and ample space for chairs. There was also a shed on an angle at the bottom of the garden, this had a stable door and I remember Squash being served [at a price] — and raffle tickets. It was a great success and most of the Mums and Dads of the neighbourhood attended. Mentioning the event to my sister recently, she recalled it was in aid of the Lynmouth Flood Disaster Fund. Checking dates on the internet I find the disaster took place in August 1952 and thirty four people died in the devastation. I guess my sisters were more aware of the news at the time — I hadn't yet reached my 5 birthday!

Saturday morning cinema was a regular treat! Gosforth Royalty Cinema on the High Street about a mile from home was a frequent place to get lost in the excitement of another era! Inside the cinema, the noise levels were unbelievable — probably a couple of hundred kids screaming, whistling, shouting and booing at every opportunity! The films were a mixture of news, westerns, cartoons and adventures. Some were serialised with a 'cliff-hanger' to get us to return the following week to see if our heroes had survived to live another day or fight another battle. It was a regular occurrence for the film to break down — to be met with a stamping of feet and loud booing from the audience! This would have been in the 1950's when cinemas were in decline. All this was before the majority had television at home, it was so magical and enthralling seeing things on 'the Big Screen'. — All for 9d.!!! Plus a couple of pence more to buy an ice cream from the usherette in the interval. In later years, many of the cinemas changed to bingo halls to attract custom, but now things have reversed with the bingo halls closing and multi-plex cinemas being well used and enjoyed. I do wonder if children nowadays get as much enjoyment as we did from those special Saturday morning shows.

The family were all avid radio listeners. The Light Programme and the Home Service were used constantly. My first memories were Listen with Mother. Later, as a family I recall endless comedy programmes (Hancock's Half Hour, Educating Archie, Life with the Lyons). Billy Cotton Bandshow, Children's Favourites, Meet the Huggets and countless others were a constant source of entertainment. Saturday teatime Dad used to check his football coupon to see if we'd won our fortune! We never did! I seem to remember Dad listened to jazz music after that — he loved Trad Jazz — we must have done other things at that time as we didn't share his appreciation for that type of music!

Television finally reached the Palmer household when I was around 10 years old. We thought it amazing. Not that there were many programmes on at that time. Children's programmes started the day at 5p.m. then television closed down for an hour before evening viewing commenced. Mam and Dad were fairly strict about getting homework done when we came home from school, so we knew if we hadn't completed that there was no television! The programmes remembered from that time were Crackerjack, Blue Peter, Vision On with Tony Hart being the most popular. As a family we loved the variety shows like Sunday Night at the London Palladium. Dad loved cricket and used to play when younger so whenever cricket was on, he'd be found in his chair watching it on TV — he couldn't understand why we girls weren't as interested as he was! Television had certainly changed family life, although we did still have lots of other interests.

Theatre visits were a special treat. Morecombe & Wise at the Empire. Frankie Vaughan, The Everley Brothers, Cliff Richard and the Shadows and Cilla Black at The City Hall. I didn't specially like pantomime as a child, but did see one or two — I cannot remember much about them.

The Majestic Ballroom in the town was the in place to go on a Saturday lunchtime. Three hour session, mainly for over 14's, starting at noon and finishing at 3pm where we could dance and enjoy the modern music — Chubby Checker and the Twist, The Shadows, Cliff of course and many others that were hitting the charts. We always had a great time. Afterwards we occasionally went to watch Newcastle United play at St. James' Park (kick off was usually at 3.30). - They had a good team then! Now, having left my home town of Newcastle far behind, I still keep an eye on the results of their matches. Now I am married to Joe, who does not have a love of football, but loves the game of Rugby Union! A very different game!

All in all I feel I was very lucky growing up in the 50's and 60's. So much has changed with new technology but is it really a more enjoyable era to grow up in? I wonder.

Entertainment

John M. Reeve

As we have described our personal Living History experiences around the table on a variety of subjects over the past months it is clear that we have shared much in common, or appreciated what others have described, because we have known about, or appreciated those things, as they were of the times in which we lived as children or young people. For example we lived during the times of the Second World War and knew about the years of austerity during the 1950's and into the 60's which followed it.

We may therefore share much in common in the area of entertainment. My own experience of 'entertainment' was therefore conditioned by what was happening in British society at those times, but more so, I conclude, by the influence that was exerted over me by my parents and by the home life that my sister and I experienced during the formative period of our childhood.

I think that I have referred before to my parents, and the sort of people that they were, particularly my mother. Both spent their own early years in Children's' Homes, (which buildings, incidentally, can still be seen from the front of Joe and Pam's house). Dad went on to serve in the Royal Navy from the age of fourteen and my mother, as I have previously described , in domestic service first on a farm in Newbold and then in London. Mum literally went from 'rags to riches' in going to London where she became a lady's companion in a wealthy household in Winchmore Hill. The family, (of three), were nevertheless 'self-made', came originally from Rochdale, were Methodists and Liberals. The young man of the family was at Cambridge University and went on to be a leading accountant in the City of London.

I describe all this because this, and her earlier experiences, profoundly influenced my mother. Although she returned to the working-classes when she married my father in 1938, her aspirations and up-bringing of my sister and I were uncompromisingly modelled on the values, and attitudes that she had learnt, and enjoyed, whilst in London with her employers. She remained in close contact with them for rest of their lives and continued to seek their advice and counsel for many years, particularly regarding the upbringing of my sister and myself. In short she was very strict, hardworking, moral, socially aware and active, upright, Christian, thrifty in the extreme, a 'manager', and very caring of the home and family. She did not have a strong sense of humour, much patience, and .. . alas, was something of a 'snob'. Dad was easier going but cannily followed in her wake,.., for over 60 years of married life.

So, with regard to 'entertainment', as in much else, our experience was very much determined. As young children my sister and I inevitably petitioned my mother for the things that other children, and their families had. . . toys, a family car. .a 'telly' .. .trips out. . . sweets.. more pocket money,.. and so on. It went something like this, "Mum can I/we have……….?". "NO". "Why not.?" "Because it's too expensive.!" "But... .". "No buts.." It was not wise to pursue the matter ! My sister, being a woman, tried another approach. .through dad. However he was just as canny. He replied that it would best to ask mum what she thought.

Entertainment as conventionally understood in those times would be common to most of our experience. One was, of course, the radio, (or wireless). We had one of these and it was listened to quite a lot. Programmes that I remember were 'Workers Playtime', 'Wilfred Pickles and Mabel', 'Archie Andrews', 'Two Way Family Favourites', 'Billy Cotton's Band / Show', 'Mrs. Dales Diary', 'Sing Something Simple', 'Henry Hall's Guest Night', 'Hundred Best Tunes' (following the God slot on Sunday evening) and of course 'Children's Hour' with

Uncle Mac. 'Round the Home' was censored because it was thought 'rude', 'Dick Barton, Special Agent' too violent and frightening, 'The Goons Show', stupid.

Television was also a definite 'no-no', for years, (well into the 1960's). It was thought 'time wasting' with 'rubbish' for programmes. However I was granted a concession to watch 'The Grove Family' on a Friday evening in Mrs. Everitt' s house two doors away, and 'The Mounties' at Mrs. Griffiths house who lived near in Percival Road. But as a young teenager I became great friends with a boy called John Lewis and through him his large family of parents, brothers, and sisters. They were avid 'telly addicts' and watched it, in the dark, through Saturday afternoon and evening. When I visited, as I did regularly on Saturday evening I was greeted by, "Come in, Sit down, Shut up. It's on I ". I loved these times.

Going to the cinema, (or the pictures' ,or most commonly, the flicks') was also a no-go area. Mum seemed to have the attitude that the more the masses went to something the more vulgar and common it was, with lower tastes and standards. Nevertheless people at that time went in droves by foot, bus, and cycle to the cinema, and waited for hours in queues in all weathers. We had three picture houses in Rugby at that time, the Granada, the Regent and the Regal. Saturday morning pictures were shown especially for children. This was the 'pits' as far as my mother was concerned and only once did she permit me to go. That was as a birthday guest of a playmate who was a 'Gandy', (a paid up member of the Granada's Children's' Club). In this instance mum's instinct was correct. It was a noisy bedlam all the way through, with children going berserk. My friend and I had the privilege on this special occasion of sitting in the front row of the balcony, over which we threw rubbish on the kids below. An usher who the children called Tex went through the motions of keeping order but seemed to take the riot in his stride.

On special occasions however we were taken to the cinema. I recall seeing a film called 'The Red Shoes' with Moira Shearer in it, and 'Dumbo the Elephant'. I remember being scared by both of them. Several years later my father took me and two friends to see 'The Cruel Sea' starring Jack Hawkins, possibly hoping to damped my youthful aspirations to go to sea. It had quite the reverse effect, although I was mystified at that time to know what the reference in the film was to 'leaving a bun in the oven'.

My parents nevertheless gave me much support and encouragement to engage in pursuits that they considered morally and religiously beneficial. Mother particularly facilitated these, and as I was generally compliant, I 'complied' and remained so for the years of my childhood and youth. Perseverance and loyalty were other virtues that were inculcated into us. Therefore I went to Sunday school, became a member of St. Andrew's Parish Church choir, (for seven years), joined the Scripture Union and later The Crusaders Bible Class. These, plus the increasing amounts of homework as I grew older, took up most of my free time from school. There were many instances of enjoying oneself in pursuing these activities but not necessarily being entertained.

By far the greatest source of entertainment in my childhood and youth came through what I made and enjoyed for, and largely, by myself. This was not all that unusual in those times, but is believed to be considerably less so nowadays. What nowadays may seem to be a disadvantage transpired for me to be quite the opposite.

I was wholly and enthusiastically devoted to 'play'. I moaned if activities such as visiting my mother's friends and practising the piano interfered with it. This was one pursuit that I did have the approval of my parents. An additional advantage was that our family home, (described last time when we considered buildings that we knew), was situated very close to the countryside south of Ashlawn Road and bordered by the (then) L.N.E.R. railway and the triangular sector, or 'green lung' of land owned by Rugby School. Even today, some sixty years on these areas remains virtually unchanged. Having not moved very far from this location, even now as I continue to live in Hillmorton, I still refer to this to my friends as my 'childhood play area'. It contained, and still does, allotments, trees and spinneys, hedgerows and bushes, fields, embankments, lanes, a canal. When I was a child there were also ponds, a decaying country mansion,(being used as flats), more farms, farms buildings and traditional farming activity and less motor traffic. Steam trains also thundered along the railway line day and night. I also had the back garden of the house and those of my mates to play in, but mum disapproved of playing in the street, especially on Sunday when it was prohibited.

A feature of children's' play is that it is imitative of experiences they have had or things that they have learnt about the world around them. My friends and I were no exception. We played cowboys and Indians, (being 'dead' for the count of 20 then being resurrected to fight on). After seeing a film of Ivanhoe, my friends and I enacted a tournament in the street. We pinched bean poles for lances and rode at each other. When, as in the film, we became dismounted we set to in mortal combat with dustbin lids as shields and coal hammers as axes, whacking away at each other with determined fury. The noise and commotion drew my mother to see what was happening. She immediately stopped it, cuffed my ear and led me indoors where I was grounded. She also told dad, so I had a good telling off. Another time I used my sister in an enactment of William Tell. Unfortunately I missed the apple on her head and caught her on the eyebrow. She still bears the mark to this day. I received a good hiding for that as well.

All these locations provided a rich source of materials for uninhibited creative play where my imagination ran riot. I hated nature study at school but loved the qualities of the materials that I experienced: texture, shape, plasticity/rigidity, colour, smell. I could also interact with them using them to build or shape things/environments of my own imagination. There was also the element of risk and danger. Mum used to resign herself to regular visits to the Accident and Emergency Department of St. Cross Hospital some time during the annual summer school holidays.

These experiences were heightened and reached, for me, their greatest delight, when we went annually to my uncles and aunts farm near the Wolds in North Lincolnshire, and to the seaside at Worthing on the south coast. I recall the many years of visiting the farm as the happiest experiences of my life. In post war times it was a traditionally mixed farm, labour intensive and idyllically rural. I enjoyed a 'Cider with Rosie' world out in the fields, streams and ponds, with my cousins, farm workers and the local children. We played in the farm yard, the hay ricks, the barns and went fishing, rabbiting (with ferrets). As children we saw and mixed in with the everyday life of the farm amongst animals and seasonal activities like harvest, haymaking and potato picking. The adults teased us and told us 'rude' things which we barely understood. We were even taken shooting. 'Health and Safety' regulations were unheard of then and we would be shown how to drive tractors, ride in wagons and on tow bars. But we survived. All I suffered were cuts and bruises and once a broken arm, (through falling out of a tree into a stream).

We were also fortunate to have an annual holiday by the sea. This was always Worthing on the south coast where my mother's ex-employers had retired to. This was directly after the war when the costal defences were being slowly dismantled, (tank traps and cement pill boxes), and the first jet aircraft were being tested along that strip of the coast. We had the use of an old bathing hut. There were few holiday makers there at the time but we were completely happy to enjoy the sun, the sea, the shingle and the shore line. Occasionally we walked into Worthing itself. I have clear memories of enjoying the power boat lake, the paddling pool, walking along the pier, but what I loathed was going to a genteel café and having afternoon tea with my parents and 'granny and grandpa'. We also met them at the immaculately kept bowling green where we also met their, also genteel, friends. My sister and I did well from presents of half-crowns, (which mum later took from us to put into our National Savings books!).

I have just read an article in the recent issue of the National Trust magazine called 'A Timely Truth'. It discusses the advantages of children's contact and inter-action with the natural environment. A quotation, "... .research suggests that cognitive development and creativity are stimulated by childhood experiences in nature; that spending more time outdoors can help reduce myopia, and that greener neighbourhoods are associated with fewer cases of child obesity...." There is nothing new under the sun

John Reeve

March 2011

1950 -1965

Home was a quiet place. No record player (or Gramophone) and my parents weren't musical at all. Dad had a violin but couldn't play it and we had an Auto Harp that my mother referred to as a "Zither". Whenever I took it out to play (at the age of 5) I would be asked to put it away.

We had a Radio. It was a Rediffusion system that was fed from a wire that went from house to house. It didn't have batteries and it wasn't

plugged into the mains – in fact it was just a speaker connected to a central radio somewhere out there. One knob on the front had four positions, "Off", "Light Programme", "Home Service" and one other that was probably the "Third Programme". There was a volume control but that didn't work. Sometimes I was allowed to listen to the Light Programme but that was not often. (I've tried to find out about this system on the Internet and can't find anything – maybe this is the only record of that early technology).

My Grandmother lived next door and she had a piano. She played it sometimes but not well. So "Entertainment" at home as a young boy was limited to reading books and comics. No one had a Television and the first time I saw one was when all the children in our street were invited into number 19 to watch the coronation in 1953. I would have been 6 then. We got a proper radio at about this time and I used to settle every afternoon to listen to "Listen With Mother", with my mother of course. I also liked listening to Mrs Dale's Diary but again that wasn't encouraged. Not really suitable for a young boy! I remember listening to the Goon Show and Dick Barton but my mum couldn't understand the humour or the excitement so it wasn't encouraged either.

When I got a little older (8 or 9) I used to spend quite a lot of time at my friends' houses. It was there that I was introduced to records. That was before what could be called Pop Music so really records were those things that *old people* listened to. That was until this guy called Elvis Presley recorded a song. This was different. I had to have a guitar so I could stand behind it and pretend that I could play it (rather like Elvis did in those early days).

So, in 1957, aged 10 I got my first guitar and it stayed in my room untouched for a couple of years that was until *The Shadows* came along. They were Cliff Richards' backing group who began recording instrumentals including their first, "Apache" in 1960. I learned to play this on my guitar.

 That was the start of my life as far as entertainment was concerned and also the end of my life being entertained. I would meet up with my friends and we would play Apache together. Other tunes followed and so at the age of 13, three of us played together on Saturday mornings when the Scout Hut opened to sell coffee to those who were out shopping. We played our three or four tunes over and over again as people came and went. As far as they were concerned we had a big repertoire because our four tunes lasted just as long enough for them to finish their coffee.

Our "group" went from strength to strength and we spent a couple of nights each week practicing together and finally got a regular booking playing at a seaside hotel in Whitley Bay every Saturday night.

This story is about "entertainment" of course. The reason I have gone into my early days playing the guitar is because it replaced "entertainment" for me. I no longer went to the cinema on a Saturday morning as I had done when I was 9 or 10, and I never went dancing like others did. My friends and I would go to dances but only to listen to other bands that were playing. There were over 200 groups in Newcastle in the early sixties so there were lots of bands to see. But no dancing for us. Just reviewing the competition!

Now during this era our quest to see other bands did enable me to see some class acts. I just remember seeing Cliff Richard and the Shadows at the Empire in Newcastle and I remember seeing the Beatles at the City Hall just before they had released "Please Please Me" their first No1. I had forgotten the details of this concert until I

remade contact with the drummer of our group who I hadn't contacted since 1966. He reminded me of our visit as follows (His words).

I remember lucidly - .March 1963 you asked me if my father could get us into see the Beatles as he knew the twin ushers on the door. I'd been fishing on that Saturday afternoon and hadn't long been back when you knocked on the front door. I'd not asked the old man but he was in the house for once and took us both down to the City Hall and went in telling us to wait outside. A couple of minutes later he came back with his mate who said "follow me and look like you should be here".

We walked down the far left isle and all the way down to the doors leading to the stage where he told us to get seats behind

the Beatles. We went past the drums a couple of rows back and sat about 12 ft from Ringo's left side. I remember that Ringo's snare drum had a velum (calf) head and the head and hoops were almost flush as it was over stretched. They were playing "Love me do".

From the stage looking out Paul, far right; George middle; and Lennon left. Harrison wandered between the other 2 harmonising with whoever wasn't singing the lead.

Chris Montez followed wearing a yellow silk shirt and had a pink srtat. He got nowhere. The crowd were chanting "We

want the Beatles". He walked off the stage but was literally pushed back on. He was putting his hand out to a group of fat lasses in front of us. One got his hand and he was yanked over the amps strat and all. The stage hands ran on to rescue him and that's when we decided enough was enough.

That concert marked the start of the end for us as entertainers. The problem was that the Beatles were too good. We could play the Shadows music and quite a few other groups. We could even sing Cliff Richards and Elvis Presley songs but the Beatles (and those that followed them) were a step change in quality and we just didn't have the collective skill to emulate them. We lasted until 1965 when everyone left the group and found other bands to join.

So, since then I've been entertaining people with Folk Music. It is interesting that all the members of our group continued with their music. One became an agent for Country and Western acts in the North-East, the Drummer spent years as part of the band on Cruise Ships; the Bass Guitarist continued playing with various bands and was still at it in 2000 when I last saw him and another of our guitarists is still making records.

Joe Heckels

30th March 2011

Our Living History

Absent Parents

Absent Friends/Family

When my mother was born in 1917, adoption was not a legal process. The Act of 1926 made adoption legal and binding, but informal adoption carried on into the 1930s. She was "taken into the care of" the couple who were to become her much loved parents and my adored grandparents. I don't know whether she ever wanted to trace her birth parents. In the days when she might have tried it was not as easy as it has become now. She never expressed any such wish to me and I don't think she discussed it with my father either. However, she must have wondered what her mother was like and who her father was – his name was omitted from the birth certificate.

My Mum loved shopping and she would take herself off to Leicester or Northampton on the bus one day a week – it was her treat to herself! She would come back loaded with bags and we'd eagerly await the unpacking – sure of a little treat!

When she went to Northampton the bus would pick up passengers from some of the villages en route and my Mum got quite friendly with a lady and her mother who got on from one of these villages. They met up perhaps once a fortnight and chatted on the journey. Then the two ladies stopped coming. My Mum knew them well enough to comment that she hadn't seen them and wondered if they were alright.

A few weeks later we read in the obituary column in "The Advertiser" of the death of a lady who almost had to be my Mother's birth mother. There were three first names all unusual and it would have been a chance in a million for it not to have been her. The village where the funeral was to take place was the village where the mother and daughter got on the bus for Northampton.

Sometime after my Mother met the daughter in town and asked after her mother – to be told she had died at the same time as the obituary notice had been seen.

We think that my mother had met, travelled with and talked to her birth mother. We didn't know what to do – did her new family know that they had a half-sister? It was too late for my mother to identify herself to her birth mother, but we wondered if that old lady had any idea that she was possibly chatting with her daughter. We decided not to contact them in case we upset them. What would you have done?

"Absent Father"

My parents were married in 1940. My father had avoided conscription by being in a minor reserved occupation, but sometime before my birth in January 1942, he finally got his call up, and served through the rest of the war keeping his head down as a squaddy/clerk in the RAOC, based, I believe, in Bicester.

He later told me about a favourite dodge amongst the less committed conscripts – walking around the camp all day with a wheel barrow – looking busy! He was far too conscientious to follow their lead, I'm sure, and just got on with what he was assigned to do.

Fortunately, he was never sent abroad, so did not see any action, but he was absent for most of my childhood up to the age of 3.

He must have come home regularly on leave, but I was too young to remember. I do have vague memories, however, of this strange man in a huge thick khaki great coat with shiny buttons, who appeared a few times, bringing me presents.

Toys were a rarity during the War, I remember having a rusting Smith's Crisp tin, kept in the pantry cupboard, which contained my 'toys'. Amongst these were: conical Bakelite electrical components which stood in for building bricks; soft almost 2 dimensional lead soldiers, which I could easily bend and snap off their stands. These I think had been my father's. And a broken banjo.

To pass time in the barracks, my father, who was no handyman, and 'couldn't even hammer a screw in straight', made me a couple of very crude cars out of rough wood. However, I had an uncle who was a joiner, and he made me a wooden scooter and sac truck – both of which I found rather boring!

My father used occasionally to bring brown tins of boiled sweets and also 'surplus' Army supplies such as a webbing belt with brass fittings, a forage cap, odd cap badges, some red MP arm bands and a pair of desert sun goggles in a tin.

So, my father was a virtual stranger until he was demobbed, just after my sister was born.

As well as being absent most of the time, like many men of his generation, he was uncomfortable with emotions, and as a result, we never really bonded.

He never played sports with me – I still do not know the rules of football, and wasted hours standing around on the school football pitches waiting for someone to kick the ball to me! I am proud to claim that I have never in my life been to a football, cricket or any other form of organised match! My TV automatically changes channels if a ball is shown!

Although he only had a basic state education, he had a thirst for knowledge which rubbed off on me and has made me what I am. He introduced me to museums, History, Dickens wonderful characters and so much more.

Still, as a boy, I never felt that close to him, and always felt the need to impress him. This need to prove myself has dominated my life ever since, and fuelled any achievements and successes I have had.

I finally developed a really close relaxed relationship with him after my mother died and he had a stroke and needed me.

John Duffield July 2013

My Absent Father?

I had never considered that I had an absent father until tasked with this project, but on reflection my father could be described as such for some of my upbringing.

My parents met at Blackpool about 1938 when both of their families were on holiday, my mother from Burton on Trent and my father from West Bromwich. They continued to see each other and married in 1942 by which time the war was in full swing and my father was in the RAF. My mother continued to live with her family while my father was away and my sister was born in 1946 whilst they were still living in Burton on Trent with my grandparents. On leaving the RAF my father was employed by the Civil Aviation Authority doing similar work to that which he had done in the RAF and was posted to a variety of places in England by the CAA.

By the time I came along in 1950 they were renting a house in a rural part of Burton and my mother was left at home most of the time, while Dad worked away, to raise two small daughters and care for an elderly aunt, who lived with us. I lived in that house for over four years and at no time can I ever remember my father being there. Obviously I was only very small and the memories of that house and those times are very vague and very few, but none of them included my father. There are old photographs of dad with all of us at that house but I can't remember him being there. Consequently he had little part in bringing me up for those first four years of my life.

We moved from Burton to Rugby in April 1954 when my father was posted by the CAA to work at Pailton Radio Station, an aviation measuring station. I later found a copy of a letter to the CAA from my father requesting a permanent posting as he had never been able to make a home with his wife and two young daughters, due to constantly moving around the country. He was almost begging for this permanent posting which he was granted. He then bought his first and only house in Newbold.

However this did not put my father into the most advantageous position as a father figure because he continued to be absent for some of the time for the rest of his working live. The Radio Station was manned 24/7 every day of the year and those who worked there, worked shifts to achieve this. Therefore my father was often not at home in the evening, during the night, at weekends and public holidays, including Christmas, as most fathers were. I can remember having our Christmas lunch without Dad and him not being there when we opened our presents and mother not opening hers until dad came home when they opened them together sometimes on Boxing Day.

It is only on reflection that I can see what effect this had on my upbringing. I was never very close to my father as a child or a teenager and often resented his presence, knowing that my mother was the person really responsible for my wellbeing. My father had had a strict upbringing and to a degree thought that children should be seen and not heard. He expected more from us than he ever got in terms of respect. I wasn't used to being told what to do by him and much preferred him to be at work. I even resented the times he had been on nightshift when mother told us to play quietly while he slept during the day. I also disliked it when he was at home in the evening and wouldn't let us stay up as late as mother did. Mum let us watch Come Dancing on a Monday night but only when Dad was not there. He never seemed able to relate to us as children, and as teenagers things were even worse. The idea of staying out late at night, going to dances and having boyfriends was quite alien to him.

He also had a very keen and active interest in the theatre, and with his difficult work patterns I don't know how he managed it, but he appeared in many plays at Rugby Theatre which involved a week of shows preceded by a full week of rehearsals and prior to that ad hoc rehearsals. I remember going to see most of his performances and sitting on the front row of the balcony watching him running around the stage in Brian Rix farces. When he was in a play that meant more opportunities to stay up late as long as we were in bed by the time he came home but an occasional late night was approved because he called at the chip shop after rehearsals and we all had a chip supper, one of my childhood highlights as there was no chip shop in Newbold in those days.

I paint a picture of a difficult man but I think it was only that we were just not used to each other and the instances of him not being there had been too many for us to develop a good relationship in my youth. There were good times, we always had a holiday by the seaside together and did have fun together as a family but things could have been better. Did his frequent absences contribute to the rift as a child and a teenager?

Things changed when I met my husband and we were courting. Dad liked my fiancé and was happy to be involved in the wedding and in us creating a new home. We got on so much better when I was an adult and we had family get togethers, playing adult games. My husband and I went on holiday with my parents, we took them on their first holidays abroad and things were pretty good. But unfortunately there was a family rift initiated by my sister and mother with the family drifting apart. I had no contact with my mother and sister for ten years but my father always kept in touch and visited me and my family during those ten years until, on his seventieth birthday, he said he had had enough of the family row and he wanted us all to celebrate his special birthday at a family lunch in a restaurant and we all tentatively attended which started the slow return to normality between the family.

Consequently I was closer to my father now than my mother and this continued until their deaths, in fact I was very close to Dad in the final years of their lives as I had to give them a lot of time and help when mum's health deteriorated until she had to spend her last year in a home with Alzheimer's which dad could not cope with. The strain of caring for mum had taken his strength away and when she died he was a mere shadow of the man he was. We tried to rally him round, took him on holidays and on outings but he had lost interest in most things and one night he passed away peacefully in his sleep only six months after mum had died.

I was distraught. The man with whom I had such difficulty relating to and with whom I had so many disagreements as a child and teenager had become so close to me and my husband, we were deeply saddened when we lost him. He did leave me with a legacy of many of his old family photographs and documents. which I never knew he had, which helped me to see the kind of difficult upbringing he had had and this explained so much of why he held such alien values to me when young. It started my interest in family history and past times and revealed a side of my father I never knew.

So from being the absent father, with relationship problems between us, I learnt what an intelligent and interesting man he was and became very close to him and I think we had a great respect for each other.

Absent Family Members

How often do we think 'what if'...? What if fate had not intervened to turn one's life in a particular direction. Perhaps for some people nothing much would have changed but for me things could have been very different. That's not to say it's been a bad life for me, in fact, in the main I've been very lucky but it's just that it could have been very different and this is due to an absent family member – my father. My father died in September 1944 when I was three months old so I have no recollection of him and never had the opportunity to share a relationship with him.

My mother remarried (a family friend who had been widowed with three sons) when I was about eighteen months old and instead of being brought up in Norwich, where I had been born, my childhood was spent in Hertfordshire with my brother, my step father and step brothers.

I always knew that this was not my family of origin, not least because there was never any suggestion of a change of surname for my brother and myself but I don't think I was encouraged to question what had happened and so I just accepted it. Perhaps I was not a curious child or perhaps I developed a sensitivity at a young age that asking questions would upset my mother. It was probably only as an adult, in fact, in relatively recent times that I have started to wonder about my father as a person – where his career as an actuary might have led him, which characteristics of my personality I have inherited from him and where I would have ended up had he lived.

My paternal grandparents, my step-father's parents and my maternal grandmother had all died before I was born so the only grandparent I knew was my maternal grandfather. He lived with his two unmarried daughters, my maiden aunts, with whom I spent holidays. My

RUGBY

memories of granddad are scant but quite clear but what I do remember is the night he died. It was the October half term just after I had started school. I wasn't aware that granddad was ill although at 82 he did seem to me a very, very old man. I'm not sure whether he had a heart attack or a stroke but it was sudden and fatal. By way of explanation I was told that granddad had gone to heaven. Whilst I cannot remember the detail of what followed I can recall the atmosphere of sadness and loss that enveloped the household.

Being the youngest in the family by some twelve years meant my brothers were adults while I was still at school so there were a lot of comings and goings with two brothers doing National Service and others working away from home and then two of them were married by the time I was thirteen. These absences, some temporary and some permanent clearly altered the dynamics within the family but overall the memories are positive ones.

One family member that I didn't mind losing was the dog 'Zen'. Zen was a Samoyed, a husky like dog with long white fur and a bad temper. Granted she couldn't really be blamed for her irritability because she had suffered two accidents, one on the road and one on the railway, and these caused something of a personality change in her. She belonged to my brother Julian and was only friends with him. Everyone else gave her a wide berth and no one (except Julian) was too upset when she had to be put down.

Missing Family Members

The missing family member that I actually miss is my brother Eddy. He is missing in that he lives in Australia so I don't get to see him that often. He is the sibling nearest to me in age he is 13 months younger than me, so we knew each well when we were growing up. Also I got on very well with his wife and still do. There is more of a gap between us and the other 3 siblings.

We email each other and speak on Skype regularly but this is not the same as sitting having a chat over a cup of coffee.

He had heart problems a couple of years ago but didn't tell me until he had recovered. He said I could hardly drop everything and rush over just to see him. As I am retired I didn't really have much to drop but going to see him is not like getting in the car and going to somewhere in the UK. We did get over to see him last year though when he had recovered.

My husband and I are going over to see again him next year.

I miss him because we used to have long discussions on different topics, we still do when he is here as he always stays with us when he comes to the UK. We also have some interests in common such as walking and we both used to play badminton. We are also both tone deaf so we both have a moan about my husband Trevor's music. Trevor likes to play it loud.

When we have family do's he is rarely present. We do sometimes get to arrange things for when he is coming over.

On his 40th birthday Trevor & I had a bbq, videoed it and sent Ed the birthday cake with melted candles all over it, squashed into a jiffy bag. It wouldn't get past the Australian customs these days.

Absent Parent

I escaped the problems of one of my parents being away during the war because I wasn't born until 18 months after World War 2. However, that didn't help matters.

Whether it was the strain of looking after me or because my mother was somewhat older than the fashion when I was born or whatever the circumstances were, when I was about 3 years old my Mum developed TB and was sent off to Garrilgall Sanatorium. This is a place out in the country where patients with TB were exposed to as much fresh air as possible. The cure took a long time and I think it was at least a year before she was returned to live with us again.

By all accounts, my Dad did not cope well at all. I was told in much later life (after both of my parents had died) that he "went to pieces". I was unaware of this at the time but I did grow up being particularly close to my Grandmother.

I have no recollection of staying with her but I suppose I must have done. My first real memory of life was moving house. We moved into the semi-detached next to my Grandparents. A doorway was made at the top of the stairs so it became possible to move from one house to the other by climbing one set of stairs and descending the other.

When I started school I really noticed the difference between my home life and that of my friends. My Mum was not as fit as theirs and would go to bed every afternoon between 2 and 4 pm. I remember the routine of returning from school at the age of 5 or so and running up the stairs to ensure my Mum was still there in bed. I suppose I felt that one day she would be taken back to the sanatorium.

As a result of all of this I spent my formative years very much as a home lover and the thought of leaving home, and my Mum filled me with dread. It is amazing how one matures though. By the time I had reached the age of 17 I was off to join the Army. I suppose by then I had come to believe that my Mum was really home to stay.

Dad pulled himself together long before I noticed but of course he was always out at work. We had great weekend and holidays though.

Absent Parent

My father was 39 years old when war broke out, I was three and my brother was ten. Dad was a GWR driver and in a reserved occupation with extra cheese and protein coupons in his ration book. At the time he was driving goods trains out of Tyesley goods depot and often away on "double home" where the ammunition trains were driven where required and he would have to stay overnight and come back next day.

His absences left mum completely in charge of two children having to make sure they were safe during air raids. I had to be carried to the shelter under the railway bank and my brother would walk alongside .On several occasions in the complete darkness he curled up and went to sleep on the side of the path. Then mum had to leave the main shelter and go and find him. As we had a fish pond in our long garden the thought of him drowning was foremost in their minds and so it was decided that if a raid was predicted we would go en block up the road and stay the night with friends in their shelter.

At this time my brother had taken his 11plus and passed for Yardley Grammar School where he went in September 1939 only to find that the school was centred in a target area, adjacent to the marshalling yards and in between factories providing accessories for war vehicles and planes. So the whole school, teachers, blackboards, books etc. were uprooted and went en block to The Forest of Dean. Dad had previously suggested that Trevor be sent to Canada to stay safely with his brother in Edmonton, but one ship carrying evacuees had been torpedoed.

Trevor was the youngest child to go and they were billeted in Lydney. Unfortunately he was moved around several times as he used to sleep walk and caused accidents in his foster homes. The one good thing that evolved from this nightmare was his deep love of the countryside and a passion for butterflies and birds.

On the opposite side of the coin I was left at home as an only child in a three bedroomed terraced house where one bedroom was unoccupied. As I was only three years old all this decision making had little effect on me. I was not frightened by events or trips in the night to the shelter or the absence of my brother. I remember visiting him by train and being terrified we would get off at the wrong station because there were no names on the platforms and no lights at all. Dad counted all the stops to ensure we vacated the train at Lydney but if it was held up at signals it was difficult to count correctly.

We now had a spare bed and immediately had to register with the billeting department to accommodate temporary war workers. We had two farm girls from Ireland who called dad Mr Gunn instead of Mr Hunt, they held their cups around the circumference instead of the handle, Mum explained that they worked in the fields at home and it warmed their hands and we were definitely NOT to copy them Every time they sat down to a meal they crossed themselves because one of the Victorian houses in Oxford Road had a crucifix shape on the apex of the roof.

The following lodger was a nurse working at a local factory and this was a story in itself. She had a boyfriend from the other side of the city who used to visit after work. One day my aunt and uncle from the same area were visiting us and we were having tea in the dining room when he happened to walk through to put the kettle on. When he had returned to the front room my aunt retorted, What's he doing here? Mum explained that he was walking out with our lodger and it seemed pretty serious. Oh is he indeed said Auntie Ann I can tell you he lives at the back of us, is married with young children. When confronted with this our lodger vowed she did not know he was married and my father, an upright correct gentleman, said she had better find alternative accommodation or stop this futile relationship.

So she vowed she had and so she stayed on and he no longer came to visit. One day a beautiful bunch of flowers arrived and mum asked who had sent them. She vowed she did not know but mum did not believe her, so the landlady issued an ultimatum .If they are from him and you are still seeing him they will be dead in the morning!   Sure enough the following day the flowers drooped in the vase. On her return from work A broke down and admitted that she had lied and she still loved him. So father being law abiding told her to go!   Years after when mum told the story she admitted pouring boiling hot water into the vase because she knew she was lying.

The next chapter in this lodger saga was that mum heard that she had had a baby and was living in poverty not far away from us. So off she trooped to see for herself and then pleaded with dad to take her back so that she could take care of the child whilst her mother worked. She came back and I must have been terribly jealous of this cuckoo in the nest I recall kicking the pram to wake her up .She did stay to the end of the war and then returned home and eventually got married later.

When my brother returned to Lydney we already had lodgers and this completely revised my brother's character. He became morose, badly behaved, breaking milk bottles in the street and nearly getting expelled from school through bad behaviour. I was in the middle of this and received bullying like behaviour. He so disliked me, the favourite who stayed at home. We were always at loggerheads until he married a lovely young lady who became like a sister to me.

So the effects of absenteeism rebounded on my young life and even if I did not know it at the time, played havoc with my emotions. I realised why my brother disliked me so much on his return in to the family and I would probably have acted the same in his shoes.

Absent Parent

RUGBY
U3A

Quote from Britain's Century D and K

(Some of the youngsters especially those from London's East End have never seen the countryside before. Some are also finding it hard to cope with an unusual though healthy diet. Their billeters are similarly finding it a challenge to cope with city habits and language. Evacuation may save many lives, it may also have profound sociological effects)

Christmas
and
New Year
Celebrations

Living History

Christmas Remembered

Is Christmas Better Now?

Looking back Christmas was always a family affair. We would all get together. But now the families have dispersed. The young ones keep the tradition with their own families but some of our grandchildren have six (or more) grandparents where the genetic grandparent couple have

Family Christmas 21st Century Style

divorced and remarried. There are also the countless aunties and uncles with their cousins to gather together for the traditional Christmas.

There is a great temptation to "go away" for Christmas to some foreign country. This can save any difficulties about who is going to travel to where and spend Christmas with who. There is little fun to be had in watching television all day (the programmes are very poor on Christmas Day) and of course, it's not the done thing get on with jobs round the house or do some gardening! And everywhere is closed!

Extended families are wonderful things but the Christmases of yesteryear may have gone forever!

Do we remember the sort of presents we would buy for our parents and grandparents? Usually of small value in real terms but how long did it take to save our pocket money to buy them? There were also the home

Christmas

made presents. We can remember making them and receiving them. We can also remember the joy they brought. Is it that we haven't got *time* now? Or have we lost our imagination. When money was short we made our own entertainment and never remember going hungry at Christmas time.

© Picture: Murray Sanders. Hair and make-up: Alice Theobald

Traditional Christmases today are as good as they always were

55

made presents. We can remember making them and receiving them. We can also remember the joy they brought. Is it that we haven't got *time* now? Or have we lost our imagination. When money was short we made our own entertainment and never remember going hungry at Christmas time.

© Picture: Murray Sanders. Hair and make-up: Alice Theobald

Traditional Christmases today are as good as they always were

Our Recollections and those of Our Friends.
Birmingham

The recollections of our Christmas Customs in our Family from Birmingham 1936 onwards.

We always believed in Santa Claus mum said, "Well please yourselves but he never comes to people who do not believe in him".

We always hung one of Dad's long woollen socks on the end of the bed on Christmas Eve. This graduated to a pillowcase as we got older. We always wrote a letter to Santa in Greenland early in December and posted it at Lewis's Department store in the grotto. Every year we queued up four flights of stone stairs to see the magnificent grotto at Lewis's in Bull Street. It was fabulous with a new theme every year, a long walk through elves pixies all moving and busy making the toys for the boys and girls. We even visited when we were grown up.

Every year about the middle of November Santa drew up to Olton station in a horse drawn coach and then he boarded the train and came by our house on the way to Moor Street Station and thence to Lewis's store. All the shop windows were decorated and seasonal after the war and were well worth a visit.

Christmas Eve a mince pie and a carrot and a glass of sherry were always left out for Santa and in the morning the carrot was gnawed and a bite taken out of the pie whilst we were in bed. We always wriggled our toes to see if he had been but never dreamed of touching the presents before morning. There was always an apple or orange a new penny some nuts and a few little toys in the stocking.

On Christmas morning we all sat down together for a pork pie and ham breakfast with pickles and toast. Our main presents were opened and given after the first meal. Grandma was always up early waiting for the children to awake and then she was in to bed with them opening the presents with great whoops of delight.

Dinner was prepared the night before, puddings were made in October and every one had a stir in order to make a wish which had to be kept secret or it would not come true. We nearly always had a cockerel which dad had fattened up in the duck pen under the railway line. He killed it and mum would have to feather it and draw it and then burn the bits off it with a taper. The oven was small so it often had to go in early so there was room for the vegetables.

One year as mum liked new potatoes for the dinner dad grew them early in the year and buried them in a cake tin up the garden. Mum had forgotten this and as there was no marker put in to show where he had buried them she was to be seen prodding around with a spade until she found them. Dad also experimented with red Brussels sprouts and no one would  eat them. Dinner was at one o'clock with the table laid with serviettes and crackers. Everyone had a silver sixpence in their pudding and we all waited for dad to be sick when he got his and a pile of coins would ensue too much hilarity. The men were supposed to wash up and every one snoozed or played quiet games for the afternoon.

After a tea when there was always raspberry trifle and Christmas cake we would play darts on the pantry door or cards New Market Rummy or Crib.

On Boxing Day we went to Uncle Jim's farm in Fillongley. He had a big farmhouse with two staircases and about 68 acres of farm land. We arrived mid-morning and went down to the pub in Old Arley with a hamper of turkey and stuffing sandwiches I t was a sparse country pub with quarry tiles and a smoky atmosphere. We returned to the farm for tea and Uncle Jim went off to do the milking and then Santa was to be seen riding on a white horse coming down the lane distributing presents to all the children. After tea we would play lots of games like charades and sing songs around the piano then everyone had to do a turn or pay a forfeit. Wc lovcd to play sardines and climb under the big high beds and up the two stair case or go inside the huge wardrobes.

Some Recollections from Bilton House

Christmas was a special time, but not as hyped up as it is today. Things were much simpler, but there was still the excitement.

Preparations began in November when the cakes and puddings were made. The pudding was usually made on the kitchen table with

everyone having a stir and making a secret wish. Small items were put in the pudding – silver threepenny bits or thimbles. These were sometimes washed and used again the following year! During the war families saved and swapped coupons for the ingredients for the pudding – sometimes carrots were grated and added to bulk out the mixture.

Before Christmas decorations like paper chains were made and strung up around the room. These often came unstuck and hung down like long snakes! A Christmas tree – usually a real tree stood in the corner and had home made decorations hanging from it.

The story of Father Christmas featured in everyone's memory of Christmas. Some of the group as children were afraid of a stranger coming into the room, one little girl hung her stocking up in her parents' room! Members of the group remembered being told to be good or "he" wouldn't come. As one got older awkward questions began to arise – "How does he get down the chimney?", "How can he get to everyone in one night?" These were questions which were ultimately raised by our own children and had to be answered. Even once you found out there was no real Father Christmas you wanted to still believe in him and would pretend you still thought he was real!

Children through the ages have woken early on Christmas morning to see if "he" had been. A sock, a stocking or even a pillowcase would be left and it was exciting to feel to see if you could find out what was inside. Long ago it would be a penny, an orange and some nuts. One member remembered having some cordial, another a crock doll, comics like "Tiny Tots", "Tiger Tim", "Girls' Own" or "The Children's Newspaper" were popular and most comics had an "Annual", which came out in time for Christmas. There might
be a box game, a jigsaw puzzle, a doll or a pram (not usually both!). One member remembered having a black crock doll with hand knitted clothes, others remembered flat cardboard dolls with paper clothes which could be hung over the cardboard shape with tabs which folded over. The lady who remembered having the dolls' pram said she used to push the cat around in it!

Christmas morning breakfasts were special, with people eating pork pie, ham or gammon, pickles and toast.

Most of our members came from Non-conformist backgrounds, so church featured early in the morning. Members spoke of pumping the organ in church, another of playing the organ and having parents who sang in the choir. Midnight Mass seems to be a more modern tradition.

After church it was time for Christmas Dinner. Usually it was chicken – turkey did not seem to feature at all – which was a special treat then. It was often reared at home in the back garden and the vegetables were often home-grown. After dinner the washing up had to be done – no dishwashers then!

Then all the children had to be quiet for the Kings' Speech which was  on the radio at 3 o'clock. After this there might be some games, like charades. One lady, who was an only child, remembered all her cousins coming at Christmas. Then came tea with mince pies and Christmas cake. It was one of the few days in the year when the "front room" was used. It was heated by a real fire. One lady's father was a coal merchant and he was especially busy before Christmas making deliveries.

New Year did not feature strongly in the Midlands. The further north you went, the more it was celebrated and in Scotland it had precedence over Christmas. Most people remembered church bells being rung to welcome in the New Year. One member of the group was serving in the merchant navy and he was the youngest member of the engine room and was allowed to strike the midnight bell twelve times (instead of the usual six). Ships in port let off emergency rockets and sometimes sounded a siren to welcome the New Year.

As a young, dark and undoubtedly handsome man one member remembered going first footing and staying the night at a party and having to sleep in a camp bed in the shed. He was nice and cosy until he awoke to find it had snowed and the snow had come in through the gaps in the corrugated tin roof!

Around Christmas and the New Year were Pantomimes and special radio programmes like Tommy Handley and "It Ma". These were later replaced by shows like "Morecombe and Wise" or favourite films on the television.

Northern Ireland

My earliest recollection of Christmas and what the visit of Father Christmas meant to me was when we lived in Northern Ireland. It was a few years after my sister was born in 1950 and we lived in an end of terrace house surrounded by plenty of neighbours. Dad worked in the Linen factory in Bessbrook village, at one time a major employer in the area, since the troubles it has been run down.

This particular Christmas Elaine and I had a Doll each, mine had long blonde hair and Elaine's had dark brown hair and a stocking with a few

 sweets, orange and a small bottle of orange cordial. We were thrilled and the dolls were with us for many years. Thinking back now I realise that my parents always did us proud for all the relevant celebrations. With money not being very plentiful for most of my early years we always had toys and my parents never went into debt to provide them. I clearly remember my mother saying to me that on many occasions the "Tally Men" would call on her to try and persuade her to buy their goods, saying "I know your family and I know you will pay me next week" Mum

retorted "how if I cannot afford to pay for this now will I be able to afford twice next week" I can only imagine they were sent away with their tails between their legs. Mum never minced her words so I guess they would never be rich from her business.

We moved into a prefab behind our previous house sometime later with more room to play as we had a larger garden backing onto a field where goats grazed. Mum and Dad always took us to Belfast to the shops where we could visit and talk to Father Christmas, what a treat this was, as this involved a train journey, this was quite a magical time for us. One Christmas I can clearly remember looking forward to a visit from Father Christmas that I was so excited I couldn't get to sleep, seeing him in the room I became frightened and Mum had to console me. However I was not disappointed and all was well after that.

I don't remember family gatherings at Christmas, although there must have been as we lived there for many years. School plays, carol services and the celebrations associated with this time of year were not events I can recall, although being regular church goers I can only imagine we must have had a great time.

When we moved back to England my memories are more vivid, being nearly 5 years older than Elaine I had to keep the pretence of there being Father Christmas, this was not difficult as I really enjoyed Xmas and deep down I always wanted to live in this fantasy world for a little longer. Many times very early on Christmas morning Elaine would wake up and shout out to me "he's been" and promptly set about opening all her presents, only to be told by our parents to go back to sleep as 'he' hadn't finished his deliveries, but wouldn't call back if we were awake. We were very lucky and had all the usual presents, bikes, clothes and plenty of chocolates.

The house was always decorated with the usual trimmings and a real Christmas tree with real candles!!!! I shudder now as Health and Safety Laws were never heard of then, thanks goodness!! We would invite the neighbours in for a celebratory drink on Christmas morning before tucking into our lunch. We always had poultry, a gammon joint and a beef joint with plenty of fresh vegetables; dad always grew them especially for Christmas even without the help of a freezer.

When both Elaine and I didn't believe in Father Christmas it lost a lot of magic, we would wake late, open our presents, go back to sleep for a while, then watch Max Bygraves on TV handing out presents to ill children in hospital. Then at 3 o'clock settle down to listen to the Queen's Christmas message followed by playing board or card games or whatever interesting games we received as presents.

New Year celebrations for me never came into their own until I was a lot older and we would go out to the main ballroom and celebrate until the wee small hours. What does stick in my mind is my parents opening the front door letting in the New Year, first footing and always had coal brought into the house too. Not sure what significance this had but I clearly remember this happening when I was home on New Year's Eve.

The magic of Christmas returned when I had my own children, keeping the presents secret and telling them Father Christmas would only visit well behaved children. Seeing their eyes light up when they received all the presents they requested and not being able to wait to try out their new bikes. The magic will again return when we share celebrations with our grandchildren who will soon understand what this fantasy time means and we can relive past memorable experiences.

Bilton House: Reminiscence Groups

The members of the group were asked about their recollections and memories of celebrations and traditions of Christmas and New Year that they experienced, or knew about when they were young.

Most of them either hung up stockings or pillow cases in anticipation of presents. But unlike recent and modem times the expectations were

modest. Nuts, oranges, and in one instance, cordial, were traditional in the stocking. Usual for the girls was a doll, and sometimes a pram or pushchair for it, but not doll and pram together: one had to wait. Some' dolls' were flat two dimensional ones that could be 'dressed' as one desired from a collection of flat cut-out clothes, having tabs that could be hung over the shoulders of the doll. Books were also given, especially' annuals' which were published especially for Christmas time. Examples were 'Boy's Own Paper', 'Chums' and, in the 50's, 'Girl', (given then to their daughters). Simple box games and cardboard

puzzles were also favourites. Occasionally individual members remember receiving memorable presents. One gentleman received a lorry from his uncle in America, complete with left-hand drive. It came in the form of a construction kit. Another lady was given a camera when she was fifteen years old.

Presents were usually opened early Christmas day morning, although many
people throughout the country adopted other practices, e.g. on Boxing

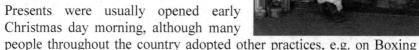

Christmas

Day. The myth of Father Christmas provoked lively discussion. Whilst all experienced its magic when young it was inevitably questioned as they grew older. Not least were awkward situations they experienced when having to come to explain matters to their own children. Having nurtured and embellished the myth to the point of belief they were confounded by the clear logical questioning of their own children as they grew older, e.g. how could Father Christmas visit ALL the children in the world in one night, how could he possibly get down a chimney, who made all the presents and how long did it take....and so on. They described how they stretched credibility to the limits by creative explanations, but eventually admitted defeat. One lady described how her son said that he would believe in Father Christmas for that year but not the next one!

Not only was Father Christmas a figure of excitement and anticipation, but one lady regarded him with fear, i.e. a stranger coming into her bedroom. This was so strong that she hung her stocking in her parents' bedroom. Church worship on Christmas day was usual. This was before the more recently fashionable 'midnight mass' celebrations. Services were held on Christmas Day morning.

The eating of, usually large, quantities of food was a common feature of Christmas day celebrations. Pork Pie and gammon was eaten for breakfast. The main dinner was at mid-day and was of traditional fair. In country districts fowl and  vegetables were locally produced, if not direct from the home. Christmas puddings and cake was also usually home made. This was not so much in town and urban areas. From their mainly nonconformists backgrounds members recalled that there was little or no drinking in the home, and Christmastime was no exception. The common location for people that did drink was the public house. Brandy did however appear to light the Christmas pudding

It was affirmed that New Year celebrations were mainly a regional and geographic affair. The further north one went in this country the more importance was attached to them, especially in Scotland where it had precedence over Christmas. Members did however recall some 'footing', and church bells keeping them awake. As a young man, with then, black hair, and doubtlessly handsome, a member was invited to cross the doorstep. He was attending a gathering and was obliged to spend a night on a camp bed in a shed. He found this a pleasant and cosy experience, until he woke up next morning covered in snow which had driven through the gaps in the corrugated roof.

Another gentleman who had been at sea, or rather docked in the port of Middlesbrough at the time, whilst serving in the Merchant Navy, recalled a traditional experience in which he was directly involved. As the youngest member of the engine room crew he was allowed to strike 16 bells, (as compared with the usual eight), at mid-night. The 'bell', as such, was the truncated and turned end of a gas cylinder and the clapper a large spanner. Ships in port also let off emergency rockets and sounded their sirens at the same time.

The Christmas period was also the occasion for an annual treat to the Pantomime, and/or listening to a special seasonal favourite wireless programme, such as Tommy Handley and 'It Ma'. Later this would be replaced by the same on television, especially the Morecombe and Wise Christmas show ... and not to mention the endless repeats of films such as 'Bridge over the River Kwai' and 'Mary Poppins'

Christmas Games

Before the times of television games were played by the family, or with friends at Christmas and at other parties. On Christmas day, Boxing Day or New Year's Day children were allowed to 'stay up' as a special treat. Where succeeding generations met together favourite games were sometimes handed down and continued.

There were different sorts of games.

Hunting' Games.

An object was hid, e.g. a thimble, numbers on pieces of paper, a person, and the challenge was to find it, him or her. The first to do so won a prize. A variation on this was to hide the object in a room whilst a person was 'out', then when he/she came in to guide the search by indicating in some way, by sounds e.g., music, whether one was 'hot' or 'cold'. R. remembered a red thimble being hid on his grandfather's bald head and not being discovered for quite a time.

A well-known game, that could have romantic adaptations, was 'Blind Man's Buff'. Another was 'Murder in the Dark'

Board games

These included, Ludo, Snakes and Ladders, Monopoly, Draughts. Sometimes there was a big new jigsaw which was left out for people to fit in pieces.

Cards games

'Snap' was a favourite. The cards were shuffled and dealt out. Each player put down a card in turn. 'Snap' was called if two pictures were the same. The first to call out picked up all the cards. The winner was the one to have all the cards in their hand.

'Happy families'. This was played as a group. The cards were in sets of four with Mr., Mrs., Master, and Miss for say, an animal family. Each player could ask his neighbour if he had a specific card, as he tried to build up the collection for the specific family. If that person did he had to hand it over. The first person to collect all the families, or the most families, was the winner. The trick was to work out who would have what cards.

Surprise games

There were games that relied on the majority of people present not knowing the trick. Those that did usually arranged and conducted them whilst the unsuspecting were 'out'. 'Shaking hands' was where a blindfolded person was invited to shake hands in turn with people and guess who that person was. At the end of the line was a rubber glove filled with water !!

Another was, 'Ride to the Ceiling'. The unsuspecting person was blindfolded, led into the room and guided to step onto a small platform e.g. a tray. They were told to rest their outstretched arms and hands on the shoulders of another person in front of them. They would then be taken on a 'ride to the ceiling'. But in reality the platform remained at the same distance from the floor but was wobbled by those that held it. The person on whose shoulders the arms and hands rested gently lowered themselves by crouching down. Then another person would tap the unsuspecting victim on the head and shout, "Jump!" The terrified victim would scream and anticipate a long fall to the floor whereas, of course, it was only a few inches from it. Many hands were ready to catch the shaken victim. This was always good fun with children who are usually trusting, innocent, and a light weight!

Circle games

Another sort of 'surprise game' as well as a circle one was the favourite of 'passing the parcel'. When the music stopped the person in the circle started to unwrap a layer but had to pass it on when the music resumed. Sometimes a small gift was enclosed in each layer, but usually the big 'surprise' one was reserved for the end.

'Winking' was a circle game of chairs where people sat on them but with a partner behind. One chair was empty and the person behind it tried to fill it by winking at another person. If that person caught the wink they would try to rush to the empty chair, but their partner would try to grab them to prevent this. Once out of the chair the person was successful. The person behind the empty chair would then continue the game.

Musical chairs was another sort of circle game where chairs were progressively withdrawn as the game progressed. Those that failed to get sat down when the music stopped were 'out'. This progressed until one chair, (and usually two markers) remained.

Team games

There were games where teams would compete with one another to be 'first'. These games were usually hilarious with ludicrous things being done.

Favourites were passing a balloon from person to person without touching it with the hands. Another was to thread a spoon tied to a long length of string from person to person passing it down the inside of one's clothes.

Guessing games

Charades was perhaps the most popular of this type. Without speaking a person or persons in a small group would act out a word, a tune or book. The audience would then try to guess what it was. A similar one based on a popular radio and television series of the 50's was, 'What's my line?' and 'Animal, vegetable or mineral?'

Group games

These were where people played as individuals within a group solely for the fun of the game, exercising a skill or aptitude that they might have.

'Chuckie' involved taking it in turn to flick a playing card towards a target composed of a bucket placed on a piece of newspaper. Each person had six goes. If a card landed on the newspaper there was a score of 1, if in the bucket then 6. The person with the highest score won.

'Chocolate Dinner' was another game. A bar of chocolate was placed on a plate which was then set on the floor. A knife and fork was placed either side of it. A dice was passed round and if a player scored a six they donned a scarf, woolly hat, and gloves (provided) and tackled eating the chocolate with the knife and fork. They continued doing this until another person scored six, and the process was repeated. The longer the spell between the six being thrown the longer the player had to get at the chocolate.

Miscellaneous favourites

These included pleasant time fillers such as darts, bagatelle and 'ping pong'.

Christmas And New Year Memories From 1930 Onwards In Kettering

Waking on Christmas morning with a pillow case on the end of the bed with presents one new penny an orange sweets and nuts. Certainly not the amount of gifts children receive today. Breakfast was always pork pie on Christmas morning. For dinner we had a lovely roast with capon chicken which was a real treat. We hardly ever ate chicken at any other time. This was followed by plum pudding and custard.

We always had to be quiet and listen to the Kings Speech on the wireless. The day was spent playing with our toys and friends,

neighbours and family popped in to sample the bottle of whisky and port and to have one of my father's cigarettes Players in a box (There was no cheap packets on this special day)

On Boxing Day after dinner, mums family congregated at grandmas. As this was a special occasion the front room was opened to accommodate us all. The men played 'cards whilst my cousins and I amused ourselves and the women prepared the food for later. The adults always ate first and then it was our turn to be waited on. In the evening we went into the front room to play games such as Pass the Parcel. Can You Say Hum Hum, A Man and his Object and other games. As I was the youngest, I was put to bed to stay the night with grandma in her lovely warm bed by candlelight

The War Years

As grandma had now died we stayed at home for Christmas and our evacuee was 5 years younger than me. Her mum was a secretary at The Admiralty and her father was a butcher so sharing rations we were never short of food. We had a really happy time until he was called into the army.

Newcastle

When I was a child Christmas didn't arrive till Christmas Eve when my Dad brought a Xmas tree home. We all took part in the decorating of it using lights with nursery rhymes on, if I remember correctly, and lamenta (strands of silver threads) and other ornaments which my sisters and I had made   old and new. Christmas Eve we left our

stockings at the bottom of our beds and were hopeful of Santa's arrival in the early hours   the sooner we got to sleep, the sooner he would arrive!!!!!   I remember often waking to find it was too early, then later waking and shuffling down the bed to find lots of super things. Orange, apple, nuts, colouring book and pencils and a few other surprises. We were always overjoyed and felt so lucky! Main presents were not given until we had been to church.

As I got older, and Santa wasn't part of the traditions we occasionally went to midnight mass. One year I recall my sisters and I thought it would be a good idea to open presents on our return. What a bad idea that was!! Christmas Day just wasn't the same!! No real excitement!! We never did that again.

Dad worked in the power station and did shift work so wasn't off for Xmas Day very often. Mum used to arrange the Christmas dinner around his shift. There was always a turkey and all the trimmings. Usually a houseful with family friends sharing our feast

New Year's Eve, with living in Newcastle was always followed by Bank holiday on New Year's Day   so a big celebration! The party always started at the bottom of the street. Sometimes just popping in for drinks and games. It always seemed to finish at our house to celebrate at midnight. The carpet would be rolled up and the piano and dancing began. 'First Footing' was almost always carried out by my Dad. He was tall, dark

and handsome   he went outside armed with a piece of coal, some salt and whiskey. The significance being coal for warmth, salt for wealth and whiskey??? After the stroke of midnight, he would be allowed back in the house with his 'gifts', which would, supposedly, bring us luck in the following year!!!

North London

When I was six my Father was taken very-very ill. He had TB and he had it badly. We lived in North London and he was taken into a hospital called St Mary's in Paddington. He was there for eighteen months the first time – I think he came home for weekends when he was getting better but he was in hospital for many of my early years. In those days children weren't allowed to visit people in hospital but because my father was so ill they thought it would be beneficial if they allowed us to visit some weekends. I would go on a Saturday and my sister would go on Sunday. We had to go up the fire escape at the back of the Hospital and Sister would open the door and make us creep along the corridor into my father's room. I suppose he was in a ward some time but I only remember him in that room.

In all we had three or four Christmases with my Father in hospital but there was one I particularly remember:

We had gone into hospital on Christmas Day (it might have been Christmas Eve or Boxing Day) and my sister and I sat on my father's bed while they wheeled it along the corridor and into the main ward. When you're a child everything seems big but this was a huge room with all the beds in rows (no cubicles like you get today) and at the end of it was the hugest Christmas tree I had seen in all my life and that was all twinkling as if they were real candles on it.

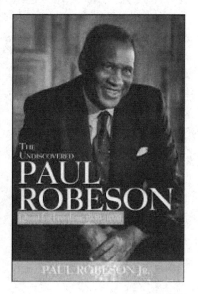

Christmas

It was quite dark so I suppose it must have been late afternoon and the nurses all came in with their capes on carrying lanterns and singing carols   Right in the middle of these nurses was the biggest black man I have ever seen. I know I was a child and everything was big but he was a BIG man. He sang with the nurses.

That man was Paul Robeson. I didn't realise the significance of it then but I grew up with my Mum reiterating that story.

Portsmouth

As an only child, I lead a very insular life. Christmas was just the three of us, if people called in have no recollection. My father's family lived on the Isle of Wight and he rarely saw them, sad from choice. My mother's mother was dead and my father did not care for his father in

law. It was not really as bad as it sounds to me now. It is simply the way it was. In many ways I was a disappointment to my parents, although dearly loved, my father would have liked me to have an interest in sport, although to be honest he never made an issue of this. My mother, however, had always wanted to have dancing lessons and was not allowed. So, I was going to be a second Shirley Temple — for which I was totally unsuited by temperament and ability. Every Christmas

Day we listened to various programmes on the radio. Wilfred Pickles (Have a go!) always interviewed children who had done amazing things, and one child always sung. You can guess the comments, I dreaded that programme and it always coloured the day for me.

I have no childhood recollection of New Year's Eve, I don't think southerners made so much of it and Portsmouth was as south as you can get. Although I had heard of First Footing, but this was something other people did, and bringing in a piece of coal for luck. This appealed.

However, after I was married this changed. David was in the Royal Air Force, Promotions were announced twice yearly on 1 January and 1 July. There was always a party in the mess, in my opinion the very best of the whole year, and there were a lot. On the stroke of midnight the list promotions was pinned up and then the evening just took off. It had a totally different atmosphere to any mess function I remember. Christmas and New Year have distinct flavours for me, one is family and the other a looking forward and back. These days we rarely stay up — but there is a forward looking freshness to 1st January

At Sea

I share a lot of your experiences but when I went to sea all that stopped. I enjoyed Christmas with my parents in Rugby and remember especially the religious celebrations, being in the choir. I used to spend a lot of time going to Church on Christmas Day' but all that stopped when I went to sea.

I was in a tanker when I first went to sea with the Shell Tanker Company. This was about 1958 -59. The merchant navy was a very different place then to what it is now. I was an Apprentice Cadet Engineer. I was in a ship called the Axina based in Liverpool (a pretty grim place) and we went from there, round the south coast of England to Middlesbrough. I would be missing Christmas at home for the first time.

So Christmas day came and we were sailing up the English Channel. I was seasick. Now if you haven't been seasick you won't know just how bad you feel. This was the first time I had been seasick and, thankfully, it was the last, but I felt awful. There were celebrations going on but I had to go on watch. Of course the ship doesn't stop and anchor up just because it's Christmas day so I had to go on watch just like any other day. I remember a Coxswain saying to me, he said "Joe boy". There was a reason he called me that even though my name is John. It's short for "Holy Joe", a hangover from my days in the choir but they dropped the Holy bit. The Coxswain said that the best place to be was the lowest part of the ship. Deep down in the engine room where there was the least movement anywhere on the ship. So that's where I spent Christmas day. Deep down in the bilges and instead of eating turkey I munched on dry biscuits.

So that was Christmas day. By New Year's Eve we had arrived in Middlesbrough. I won't describe Middlesbrough – it may upset some people – but it's a grim place. We tied up in Middlesbrough and observed the tradition that the youngest member of the crew "strikes in" the New Year. I was the youngest member of the crew.

We had a bell on the ship but it wasn't the traditional ships bell. This one was made from a gas cylinder. The top had been cut off and it was turned on the lathe to make it into a bell. Instead of a Clapper, it was hit with a spanner. On board ship each four-hour watch is signalled by the sounding of a bell. One ring for every half hour. The end of each watch is signalled by sounding eight bells. However, at New Year Eight Bells are sounded for the end of one year and a further eight for the start of the New Year. So it fell to me to hit the old gas cylinder sixteen times with the spanner. As in every port in the country, if not throughout the world, all the ships then blew their sirens. A wonderful plaintiff sound echoing round the port.

Shopping

SHOPPING MEMORIES OF CHILDHOOD

The Grange Park shops were the nearest to home – 5 minutes' walk away. Crossing over the main A1 was a lot easier in the early 50's – now traffic is busy and there has been a pedestrian crossing installed for peoples' safety.

The Co-op was the main store for everyone's requirements in butchery and grocery. The butchers shop was separated by an open doorway to the main store. Large wooden butchers blocks and sawdust on the floor. The butcher and his assistant always smart – even if a bit bloodied – in their white coats and striped aprons. Through into the main store was the bakery and confectionary, the fruit and vegetable counter and the dairy products and cooked meats and bacon. Along the right hand side - baking ingredients and tinned goods. I always watched in awe when the bacon slicing machine was being used – feeling sure that one day I'd see one of the assistants cut off their fingers! The Butter was barrel shaped and the required amount cut off the slab and weighed, put onto greaseproof paper, then wrapped again in brown paper. All dry ingredients like flour, sugar, dried fruit etc. were all weighed and packed into blue cone shaped bags. Nothing seemed to be pre-packed. Always separate queues for each counter. The was a small kiosk in the centre of the shop floor for the cashier which doubled up as a tobacconist serving point.

Next door from the Co-op was the garage – both petrol and repairs. The Ebletts newsagents followed on, another butchers shop, another greengrocers, the Post Office, Fish and Chips, the Off-licence, the Florists, Mr Burman the Dentist (above the shops) and finally the Chemist Shop. All our shopping needs for the essentials could be bought in these few shops.

Shopping

RUGBY

Gosforth High Street with loads of shops was the second port of call for other requirements. Whenever we went there we referred to it as 'the Village'. It took about 10 minutes to walk there.

Newcastle was 3 miles away and we always took the bus – the trolley bus. We referred to that as 'the Town'. It had everything you could possible want and more! It still is one of the best cities for shopping in the country in my opinion. We had Fenwicks, Binns, Bainbridges, Co-op – all large department stores. At Christmas, Fenwicks always had the most beautiful window displays with a Christmas theme – usually animated. It still keeps up this tradition giving so much pleasure. In Northumberland Street, which was the main street in town from the Haymarket, there was always lots of traffic - now, of course, it is pedestrianised.

In all shops the assistants were behind counters waiting for your custom – Self Service stores were well into the future! An exception to this was the clothing stores. An enthusiastic assistant would appear from nowhere as soon as you entered the store asking if you needed any help. Mam didn't much like the 'pushy' stores where staff – possibly on commission on sales – would tell you that you suited anything for a sale!

Thinking back I feel that we used to buy far less in days gone by. Our parents always seemed to manage to clothe and feed us very adequately. Clothes were often hand me downs, with the exception of shoes. Often material bought for new dresses to be made and clothes altered to fit or make something new. All the families we knew seemed to have much the same lifestyle as our own and not a thought of us feeling envious of what they had.

SHOPPING

In our lifetimes we have seen a fundamental change in the way that food and consumables are distributed and thus the way we shop.

This has had a profound effect on the environment and even the community in which we live.

Our grandparents, even out parents, would have shopped in their corner shop or local vibrant High Street with its variety of local shops, open from early in the morning to late at night, and supplying all their daily needs. (Scrooge was able to buy a goose on Christmas morning!)

Although coal, bread, milk and certain other products might be delivered daily or weekly by horse and cart, most people did not have cars, and shopping had to be carried in your own shopping bags, so it was generally necessary to shop locally more or less daily.

There was very little pre-packaging and most things were sold loose – even eggs, biscuits and butter, so your own range of stout shopping bags, particularly for potatoes, was essential.

With the absence of domestic refrigerators in ordinary homes, the only form of storage for meat was the 'meat safe' placed in a cool area such as the cellar head.

The High Street might contain a few national banks and stores such as Boots the Chemists, and later Woolworths. (My father used to say that you knew you had reached civilization if there was a Woolworths!) Then there would be the local Co-op, Grocers, Bakeries, etc.

Of course for long periods in the 20th. Century there were shortages and rationing and hours of queuing outside shops was a daily necessity for most housewives.

The absence of our everyday domestic appliances meant that the housewife was literally ' a housewife', who generally stayed at home doing all the weekly rota of heavy repetitive housework, for example, Monday was generally washing day when the laundry was done by hand using a copper, dolly and mangle.

The husbands were the bread-winners going out to long hours of work, often in appalling conditions. There was no such thing as job security then, and certainly no Health & Safety considerations. Industrial injuries, deaths and disasters were common. My own paternal grandfather worked as a signalman for the GWR and lost a leg in a train accident in 1919. He was generously offered £100 or a job for life. Having a wife and 4 young children, he chose to spend the rest of his life as a one-legged platform ticket collector with a crutch.

As for Shopping, everything changed when car ownership became widespread and the Supermarkets appeared, often cleverly sited on the outskirts of the town, sucking the life blood away from the High Streets which are now transformed into pedestrianised urban wastelands of card, shoe, charity and empty shops which die every evening around 6.00.

Life and shopping might be much easier, less onerous and more convenient for us today, but in less than a century we have lost a complete way of life dating back to time immemorial, the vibrant social community life that existed in the High Streets of the past.

Our ancestors would not recognise today's High Streets, they are completely alien to their way of life.

John Duffield July 26 2011

SHOPPING.

L.G. Bond.

I have spent nearly 50 years of my life working in a shop (a pharmacy) and so after retirement the idea of "going shopping" has never filled me full of joy. However shopping as such has changed dramatically over my 70 plus years.

As a wartime baby my first real memories of this activity were of shortages and rationing. This was to continue for many years after hostilities ceased. As a family who had been evacuated to the country at the start of it all we were very lucky to be living in a house with quite a large garden. This would supply most of our vegetables and some soft fruit during the seasons. We also kept poultry, and father, after the war, would often return home from the pub on a Sunday lunchtime with rabbits or pigeons. This all helped stretch out the meat ration.

We had no fridge so mother would shop locally on almost a daily basis, although bread and milk were delivered to the door. Milk would be sterilised as it was easier to keep. I also remember a mobile greengrocer's van and a "pop" van. Father also received his Davenport's" beer at home". He always complained about its quality but still went on having it.

The nearest shop to us was about 10 minutes walk away and our weekly shop was collected by father on his way home from work on a Friday night. A list had been left on the Monday morning and virtually remained unchanged for years. I can still remember it now:

Sugar, tea, butter, lard ,marge., cheese, biscuits, 60 "Woodbines", 20 "Players", 6 boxes of matches, packet of "Persil", packet of "Bisto".

If mother left anything off the list it would be sent with a note to return if not required. Notice no sizes were ever specified, the grocer knew the size of families and would send whatever he felt would fill the bill.

Mother rarely shopped for clothes and I being smaller than my brother always got the "hand me downs". I well remember the braces of my trousers came up to my armpits. We were members of "The Provident Clothing Company" and we paid an agreed amount of money into a club every week. Mother would not let us have anything until we had paid in enough money to pay for it in full. "Tick" or credit was very much frowned upon, and was only used to buy furniture.

Once or twice a year mother and I would catch the bus to Birmingham for her to buy "something special" - possibly a new winter coat. The city is only 15 miles away but would take an hour to reach it going round the villages. Mother welcomed my company or so she said. Father hated shopping and so I would get a half crown (12 1 /2p) to spend on a book. I would be left at Hudson's Book Shop and I would happily browse in the section of war stories for an hour or more while mother did the rounds of stores. That shop was magic and over the years I built up quite a library. I believe it has now closed.

In 1962 I started work as a trainee manager for Boots the Chemist and this would be the time when supermarkets were just starting up. Part of our training was to assess the possible effects of this new form of retailing and what changes the company would need to adopt to meet them. I was working in a fairly large branch in London and had to visit other companies to record how they were reacting. Should Boots go "self-service" in all departments or "self-selection"? In the former, as today, the customer would help themselves to the merchandise off the shelves, in the latter customers would have the choice, to be served as in the past, or opt to help themselves. Very rapidly the policy came out firmly in favour of self-selection for all departments, subject to certain legal restrictions on medicines.

As the march for larger and larger stores has progressed, selling the widest range of products, we are seeing almost the death knell of many traditional companies in the high street as well ~ a huge growth of out of town shopping centres. Opinion is strongly divided as to whether the changes are for good or ill. On a personal level I'm glad to be out of it!

My Mums Shopping as I Remember

Milk Delivered from the farm in the milk churns and then put into jugs.

Bread Delivered to the door.

Coal carried to the outside coal bin or shed in sacks.

Corona was brought to the door in crates of four with stopper clip type openers.

Ice Cream came round with compartment of ice cream driven by a man on a cycle" Stop me and buy one" clearly displayed.

Meat Always from the butcher

Friday was pay day so a visit to the Co-op for the groceries. Check No. 6100 must not be forgotten as the twice yearly payouts of dividends were the highlights of the year.

Saturday morning Shopping in town Woolworths, Marks and Spencers etc.. The market for bargains. Woolworths had a very popular tea bar which was sorely missed – when toilet facilities were required by law where food was served, it sadly closed.

Good Friday Very early in the morning cries of Hot cross buns could be heard in the street and we would go out and buy what we wanted.

My Shopping

By now milk was delivered in bottles daily to the door.

The coal man still delivered coal in sacks to the house.

I visited a local grocer and was able to choose which bacon I wanted, how thick it was to be cut. Likewise I chose my cheese and had it cut to the size I required with a cheese wire. Biscuits were in large boxes along the front of the counter for our choice. Some got broken and bags of broken biscuits, including expensive ones, were the bargains. All these had to be carried home so prams were useful. Not many cars around.

Delivery vans came in to being so orders could now be delivered to the door. With the arrival of fridges and freezers shopping became easier. All goods were purchased from specific shops i.e. Hardware, clothes, shoes, chemist florists etc. More cars by now making carrying goods easier.

Then along came supermarkets selling everything and on line shopping meant you no longer had to leave the house.

Shopping

Shopping was our favourite game, tins and cartons were brought out from the walk in pantry under the stairs. They were all neatly arranged and stacked on to a low table or plank in the living room or in the summer on the lawn. Potatoes and carrots were weighed out and bagged up for imaginary customers or any adult who was unfortunate enough to be resting nearby at the time. Prices were chalked up and newspaper bags were twisted into cones and screwed up at the bottom. In large letters OPEN and CLOSED were printed on a piece of cardboard. We played with real pennies or half pennies or buttons which were securely kept in an old tin. The customers wore different hats or turbans when they came to shop for their groceries.

In the 1940"s there were no home freezers or fridges and few home telephones. Our provisions were bought regularly from the Co-op shop on the Yardley Road because the cooperative movement supported the unions in the big strike and they had allowed customers to have goods with delayed payments. The Co-op shop displayed groceries but mainly they were kept behind the counters. The butter, cheese and bacon were cut freshly to your requirements and wrapped in grease proof paper. A payment office was set up above the displays and pods on wires whizzed overhead with receipts and change for the customers. You had to give your divi number which was written on a receipt pad and the top copy torn out and given to you. Woe betide you if you forgot your number. Biscuits were displayed in large tins along the counter and weighed out to requirements. We had no cars so prams and pushchairs came in very usefully to transport provisions. Mum or dad usually travelled by bicycle with a large wicker basket on the front handle bars.

Our milk was delivered daily by the Co-op horse and cart, also the bread with infrequent visits by the Co-op coalman carrying large bags on his back. Later after the war Corona pop was delivered weekly in crates with metal and ceramic tops to keep in the fizz. The paper boy delivered the daily paper or the Evening Mail from our corner shop and we paid weekly for this.

It was the era when shops were specialised and smelt of what they sold. The iron mongers in the village smelled of paraffin and wax polishes and had numerous boxes of screws nails glues and rivets etc. After the war the haberdashery shop had rolls of material and dress patterns. The wool for knitting was kept on the shelf with your name on so that you collected what you needed. We had Woolworths in the village it was the 3d and 6d store and sold everything from pencils to saucepans.

During and after the war I was too young to understand the rationing system but I remember as dad had a physical job he had extra cheese and bacon rations each week. He always took cheese sandwiches in his pack up so it made little difference to the family. I do remember the panic buying and stocking up and if you saw a queue join it disregarding what the prize was. The word soon got around on the jungle telegraph. I clearly remember the beige ration books and the proprietor licking the end of his indelible pencil to cancel out the strips of coupons in the book. When the book was finished we had to go into Birmingham to the Food Office and queue for the next one.

I was brought up on dried egg powder which was introduced in June 1942 when I as 6 years old. We had one tin every 8 weeks. This was about the time we started keeping chickens under the railway bank together with ducks and rabbits. I remember the queues for unrationed goods but needed to be reminded that 2lbs syrup cost 1 shilling, salt was 1 and 6 pence and butter 1 and 7 pence. I remember the British Restaurant in the village where we ate occasionally, it was only 2 pence for soup, 8 pence for the main course of meat and two vegetables with 3 pence for a pudding followed by a penny halfpenny for a cup of tea.

Shopping

I still remember the secrecy surrounding the visit of Mr Fanakupan . At the time I never knew who he was or whence he came from but we never told anyone when he was due. The front room curtains were always drawn and a few chosen neighbours knocked the door to become his customers. He had a small black case containing many things in short supply like school white socks and enamelled butterfly brooches to name but two.

We were always trained to save up for anything before we purchased it. You never paid hire purchase or postage. When I started work in the fifties I bought a Harella three piece costume and coat to match and I paid weekly. The clothes shop on the Warwick Road used to hang lists of customers who had not kept up their payments in the shop window. I was terrified my name would be on the list and I was sick and tired of the outfit by the time I had paid for it, On another occasion I saw two cotton dresses advertised in The Daily Mirror, they were cheap and I nagged my mother to send for them. This was to be my second lesson, not to believe pictures and descriptions of goods for sale. My mum was right, the material was like a rag and the dye ran in the first wash. I never did forget this.

A friend of mums was a tailoress and we were always trained to ruffle up cloth in your hand before buying it, squeeze it hard to see if it was full of dress and therefore would crease when you wore it. Other lessons in shopping were learned at the Rag Market in the Bull Ring. Beautiful off cuts of material could be found quite cheaply if you knew what to look for and you had access to a treadle sewing machine. The Bull Ring market was also my mentor. Mother's rules were

     a Always walk right down the line of fruit barrows before you decide which to buy

from.

     b Watch how the barrow boy fills the brown paper bag with fruit. Does he delve to the back of the pile where the bruised and damaged fruit were hidden. These were covered up by the polished apples at the front,

c   Always check in the bag before you left the stall and then confront him with damaged wares.

At Christmas positioned amongst the numerous barrows of fruit and seasonable goods would be Santa offering us young children goodies from his sack. Crying, sulking, pouting and then my mum gave in and I can clearly remember the consequences of all the cajoling. I was handed a well wrapped parcel, a pair of motor cycle goggles and last year's calendar. Oh well I was learning all the time.

In 1960 when we were first married I used to shop at the Co-op once a week and carry the groceries home on my bicycle. When I finished work in 1963 to have my first baby I kept some household accounts. The cooker was on H P at 5 shillings a week. The weekly shopping cost about £6 10 shillings. My husband earned £12 10 shillings a week I the mortgage was £12 a month. We had little cash to spare and had bought an old Ford 10 car for £25. It had been laid up during the war with its bonnet covered with coats so the paint had corroded and the wooden floor under the drivers seat had given way. The exhaust leaked and we called it Pooh, but it enabled us to visit friends and relations and petrol was 2 shillings a gallon.

When the children were little we used to go to the market down by the station and we were always thrilled to find off cuts of towelling, trouser materials and dress materials, knitting wool etc. to make up at home. Before charity shops were born about 1976 Einbeck opened in Regent Street, the boys were teenagers and often bought second hand suits, shirts overcoats, all top quality labels. They joked about the possibility of strolling around in Himmler's coat or Hitler's trousers.

RUGBY U3A

1963

JANUARY DAILY NOTES

DATE		£	s	d	DATE		£	s	d
31/12	groceries		11	0		fish		1	9
	fish		3	0		butter		1	7d
	topside bf		8	3		meat		2	6
	papers +1/-		2	0		groceries		12	1½
	bread cake		5	6		papers		2	10
	groceries		10	0		bread		1	6
1/1/63	bread groc		6	9		bread			8
2/1/63	groceries		12	10		bread			8½
	shaving stick		2	3		meat		5	5
	papers		2	3		cheese etc		3	8
3/1/63	fish & bacon		3	6		bus fares		1	2
	writing paper		1	6		greengroc		1	0
	groc		3	0		cheese		2	6
			3	0		potatoes		4	6
	meat & butter		3	9					
	fish		3	9					
	flour out		3	1					
	Punja dub		2	2					
	phone call			6					
4/1/63	eggs 12 weeks		13	0					
	milk		8	6					
	groceries		8	11					
	bread		2	8½					
	hairdressing		8	0					
	shampoo		1	9					
6/1/63	biscuits		1	2					
7/1/63	bread			8					
	brush		1	9					
	meat		3	10					
	buses		1	7					
	bread		2	6½					
	jellied veal		1	4					
	potatoes		2	0					
	peas			10					
	potatoes		2	0					
	bread			8					
	meat		3	4					
	groceries		1	8					

164

HOUSEKEEPING ACCOUNT — JANUARY

	PARTICULARS	1st Week			2nd Week			3rd Week		
1	Grocery and Provisions	1	17	6		12	7	3	0	9½
2	Butcher		17	3		9	1		7	11
3	Baker and Confectioner		5	6		6	5		5	0
4	Dairy		-	-		1	6		8	11
5	Fish and Poultry		12	10		1	9			
6	Greengrocer					4	0		1	0
7	Chemist					3	3			
8	Beer, Wines and Spirits									
9	Tobacco and Sweets									
10	Weekly Club Sheets		4	0		3	6		3	6
11	Clothing		-	-		-				
12	Laundry and Cleaning		-	-		-				
13	Heat, Lighting and Fuel	1	0	0	1	0	0	1	0	0
14	Car Expenses									
15	Garden Expenses									
16	Wages and Extra Help									
17	Rents, Rates and Taxes	1	0	0	2	0	0	1	10	0
18	Telephone									
19	Stationery, Books & Stamps		3	1					1	9
20	Newsagent		2	3		2	3		4	0
21	Hairdresser and Cosmetics		-	-		3	0			
22	Recreation - Bk. Club		1	0		1	0		1	0
23	Gifts and Subscriptions									
24	Education									
25	Furnishings and Repairs									
26	Minor Household Expenses		8	0		5	0		3	0
27	Doctor and Dentist									
28	H.P. Cooker		5	0		5	0		5	0
	WEEKLY TOTAL	6	6	5	7	0	4	7	7	7¼
								7	7	7¼

NOTES

"26" Tax to St Cross, Salad lunch & Roses.
26 buses 7 Shampoo 9 bread

162

Shopping

We remember shops being mostly small, family concerns, where customers were known by name. We paid in cash for our goods but the shop keeper would sometimes allow customers to buy things "on tick" – to be paid for later! Nearly every corner had a shop, so no-one had to walk far. Towns had an "early closing day" to give staff a break. Wednesday was Rugby's day – the shops all closed at lunchtime. They opened on Saturdays, but not Sunday – that was a day of rest. Shop assistants added up totals by writing everything down in a list (usually in pencil) and totalling it all up. Good ones could do it "in their heads".

There were sweet shops selling sweets from jars all lined up on the shelves. The sweets were weighed out on big scales and put into paper bags (no plastic bags then!). We remembered buying liquorice sticks, parma violet sweets, aniseed balls, Pontefract cakes, dolly mixtures, sherbet dabs and gobstoppers.

Every town had a Woolworth's in the High Street. It was commonly known as "Woolies" and when it first opened everything cost 6d. It was always known as a cheap shop.

There were butcher's shops selling fresh meat with sawdust covering the floor. Mr Lissamer was the butcher at the top of Railway Terrace and his delivery boy, Maurice, who eventually opened his own shop in Bath Street.

Pawnbrokers were recognised by their sign over the door – three gold balls. People could take things in and exchange them for money and then, when they got paid the things could be "redeemed". One lady remembered being sent to take her Dad's suit in each Monday and then redeeming it on Friday, in time for him to wear it at the weekend!

Rugby had a big market in Railway Terrace, with stall holders calling out to sell their wares! Mick was a popular character, each Monday he gathered a crowd round him, many of whom went just to hear his sales patter- "I'm not going to charge you 10, not 8, not 6, not even 4 – it's yours for £2".

Many tradesmen came round the houses selling their goods. Bakers, milkmen, coal men, Betterware, bakers and Collier's (who sold paraffin, candles and the like). They usually went to the back door and came on a set day each week.

Co-ops were in most towns and had a variety of shops. Nearly everyone remembered their "Co-op number" – this was quoted on each purchase and at the end of the year a "divi" (dividend) was given. An order book could be taken in early in the morning and the delivery boy would have the order at your door by the afternoon.

Rugby people remember Lavendar and Harrison's – a grocery shop in the High Street – which had a huge coffee grinder in the window and the smell of coffee wafted into the street to lure people in!

Baker's shops often sold bread and cakes made on the premises and displayed in the windows.

Many food shops had a "Christmas Club" into which customers paid so much a week, to get a bumper order for Christmas.

During the war, and for a few years after, things were rationed and could only be bought with coupons, cut out from a Ration Book. People saved their coupons for special events and there were always those who could get things on the "black market".

Shopping

Shopping! Well I am a very unusual woman who does not like it very much, but having to think about it for this afternoon I became to wonder why.

As a child I do not remember shopping very much at all, because my mother, who was a dressmaker by trade, do you remember her yard rule, made all our clothes, skirts, dresses, coats etc. I think we bought socks and underwear from Woolworths, and I remember going to get shoes from a special shop who took the vouchers that were given to us by the National Assistance Board, but they were always awful lace ups which I hated and as I had big feet usually only one pair to choose from. The first really nice dress I had from a shop my husband to-be bought me for Christmas when I was 16.

I did work in a shop though as a Saturday girl. A general grocers, no health and safety in those days, biscuits in tins, bacon on the slicer or by hand but only by the manager, the stock room full of sacks containing currants, raisons and sugar all to be weighed out by hand usually by me. No latex gloves to wear - you served and took the money.

NO calculators to add up the money you wrote on the customers paper bag or white paper that the cold meats were wrapped in £ s d in those days, still good at adding up today.

After the shop closed on a Saturday everything had to be washed down the bacon slicer taken apart and the wooden counter scrubbed with boiling hot water. I think soda was added to the water, played havoc with your hands.

All our food shopping was done at the local parade of shops, butchers, bakers, greengrocers etc. I remember a hairdressers as well do you remember hot perms!.

After I married I still made most of my own clothes, and the children's when they came along, over the years I put on a lot of weight so once again clothes shopping was not an enjoyable experience, and I usually ended up making something myself if it was a special occasion. Later I was to discover club books where you could try things on in your own bedroom and they did bigger sizes, I still use club books today particularly for evening wear. I don't make any clothes any more have slimmed down quite a bit so am able to buy more easily, I do go shopping with girlfriends etc. but enjoy the coffee and cake or lunch out more than the trying on etc. is that because I never got a taste for it early on I wonder.

Just to finish do any of the ladies remember navy blue knickers with a pocket in them, my dad called them my Tate & Lyles because sugar used to come in blue bags, always made me remember him when in the stock room weighing out the sugar.

SHOPPING

We had two shopping areas: one about 10mins walk away, for everyday things and secondly either a 20 min walk or bus ride for a wider range of goods.   The first, referred to locally as "up the top" had an amazing range of shops.   It would take less than 5 min to walk from one end to the other, and this was only on one side of the road.   There were 2 butchers, fishman, chemist, newsagents, post office, baker, hardware and ironmonger, co-op and off licence – probably more. Apart from the Co-op they were privately owned and seemed to make a living.   I realise that for a good part of my childhood it was wartime, and rationing lasted much longer – but there was enough for our needs.

And, a meeting place for chatting with friends and neighbours.   This was situated on London Road which carried most of the buses going into Portsmouth and Southsea so it also connected you with the wider world.

The other choice for shopping was at North End, referred as "going down North End" – these phrases sound rather comical now, but were in general use by all.   This was still part of London Road but much busier with a wider range of shops.   Boots, Woolworths and Marks & Spencers were there and the rest once again were small businesses.   We had three department stores, two cinemas, the library, bus depot and a wonderful selection of smaller shops which had their own personality and their own smell.   A small department store called Melanies was perfumed, and it was rather a superior kind of shop in which to work. Cosmetics, lingerie and fashion were predominant – definitely a woman's shop.   It was such a treat to visit here.   Another treat was the Landport Drapery Bazaar – which was not in any way fashionable but when you paid for goods the bill and money whizzed across the air to a

Shopping

small box near the ceiling, where a cashier dealt with it. That was a position for a child to aspire to! There was a large baker's shop called Smith & Vosper with a restaurant on the first floor, occasionally my mother and I would go for tea and a fancy cake. I was lucky to live in an age where such simple things gave so much pleasure. The Vospers of Smith & Vospers were related to the boat building firm in Old Portsmouth.

Earlier this year we revisited Portsmouth, and travelled by bus through North End. I could have wept it was down at heel and down market. One cinema had vanished and the other a splendid 1930s Odeon was crumbling and was now a discount warehouse. Planners may disfigure an area but they cannot touch your memories.

Sylvia Edwards 18.7.

Shopping

In my first four years, we lived on the outskirts of Burton on Trent and shopping opportunities were limited. We had milk and bread delivered, as was normal in those days and fresh vegetables were available at a nearby small holding called 'Gees', run by Mr and Mrs Gee, who also stocked a small range of other items including tinned goods. For anything else we had to go down the long hill to the main road where there was a corner shop or catch a bus from there into town.

There was a good selection of shops in Burton, including a market on some days. As all towns in the early fifties it was a bustling centre except on Thursdays when it was half day closing and Sundays when all shops closed all day. There were many corner shops in Burton away from the town centre and they seemed to be open all day and every day.

Burton market 1954. Grandma (right) chats to a friend. Mum is next to her next to my sister. Auntie Beryl holds the pram where my cousin Lynn sits. I look on with my back to the camera. I was four then, my sister seven.

I remember more about Rugby and the village we lived in, Newbold. We had a post office, which also sold groceries and other items, a butchers and a Co-Op in the village. Every week my mum filled in her order book and took it down to the Co-Op for all the groceries we needed. The order was then delivered returning the book in which the items were ticked off or crossed out if not available. Mother must have gone along at some point to pay the bill and get her 'divi', the dividend which was the old way of awarding the loyalty points of today, her number was 583, an unusually short number I recall. As well as the daily milk and bread deliveries, we also had weekly rounds by tradesmen for fish (by Patchetts), for tea and for hardware including paraffin (by Colliers).

A bus would take us into town for any other items. It was quite an outing to go **'up town'** as we said, (but it **was** literally up a hill into town) but I don't remember us going regularly, only when we needed to. As mother made most of our clothes and knitted most of our cardigans and jumpers, the visits were usually to buy material or wool. Rugby had a decent shopping centre in the fifties and sixties which included a large C0-Op department store in Regent Street which had at least two floors of shopping area. It also had a strange vacuum driven system used to transport the money you paid in cylindrical tubes up to the cashier's office where the change was put into the tube and sent down again. There was another building in Chapel Street which housed other C0-0p departments e.g. furniture and toy departments, as well as their offices where mum went to have her divi book made up and cash in the money due if she wished. Asda now sits on the land where that Co-op building stood. The High Street was buzzing in those days with Woolworths, Boots, Marks and Spencers and branches of all major retailers. MacFisheries, W H Smith, Sam Robbins Department Store, Briggs, Freeman Hardy and Willis, all had branches in town. We frequented record shops at Bosworth and Carvells, and Berwicks. George Masons, Liptons, International Stores, Ben Radio and Yates all filled the town, none of them self-service as we have now. In the sixties I worked as a Saturday girl in Woolworths and then Marks and Spencers standing behind the counters. There were no empty shops then. The half day closing for Rugby used to be Wednesday.

Rugby also had a market on Monday morning and Saturdays. It was situated quite a way out of town, next to the cattle market at the bottom of Railway Terrace. It was eventually moved to Rugby town centre in Lawrence Sherriff Street by the public toilets opposite the Squirrel Pub, then again moved to the area outside Brotherhood house in Castle Street next to the current multi story carpark which wasn't there then. It also used land behind the Rupert Brook Pub (one of Weatherspoon's pubs) now used as a car park. Only in recent years has it gone back to its original home, around the clock tower.

Sometimes we went out of town to a city like Coventry or if staying with grandmother in Burton we would go to Derby. This was amazing as we visited large stores we never had in Burton or Rugby, C & A, British Home Stores and many large retailers few of which remain today. They sold racks of amazing clothes which took my breath away. Usually we were treated to something new on these very exciting outings.

I can remember a special shopping trip in Rugby when mother took me to town to buy my school uniform. I never had so many new items at once, from navy knickers to the blazer and blouses, overalls for cooking and science to the sportswear. Some items came from the Co-Op but many from a very expensive shop in High Street, the name I forget, which specialised in the individual items for each of Rugby's schools where a uniform was compulsory.

It was in the 1970's that shops started to become self-service. I didn't have to buy groceries until I married in 1970 and our local shops were old fashioned but soon followed the trend set by the large stores and changed to self-service. It did seem quicker but I thought played into the hands of thieves and dishonest people.

The next huge change was the introduction of credit cards and bank cards. We could get cash out of the 'wall' without having to go into the bank and at all times of the day and night. But the credit card made the biggest change to our lives. It took me and my husband a long time to embrace them as we wanted only to buy things when we could afford them. We had never embraced credit and rarely bought items on hire purchase. I did once have a loan from the bank to buy a car but soon paid that off. I remember in 1991 when we went to Florida for a family holiday, although we had credit cards they were just for an emergency. It caused some surprise that we did not want to use them to pay by card but in fact we were forced to pay for some things that way as some American businesses would not accept anything else. Unfortunately this has led to many people running up debts they could never pay and getting into financial difficulties. My eldest son did just that and when he had sorted his problem out he refused to have a credit card again for many years to avoid it happening again. I think he now uses cards a little more carefully but he will never be good with money. In reverse his younger brother would not use a credit card even though he was given one with his student account. He is very careful with money but when he joined us on a cruise some years ago he had to have a credit card for his on board account and so had to obtain one. He had great difficulty as he had no credit history and so no credit rating. His only option was to go to the bank where he had his student account as it was aware of his financial history.

Change never stands still and the last change to our shopping habits is of course the internet. Whist reluctant to embrace this technology, we did relent as sometimes it is the only way to get what you want, or get it at the cheapest price. I don't remember the first item we bought on line, it was probably a holiday, but I regret, that even though I do try to shop locally these days, I am driven to the internet by necessity, a sad end to our high streets.

I enjoyed the days of popping into town. Looking in shop windows for items I probably couldn't afford but would have liked to have. Our town, like many others, is full of empty shops caused by bad planning decisions and internet shopping but we still head out of town to a large shopping centre each November or December to do our Christmas shopping. I do enjoy some retail therapy but unfortunately I get tired easily and cannot keep up the pace to be a true shopaholic for too long.

Cooking

COOKING

We thought this might be a rather dull subject for our meeting. How wrong we were! It was surprising that about half of us had memories that did not include anything to do with cooking. But even that did not stop enlightening discussion about why there was no recollection.

Some of us were boys – excluded from the kitchen in those days in the middle of the twentieth century. Some of us were faddy eaters and didn't want anything to do with food. (but that just went to prove that our childhood distaste has little to do with later life). One of our group declared, "If it takes longer to prepare than it does to eat, cooking is a waste of time!"

What most of us remembered however was our parents' ability to make meals from very few ingredients. Very often the meal that we all sat down to eat together was "dinner" that was consumed around mid-day. Mothers, whose main role in life was to look after the home, would spend a good part of the morning preparing the mid-day meal except on Mondays. Mondays was cold meat day. Leftovers from the Sunday Roast. This was necessary because Monday was washday. No time for cooking.

Rationing during and after the second world war seemed to feature in most of our cooking experiences but sometimes this was most detrimental. One group member was banned for learning to cook because her mother could not afford to waste the ingredients. At school, girls were taught cooking. This started at age eleven (or sometimes younger) and went on until fourteen or fifteen on a weekly basis. We heard that now, if cooking is taught at school at all, it is restricted to probably one term during the whole time at secondary school.

Cooking

In our early days, few of us could recollect going to a restaurant. A couple of us could remember being taken out for our first meal to celebrate our twenty-first birthdays!

Read on for our individual stories.

Cooking As I Remember.

Grandma cooked mainly in the oven next to the coal fire. Her baked rabbit and roast potatoes followed by creamy milk puddings were delicious. Her jacket potatoes cooked in this way were also very good.

Most families grew their own vegetables. These were picked fresh on the day they were to be used and tasted so much better than the super market choice of today. Offal was cheap so liver, kidneys, hearts, sausages and minced meat were frequently used. Chicken seemed to be a luxury for Christmas unless a friend who kept them gave you one.

Fish was on Fridays but there was always a roast dinner on Sunday with Yorkshire pudding eaten first accompanied with gravy. Monday being wash day was cold meat fried left over vegetables with pickles, homemade of course. Tripe was popular if you could stand the sight and smell of it.

My boy friends" mother lived in the country. Her garden was like a small field with fruit trees and bushes. As she had a large walk in pantry these fruits were gathered and preserved in Kilner jars ready for fruit pies, tarts and steamed puddings served during the winter months

Spotted dick made and wrapped up in a piece of sheeting, and meat and fruit boiled puddings in basins with sheet covering the top, all cooked in water in a saucepan were firm favourites. The top covering of material made it easier to get the red hot basin out of the water.

With pigs at the top of the garden nothing was wasted when killing time arrived. There were joints for roasting, rashers for frying and chops for dinner. The head made brawn, the meat pork pies, intestines were for chitterlings and or course pigs trotters.

Cooking

Some days we had a good fried breakfast this consisted of bacon egg tomatoes mushrooms with fried bread, what a good start to the day. Later whilst camping many a splendid meal was conjured up all cooked on a Primus stove.

COOKING

The kitchen in my first house was tiny — it was built in 1930s when all that was needed in a kitchen was a sink and a cooker and a little space to work. There were no fridges or freezers, microwaves, washing machines, tumble driers and certainly no dishwashers! We did have a pantry with a stone floor, this was where food was stored and kept cool, but when fridges and freezers became commonplace cooking was revolutionised.

Kitchen in a 1930's house

Before then people shopped regularly and there were more deliveries – roundsmen from bakeries, butchers, dairies, fishmongers all delivered daily or weekly. Some shops, like the Coop would deliver an order and joy, oh joy, when you bought from them you had a "divi"(dividend) at the end of the year! Who can remember their Coop number—ours was 19627. Corona pop was delivered weekly and you got tuppence back when you returned the bottle.

Cooking

RUGBY
U3A

Corona pop delivery

Unlike the deliveries from Tesco or Sainsbury's they always came to the back door. Cooking was a daily job apart from the stone floor there was nowhere to keep food fresh.

We tended to eat a cooked meal at mid-day and then have a lighter meal at tea-time. I came home from school for dinner and my father came home mid-day; my mother didn't work so she spent her morning preparing dinner for us. I can remember my grandmother heating up a meal for my grandfather when he came home at night by putting a covered plate of food over a pan of boiling water.

I still have the fork my grandmother used to mix cakes _ its tines are worn down at a 45 angle from all the beating and I have kept it to remind me how lucky I am to have an electric mixer!

Grandma's mixing fork

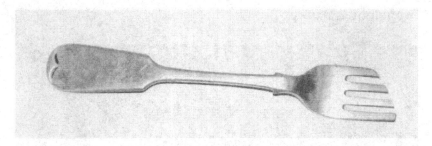

Both my grandfathers and my own father grew vegetables, so these were fetched from the garden immediately before cooking. Nowadays we would call them organic! We had the vegetables and fruit which were in season – our first meal with new potatoes was always (tinned) salmon, peas, parsley sauce and of course the new potatoes. It was often my job to shell the peas, I think I ate as many as I put in the pan. My grand-dad used to put an enamel bucket over the rhubarb to "force" it. The first rhubarb was sweet and I still look forward to picking the first rhubarb from my own garden. How we looked forward to the strawberry crop! Fruit grown in the garden was made into jam or bottled to keep it, apples were stored on trays and lasted until the winter if kept in a cool place. Salt came in bricks and it was my job with a spoon to scrape it out to salt down beans in kilner jars – a layer of salt and a layer of beans. When they were used they had to be soaked beforehand to get rid of the salt. I was never keen on salted beans, but I have never tasted runner beans as nice as the ones my grandmother cooked – I wish I had asked for the secret!

Salted beans in Kilner Jars

I don't know whether gas cookers were the forerunners or whether my mother and both my grandmothers preferred them, but we had a gas cooker during my childhood and if we weren't careful the gas, which was on a meter, would run out and we had to have a shilling ready to put in so that the meal wouldn't be spoilt.

As a child I didn't really cook, but I was given the left over bits of pastry to form into shapes – by the time I'd finished with it, it was a bit grey! I was always waiting to scrape out the cake bowl – I do that even now when no-one's looking. I suppose food was still rationed when I was growing up, soI wouldn't have been allowed to experiment in case I wasted it!

The war was over by the time I came along, but it was still near enough for me to hear tales of how inventive people were when food was scarce. We are told now that the diet was far healthier than nowadays when food has so many additives and preservatives.

When I first had cookery lessons at school we had to break the eggs into a cup before adding to cake mixture, just in case they were bad! There were no "sell by" dates or "use by" dates on food, so you never really knew how old it was when you bought it! Flour had to be sifted to sort out the lumps and there was no soft margarine to cream for cakes. Milk could "go off" quickly because there were no fridges to keep it really cold in the hot weather.

Sifting flour

My husband's family home still had a pig sty. Families kept pigs fed on scraps of food and killed them to eat the meat. My mother's family were country people who reared hens and geese for meat, but generally chicken was a treat only for Christmas. Rabbit was a popular meat, but when myxomatosis was introduced to kill off the rabbits then it disappeared from the shops. I remember having rabbit stew (casserole would be the fashionable word now!) and I think it tasted a bit like chicken.

Rabbits hanging in a butchers shop

My grandmother used to cook tripe and onions and I enjoyed this _until I realised what it was! Another delicacy our family ate was elvers _baby salmon. My grandmother's sisters came from Gloucestershire, where the salmon breed and each year we would have, a parcel through the post containing elvers.

Fishing for Elvers   *A plate of Elvers*

Most families enjoyed a roast dinner on Sundays and because Monday was always washing day, which left little time for cooking the meat was eaten cold with left over vegetables fried and pickles. This was called "Bubble and Squeak".

Puddings were always served after dinner— rice puddings, steamed puddings, covered with a cloth and put over a steamer for hours!, pies or fruit

When I worked in school I was amazed at how little cooking the young mothers seemed to do. When I asked for volunteers to come to help the children to cook panic came into their eyes and they told me they couldn't make cakes and when I offered to make mince pies one Christmas with another teacher's class she opened her eyes wide and said "Can you make mince pies?" Ready meals and frozen food and easily available cakes and pastries mean that today people don't need to cook—just heat food and the microwave is there to ensure that this is done quickly, but then most people are at work all day and don't have the time to spend preparing meals. What a shame that they never have the satisfaction of seeing a row of pots of home-made jam, or a batch of scones fresh from the oven.

Homemade jam

Cooking in the 30s
by John Hobson.

Of the skills at which I am incompetent, cooking is near the top of the list. As a primary schoolboy through the 30s, it may not be surprising that I was never allowed near fire.

Our farmhouse wasn't wired for electricity until just before the war so my mother was limited to three sources of heat, the open fire in the kitchen with a cast iron oven alongside, the paraffin oil stove in the scullery and, later, "The Billy".

This was a fearsome flat-topped monster which stood in splendid isolation, also in the scullery, supplying hot water to the primitive plumbing. For simmering the pot of breakfast porridge or any other item requiring slow heat, "The Billy" was ideal.

Otherwise it was the oil stove that provided the flames. Although two of the burners were below an oven, Mum used the one beside the kitchen open fire for roasting and baking. It required constant replenishing with coal and logs for a steady heat and the results were magnificent.

Hungry menfolk on the farm depended on Mum's cooking and my father, brother and I were well content. Ham, bacon, pork, poultry, rabbit, eggs, milk, cream, butter and all the fruit and vegetables were readily available. Not so beef, mutton and fish. The relatively few items the farm and high walled kitchen garden didn't offer were delivered to the door from the grocer's, butcher's, baker's and fishmonger's vans.

Although never entrusted with cooking duties indoors, I *was* allowed to boil the pig potatoes over a log fire within a sturdy old oil drum in a corner of the orchard. When well and truly soft, I mixed the little potatoes with pig meal with my hands. The lovely squelchy, warm satisfaction remains with me still.

On second thoughts, there was an indoor example of trust; making toast. We had a very long-handled toasting fork made by my father with strong wire, a trick (among others) with wire he'd learned as a young jackaroo on a New South Wales cattle station before WW1.

Jerry, the ancient farm cat was jet black. One cold day in 1933 she crept into the kitchen oven for warmth. The fire was almost out, the oven door had been left ajar and in she must have crept for relief from the frigid old farmhouse.

This well-meaning five year old unwittingly closed the oven door in passing, not aware of Jerry's hideaway. An hour later someone must have heard plaintive cries from within and opened the oven door. Jerry survived, wringing wet with perspiration but uncooked to enjoy her ninth life.

Cooking for Myself

My Grandmother was a wonderful cook. She learned her craft through two world wars and by the time I was five, she was responsible for feeding me. My Mum was convalescing from TB and therefore when I had walked home from school for my lunch, it was my Grandmother who provided the fare. (School was about three-quarters of a mile away and there was no question of being collected – not after the first day anyway).

My Grandmother made wonderful Broth. I suppose you would call it "Scotch Broth". Always made from bones collected from the butcher and packed with good root vegetables. When there wasn't any broth made, and as a special treat, I would get a bowl of Heinz Tomato Soup. (Only Heinz would do – I could easily tell the difference between Heinz and any other brand).

I remember one day coming home from school to be presented with a bowl of different soup. It was not nearly up to Grandmother's normal high standard. In fact it tasted ….. well just funny.

"What's this?" I asked.

"Well there wasn't enough broth left so I put a tin of Tomato Soup in with it."

"But it's horrible", (five year olds are always prone to exaggeration)

"But you like Broth and you like Tomato Soup so why don't you like them together?"

"I don't know. A small bowl of Broth and a small bowl of Tomato soup would have been fine."

Cooking

So began my life as a gourmet!

I wasn't really encouraged to cook at home. Cakes where what the family made and when we had meat it was either roast or stewed. There was also a "Beef Mould" that one of my aunts made – rather like "luncheon meat" and really quite nice. But in all these things it was women's work and young boys were excluded for the kitchen.

When I was eleven, (1958) I joined the Boy Scouts. We had an incredible Scoutmaster who had the attitude of "You look after yourself. Don't expect me to do anything for you." We grew up very quickly. Scout camp was where I learned my cooking, over an open fire. We had to collect wood from the local area and get the fire lit even in the rain! The wood always burned with filthy smoke and it would take us ages to get the pots and pans cleaned up after our meal. No brillo pads either. We had to use gravel, sand and grass. (points were deducted for dirty pans). It was amazing how quickly we learned to bake potatoes in the fire ash and meat was bar-b-qued on green wood skewers. We even had a competition to boil an egg in a paper bag. (Yes it is possible).

It was later in my Boy-Scouting days when I was about fifteen (1961/2) that we really learned how to cook good grub. It happened one summer when three of us had managed to wangle ourselves a weekend working on a sheep farm in the middle of Northumberland. We didn't get paid but the farmer's wife fed us and we slept in the barn on top of the straw bales. That was the first time I was offered *fresh* milk. By fresh I mean that it had only been out of the cow for a few minutes. Warm with lumpy bits of cream in it. A very different drink to the ice-cold milk that I was used to by this time.

It was a wonderful weekend, warm and sunny and by Saturday evening we were all pretty tired. We were walking along a farm track going back for an evening meal when right in front of us a large rabbit popped out of its hole. We were so close it was petrified and froze. My friend bent down and picked it up by the neck.

"Look what I've got!" he said as he gave it a swift chop on the neck. We now had a very dead rabbit with a well broken neck.

"First rule of hunting," he said, "if you kill it you eat it!" (A mantra I have lived with ever since).

We went to the farmer's wife and explained that we would be dining out that night, if she would give us a bit of butter and some potatoes. Armed with our rabbit, a couple of large potatoes and half a pound of butter we set out to find a quiet spot.

First job, light your fire. Easy, mid-summer and it was dry. We soon had a good blaze going and the potatoes, covered in mud, were placed in the embers.

Next, skin and clean your rabbit. Here you have to be really careful. If you nick the guts with your sheath knife the meat is ruined. The first cut is across the belly (not length-ways) when you are in you can unzip it and take the skin off like an overcoat. Off with its head and when all the innards have been stripped out it's on to the green stick and over the fire.

Basting – this is done with the half pound block of butter. When the flesh looks a bit dry, rub the butter over it.

When is it done (properly cooked) – well you don't want it to be burned. Our method was simple. Slice off a bit of nicely browned meat and eat it. If the bit under the slice we had eaten was not yet brown, continue with the butter and rotate on the spit until nicely browned again.

Eventually, what was left of the rabbit fell off the spit and landed in the embers. There it remained as we continued to pick at, now blackened, bits of meat. By the end of our meal there was only bones left. The whole half pound of butter had been used up and very little of it was used on the baked potatoes. Three very well fed Boy Scouts.

The rabbit skin was rolled up and I took it home to cure. A friend of mine had a Rabbit Fur waistcoat and I was very envious. He let me try it on once and it felt wonderfully warm (the original organic "body warmer"). My rabbit skin was pegged out, scraped, cleaned with salt (it should have been saltpetre but I couldn't get any of that) and eventually softened up with oil. I had that rabbit skin for several years but never got any more so I never got to make my own waistcoat. I remember the rabbit though. I've eaten rabbit many times since but I have never enjoyed it like that first one.

Do fifteen year old boys learn to cook in the 21st century. I suspect the good old "health and safety" would get in the way.

Joe Heckels

Cooking

No such thing as convenience foods, fridges or microwaves when I was young. So fresh vegetables and fresh meat were very much the order of the day.

Thinking back to when I was a child when we lived in Northern Ireland where food and cooking didn't have such a high profile. I don't ever recall going to a restaurant. The village where we lived just had the basic essentials such as a grocers, greengrocers and bakers shop. We had to travel into Newry, a bus journey away, if we needed anything more in a larger choice of shops. I don't recall clearly how much Dad grew in his garden, but remembering clearly when I was older when in Swindon, our garden was crammed full of vegetables so we would have never been hungry.

What I do clearly remember was that money was never plentiful when we were in Ireland so Mum never had many of the luxuries we now take for granted. Dad was always interested in backing horses and when he had the good fortune to have a winner he would hand over his winnings to Mum and this would be spent on a joint of meat and all the trimmings.

I was a nightmare when it came to food that I wouldn't eat, beetroot was my particular favourite there was always a full dish on the table, so this is where my love started. School dinners were also a nightmare for me I would never eat them as I was very picky, when my Auntie Aggie worked at the school she would pay particular attention to me and try to coax me, but alas in vain!!!

On many visits to my grandmother's house there would always be a large saucepan of Irish Stew on the range, so we were always welcome to have a meal with them. It was quite normal to have bantam chickens in the back garden so we always had plenty of eggs alongside the staple diet of potatoes. Soda bread was also very popular and Mum always kept back sour milk to make this, she continued to make this up until we all left home.

Memories are clearer when we moved to Swindon, Dad had a very large garden and was always well stocked in the growing season with all our favourite vegetables, enough to keep the neighbours fed too. The neighbours were also keen to share their produce too. As I became older I never really had a love affair with food, thinking back I really only liked vegetables and would only eat good quality meat. This is still the same today as I never liked to eat fatty meat but of course there is a more varied diet now and I never wanted to encourage my boys to be as awkward as I was.

Mum was always good at baking, coming from Wales she always made Bakestones (Welsh cakes) Victoria Sandwich and Soda Bread farls. We had a roast meal every Sunday with of course loads of vegetables from the garden. They certainly had a fantastic flavour despite the carrots being very varied in shape, how I long for that taste now. I was always sent into Swindon armed with 10 shillings which bought me a joint of meat, bread and some pudding ingredients, where are those days now!!!!!!

Domestic Science at school proved a minor disaster for me, I tried my hand at making pancakes but as many of us now experience if the pan isn't hot they turn out a little like scrambled egg, this is what happened so I didn't take anything home, Mum then refused to let me cook again unless I was supervised as she couldn't afford to spoil good ingredients. I was allowed to cook again at school but I don't recall anything I made being a resounding success. Good that Mum helped me learn to bake, as now I make a mean Lemon drizzle cake and great scones.

Choices of food were a little more varied when I married and the boys came along but it was still a battle to get them to eat healthily. I clearly remember a particular meal where the boys were given a lamb roast meal and picked at it until the gravy became cold and very unappetising, eventually ending up in the bin. Because my parents always emphasised how important a good diet was I always prepared healthy meals for the boys, however ungrateful they were and constantly I remind them of this. As one of my boys has his own family now and encounters similar mealtime battles I raise a smile and comment that it will get better, he is living proof.

MEMORIES OF COOKING FROM CHILDHOOD

I was born after the war in 1947. By then rationing was coming to an end, although I still remember sweets remained scarce until 1953. Both Mam and Dad were good cooks – Dad especially good at breakfasts and Sunday roasts. After church on Sundays, Dad's shift-work permitting, we always came home to freshly made pancakes which we could have with syrup or lemon and sugar or the full fry up of bacon, eggs, sausages and mushrooms and fried bread! Looking back I don't know how we managed to have room for the roast dinner which seemed to follow a few hours later! More about the food later!

Milk was delivered every day to our doorstep, and as we didn't have a fridge for many years it was difficult to keep fresh in warmer weather. Luckily we had a pantry with a marble shelf where it could be safely stored. (occasionally in a bucket of cold water). We had various delivery vans – Contalls the greengrocer – a very large truck which opened up completely at the side with a counter – Mum would go out with shopping bag lined with newspaper, buy potatoes, onions, carrots and greens and the odd can of tinned fruit. All the other fruits etc. were bought in Newcastle Big Market. We had a fishmonger call once a week. The Ice Cream van – Mark Tony's – with the ice cream we described as 'back street' ice cream, most delicious of all with little bits of ice in it. Far nicer than what came later with 'Mr Whippy' – far too soft and no ice!! The Pop truck, fizzy drinks, delivered once a week. Dandelion and Burdock, ginger beer and ice cream soda being our favourites. This wasn't a regular purchase in our house, only once in a while during the summer. Ringtons tea also called – loose leaf tea only as tea bags hadn't yet been invented!

Foods, especially vegetables were only available if they were in season and not many imported. We did have oranges, bananas, grapes and pomegranates which probably were shipped into the country. Usually though, we only seemed to eat seasonally. Damsons, plums, rhubarb, loganberries and blackberries all available – usually free by picking on country walks or given to us by neighbours that had an abundant supply in their gardens. These were especially good – Mum made loads of jam with our supplies – well worth all the bother of all the cleaning and preparing the jars and fruit. Many an afternoon would be spent top and tailing gooseberries and de stalking blackberries!! It seemed the normal task to Mum's generation and we were so glad it was as it tasted truly delicious. One of Mum's sisters, Auntie Norah, was into bottling and pickling especially. In a gigantic dresser at the top of her stairs she had filled from top to bottom, inside and out, with jars upon jars of all manner of things from pickled eggs, chutneys, jams and bottled fruit and vegetables. Very industrious!!

I suppose we had quite a bland diet in my childhood – At school, it was usually a set menu for the week – so knowing what day of the week it was, we knew what our meal would be! Think this was the normal pattern for most school dinners. Mum was a dinner lady for a while and worked at my school, so she always knew what we had as she'd helped to prepare it! Some of the dinners were awful and puddings even worse – especially the tapioca (we called it frogs eggs). Some things were delicious, but not many. Children didn't take sandwiches to school for lunch and only children living very close to school were allowed home at lunchtimes. We would have a sandwich and cake or scones when we got home from school. Sunday, at home would be a roast dinner. In school holidays, Monday being washday (and all that involved) we would usually have cold cuts with some veg followed by remains of a fruit pie or rice pudding. Other usual meals were stews, minced beef which was made into cottage pie, liver and onions, and fish pie. We really had plenty of nourishment, but perhaps not much variety! As I have mentioned, my Dad worked in shifts so wasn't always around at mealtime in the evening, but we always ate as a family regardless of whether he was at work or not. It seemed a very important time to discuss the day's happenings and get together.

When mealtimes didn't include Dad, he used to have a meal kept on a plate, which would be put aside to be put into the oven and reheated later. As I mentioned earlier, Dad was quite a good cook, but some of his dishes were never eaten by the rest of the family. Roasted Pigs Head and Tripe and onions to name but two! None of us could be tempted to try them!! But he couldn't be bettered at making roast beef and Yorkshire puddings. His Yorkshire puddings were still the best I've ever tasted – they would always raise tower high above the baking tins, and be light, fluffy and crispy. If there were any leftover after dinner, we would all want them with a good dollop of golden syrup. He could never make enough!! Another favourite of mine were Dad's kidneys on toast – always in a beautiful creamy sauce – heavenly!

My mam trained me well in baking. I didn't have any choice! My sisters don't recall helping at all. Perhaps Mam had more time with me as I was the youngest. Fruit pies, Victoria sandwich cake, scones, were my weekly chore at weekends. I wasn't always keen to help as I'd rather be outdoors! However, I am so glad I was encouraged. I remember having two cookbooks in the house – Mrs Beetons Household management, which was about four inches thick – very elaborate recipes – often stating to use a dozen eggs. It had the most beautiful arty pages of very ornately decorated and exotic foods. I was always paging through it – years later I remember looking at that same book to find I'd drawn inside the cover! Bero flour cookbook was the other. I still use this today – replaced over the years as new editions were published. It contained all the straightforward cakes, scones, biscuits, pies and Xmas cake. I don't ever remember making dinners when young only baking, baking and more baking!

As well as baking at home, in senior school we had domestic science class once a week. Only the girls did this – the boys had woodwork and metalwork. Very sexist! We learnt everything from cleaning, laundering and cooking. Baking everything from coconut haystacks to Christmas Cake. It was a lesson I enjoyed thoroughly and really has equipped me in life.

Now in the 21st century life sometimes feels far removed from the era I grew up in. No microwave ovens, ready meals, frozen pastry and all the non-seasonal vegetables etc. The popularity of foreign foods and new flavours has increased, probably since the 1960's, with millions taking package holidays and the influence of new immigrants to Britain. We now have access to all the worlds foods as transportation has evolved.

We now have so much choice of what we eat – but – are we healthier! Food for thought.......

Cooking childhood memories

I was very lucky that my parents were extremely resourceful and I never remember being hungry. There were never any clever fanciful recipes and serving dishes were never used. In fact we had relatives to stay once and I remember asking what they were for when the vegetables were put in them on the table.

Recipes were handed down and often scribbled on scraps of paper. Where ever possible basic ingredients were home grown, reared in the duck pen or grown on dad's beloved allotment. Being a shift worker he was able to dig in daylight during the week. The allotment Association or The Pickle Cabbage Club played quite a sociable part in my parents' life. Dad always had to go off to pay for his soot at lunchtimes when he was home and it never occurred to me that soot was a horticultural necessity all year round.

The Pickle club Show was the high light of the year when onions would be polished, kidney beans straightened, homemade pickles and chutneys and jams all brought out to compete for the prizes. Mum was always at a disadvantage when cherry cakes were required. In desperation she bought a packet mix and used this instead of the original recipe. This devious method of beating the neighbours was used when tins of bought peaches were opened and put carefully into Kilner jars sealed and displayed and labelled as HOME MADE. When questioned about her devious habits her reply was "Well the judge is a domestic science teacher and she jolly well should know the difference! Needless to say we all fell about laughing when her 1st prize certificates were awarded.

Rabbit was served regularly as a week day meal together with veg from the allotment. Chickens were killed and used on special occasions and the Christmas cockerel was fattened up early. Then dad wrung his neck and mum feathered and drew it. The baby chicks were always bought in the spring from the city market and reared in the fire place by the warm oven, even the baby ducks learned to swim in a bowl there. Then the chickens laid eggs and they found Rhode Island reds were the best layers. Fish heads and bones were bought from the chip shop up on Yardley Road and they were boiled in a cauldron on an open fire in the duck pen to make a mash. In the war you were supposed to register your eggs if you had more than your quota and then supply neighbours with the surplus. I never did think my parents could add up properly.

If it was Irish stew with a cheap cut of lamb, the rule was if anything was lost or left about dad would add it to the saucepan to add to the flavour. Often dad used his catapult if he was held up at signals in the country. He also had a shoot with uncle Ernie for pigeons or anything else that was edible. My grandma hated rabbit so I remember mum roasting a rabbit she dressed and stuffed it to look like a chicken and it was served with veg and roasted potatoes. All went well until someone found some lead shot in their meat and the penny dropped that chickens were not killed in this way.

Auntie Connie's daughter worked for Cadburys but in the war became a demonstrator working for the government food office. She showed housewives how to substitute ingredients in recipes using dried egg powder or sugar substitutes. Mum used chopped swede in a syrup for pineapple pieces. We had whale meat steaks served with fresh new stinging nettles as spinach. Rhubarb and custard was a stalwart pudding closely followed by boiled suet apple pudding cooked in a shirt tail in a large saucepan. There were plenty of windfall apples to be shared and raspberry loganberry blackberry cherry were all fruits that were bottled and kept. Mum tried drying out apple rings in the oven. Copious kidney beans were salted down in huge sweet jars beside earthenware jars of eggs preserved in icing glass liquid, together with sweet jars of pickled onions. Semolina was used with cheese for welsh rarebit evaporated milk on fruit instead of cream. She made bread and butter puddings but best of all were her bread pudding made with suet and eaten straight out of the oven whilst hot.

About 1950 we used pressure cookers at school in our domestic science lessons and went along to see how they worked and fascinated by the speed and the results of the cooking she became the proud owner of one. It was used daily for stews soups ham beetroot and a disastrous experiment with jam which shot over the ceiling.

Marrows were used as substitutes especially for jam and with added ginger were quite palatable. Stuffed marrows saved on the meat ration. Liver and onions, neck of mutton sheep's hearts and skirt of beef were served when available. Soused mackerel fresh from the sea baked in vinegar and pickling spices with onions and served with bread and butter was a favourite on holiday.

So it was no wonder that it had been installed in us from an early age that if you saw a queue after the war you just had to join it.

Cooking

I cannot write about cooking without looking at food in general. I was at junior school when the war ended, and now realise just how little food our mothers had to cater with week in, week out. I have googled some notes about rationing.

I regret to say that I was a fussy feeder! And can remember sitting for long periods of time – just refusing to eat what was in front of me. I hid bits in the kitchen table drawer, under the cloth but my mother always found them. It must have been a nightmare on the meagre rations she had to hand.

Our weekly menus rarely varied. Roast on Sunday, cold on Monday, the remainder minced and put in a shepherd's pie on Tuesdays. The rest of the week provided sausages – about 80 per cent bread crumbs at the worst, liver or stuffed heart – which strangely enough I enjoyed fish which was not rationed and then we started all over again. We always had a pudding: bread pudding, bread & butter pudding, milk puddings – which I loathed – baked apples, stewed fruit and custard. Once when my mother was queuing she overheard someone passing on a recipe which we called Queue Pudding – it was crumble, thereafter apple crumble was added to our weekly menu. My father dug up our back lawn and grew potatoes and presumably other vegetables. At the end of the garden we had three Rhode Island Reds so eggs were often available. I can remember the smell of the chicken mash which was boiled up in the kitchen. Infinitely preferable to the cat fish which was also boiled up, as there was always a cat in our house. The smell was unforgettable, I can't remember having tinned cat food until after the war. Another smell which struck horror in my heart was marrow bones a-boiling in order to make stew. All sort of things went into this stew: pearl barley, lentils, vegetables and occasionally some meat. Every now and again I would bite on what I thought was a piece of potato and it was a piece of gristle from the bone itself. Ughh!

On Saturdays, I and my friends were always sent out shopping, or should I say queuing, usually at the vegetable shop. We all went with a very ill grace, although we always had a laugh and it wasn't that bad to be out together. But, what with potatoes, carrots, cabbage and fruit the basket was heavy.

Even when I was at the grammar school, I always had to get up early on Tuesday mornings and cycle to the butchers – once again to queue – one forgets what a large part of our lives this was.

There was always cake for tea, my mother enjoyed cooking, and at the weekend we had fancies. These were bought at The Yorkshire Shop, in our nearest parade of shops. I am sure my earliest memories of going there with my mother were pre-war – because I recall an incredibly delicious cake shaped like a small rabbit which was bought for me. I have never since tasted anything so good. I recall wartime bread which, although very good for our bowels, was grey and dense. I have always had a sweet tooth, and as a child bad teeth, especially as I enjoyed golden syrup and even sugar sandwiches. Also, do you remember chocolate spread - heaven!

There were always Christmas pudding and cake, and usually worries about whether there were enough pennies for the gas meter under the stairs. Food loomed very large in everyone's lives – if anyone had predicted our throwaway society it would have been unbelievable. But I was never hungry and certainly, bar my teeth, healthy. One thing I now recall is the attitude of some of the shop keepers. There was a delicatessen not far away "Cookhams" and I can see the owner now. A large man, rather like Oliver Hardy, who had a downcast, bullied wife who helped in the shop, and he was quite frightening. We rarely went there, he made every customer feel as if they had to beg for food, and it was grudgingly handed over. I am glad to say that once the war was over, and food more readily available he closed down. This situation did give shop owners a power to wield if they were so inclined.

We had a co-op in that parade of shops. We all had a co-op number and saved with our divi. It is long since vanished, but had a good atmosphere. My mother's groceries came from a shop called Pinks, we would go in once a week and leave our order book and then the shopping would be delivered by bike the next day. I recall the assistant wrapping up sugar on a square of blue paper – this was quite an art. Butter was in pats, imprinted with a flower shape.

I think I'd better stop now or I will ramble on too long as more and more memories flood back.

Our History
In
Our Objects

'THE BROWNIE BOX CAMERA'

The camera and its owner, Dorothy May Reeve.

As told by John M. Reeve.

My mother would now be 101. She was born in 1909, and died five years ago, nearly 95 years old.

She was born in Cosford, near Brownsover, the only daughter in a family of four children, the daughter of a farm labourer, working on the Boughton-Liegh estate.

Her mother died when she was 3 years old, and the children were placed in the McClure and Townsend Children's' Homes in Charles Street. The children were visited by their father every Sunday. Whilst in the home my mother met my father, who was also in the boy's home with her brothers, next door. He was eleven, she was ten. In all, their relationship covered over eighty years until they were separated by death.

When she left school the family was re-united and she went to work as a 'farm girl' (in the house and on the farm), at Tower Farm, Newbold-on-Avon, The building is still there.

At eighteen she was more or less directed, (by a visitor to the farm), to go to work in domestic service in London.

She hated her first appointment, was lonely and miserable, BUT HER LUCK CHANGED.

Through a friend she'd met in a Bible Class she gained an appointment as a 'lady's companion and chauffeuse'. Her life was transformed, almost from 'rags to riches'. She became the 'daughter' that her employers could not have, the 'brother' that their only son did not have, and she gained a loving 'mother' that she never had. Her employers were strict and very moral and upright Methodists, Liberals, hard working, originally from Rochdale, but the 'master' had worked himself up from the bottom to become the Managing Director of Turner and Newell, then a multi-national asbestos company. They were very wealthy. My mother was very happy with them. They cared for her and she was part of their family life. She stayed with them for ten years, (throughout the 1930's), until she left to marry my father in October 1939. She remained in weekly touch with this couple, and we visited them every year in Worthing, until their deaths.

Whilst living with these people my mother joined the G.F.S. (the Girls' Friendly Society), which was a Christian Mission to girls in domestic service. My father called them the God Forsaken Spinsters, which never failed to annoy my mother.

She made good lifelong friends with about seven of these 'girls'. In the early 30's one of them gave her a Brownie Box camera. Amongst the various things that they did together, they went on holidays. They graduated from the Isle of Wight to going abroad.

In 1936 they went to Germany and the Rhine land. She writes, 'In Hitler's Reign'. (they are in their 20's). They went to Obserwesel, swam in the Rhine, saw the flags flown from the houses in the streets, (Swastikas), and saw the air ship Hindenburg. They also go to Rudesheim, and other places that I cannot read (my mother's writing was atrocious). They attend and photograph a meeting of the Hitler Youth Movement, and witness youngsters running through 'fire and water for Hitler'. They also go to Wiesbaden and mix freely with local German people and staff of their hotel. Mum was impressed by the traditional leather shorts as worn by the men, and approves of German cleanliness and efficiency.

Another holiday, (not dated) of that time is to Tenerife, where again, she photographs the airship Hindenburg, and a 'young fascist' (Franco ?). My father who is in the navy at that time was hunting down gun-runners in the Spanish Civil War.

In 1937 the girls are back on holiday in Germany again. This time in Hoenschwangau, in Bavaria, staying at an imposing luxury hotel.

They go climbing the Savling and the Obserdorf mountains. Happily, 'with our German companions', (two years hence the countries are at war, and 'companions' become 'enemies'). Other places visited are Garmisch, Mittenweld, Oberammergau and Innsbruck.

In 1938 they go to Bavaria yet again, to Hoenswchangua and Swahangau. They visit the Ludwig's castles. Again they are photographed happily with German people.

However an anecdote was told by mother covering this last time. Increasingly they were greeted by the raised right arm and 'Heil Hitler'. One young lady of the group became so irritated by this that she replied, ".. .and God save the King!"

No more pictures were taken by the Box Brownie until 1945.

John Reeve

November 2010

Family Bible

My old and battered Irish bible that belonged to the Breasley family gave me the confirmation of information that I obtained from various genealogy websites. As with many bibles of the time this one was a prize' from Sunday School in Drumcondra, Dublin in 1859 and it belonged to my great-grandmother Emma Shore, given to her when she was 6 years old, and handed down to her son, my great-uncle George.

The pages are very brown and brittle and really in need of some restoration but containing such valuable names and important dates. The most significant information was the date of her marriage on 15 September 1872 to Thomas Albert Breasley in Drumcondra Church and the subsequent births of my grandfather Thomas Charles on 30 January 1874, Emma Jane on 27 February 1876 and George John on 1 July 1879. Their address in Dublin was given and the date of the death of Queen Victoria, obviously a significant figurehead at the time.

Emma or George must have been a regular churchgoer as there are eight bible verses quoted together with childish scribbling. They may have found the bible hard to read, as the printing on the pages is extremely small and may have distracted them from their studies.

I feel very fortunate to have a link with my Irish ancestors, with the bible being over 130 years old and in my possession I found many coincidences with my family. Firstly, Emma and Thomas's marriage on 15 September, the same date as my first son Haydn's birthday, their son Thomas Charles's birthday was 30 January 1874 exactly 100 years before my second son Kenton was born and their first daughter Emma Jane was born in February the same month as my sister's daughter Sarah was born.

I look at this bible and think my family handled it all those years ago and how significant it has been to me now.

MY MEMORABLE OBJECT
SHOE LAST

A very odd object to have some significance in my family you might think. I can only imagine that coming from a large family of 11 children in Ireland in the early 1900's the family were taught basic skills and probably on every street corner was a cobbler/shoemaker, which would have drawn some interest from my Dad

When we moved from Ireland in mid 50's and set up house in Swindon this was when I became aware of my Dad's shoe last. He was always working in the shed mending his working boots and shoes. At this time it was viable to repair footwear, shoes were much more sturdy and of course expensive in relation to modest wages at the

time. Dad was able to buy small sheets of footwear leather that was carefully measured and nailed to the worn sole. The last had 3 different iron moulds that fitted all the shoes he had to mend and help him make a professional finish.

I distinctly remember him mending all the family shoes as well as his own, but our shoes didn't always need a leather sole so he used rubber soles that were glued on, so our footwear was always as good as new.

Sadly when footwear became more affordable and not sturdy enough to be mended, the shoe last was confined to the top shelf in the shed and never saw the light of day. I have kept it until anyone in my family has the right setting in their home to make this a conversation piece.

I wonder if it could talk what tales it would tell and hopefully plead 'do not discard me'

MY MOTHER'S CAKE TIN

It all started when I took my mother's cake tin to the Living History group as an example of my family history.

Then, I began to think of the kitchen decorated in green and cream paint, which was considered a very suitable colour scheme, and echoed throughout the land. Linoleum on the floor, plus coconut matting. Check curtains at the window and the back door.

The cake tin lived at the bottom of the dresser, together with patty tins, saucepans and roasting tin. On the first shelf were cooking ingredients: flour, white sugar, rice (pudding only) and macaroni for the unbelievably revolting macaroni pudding we eat during the war. If lucky there were glace cherries and dried fruit. Usually baked beans and dried butter beans. Margarine, butter and lard, milk, eggs and meat were stored in the pantry. On the floor of which stood a large pot, filled with isinglass, where eggs were 'put down' and into which I resisted plunging my arm.

Apart from Sunday tea, we eat in the kitchen, I did my homework there. My mother removed the light bulb, plugged the iron into the overhead fitting and then ironed on the kitchen table.

I disliked Mondays, the feeling of the kitchen changed. A small metal bath stood on the gas stove to boil the whites. The room was steamy and on a wet day washing was strung out to dry. When ironed it was aired on the plate rack over the stove. Unusually for the times we always sent the sheets to the laundry.

In the glass fronted cabinet above the dresser china was stored. Everyday things to hand, best plates on the top shelf. Incongruously we had four cocktail glasses. My parents had a glass of port at Christmas; I have no recollection of them drinking at any other time. Maybe these glasses represented a dream? Beneath stood a fruit bowl, and on the right hand side were the newspapers, and a small tin containing my pocket money. One drawer contained tea towels and the other the cloths on which my mother ironed.

I am amazed at the details that have come to mind.

Panduffra's Box

Like many people of my generation, my father was absent fighting the War, so I didn't really know him until I was about 3.

They both died some 30 years ago and I inherited this biscuit tin which contains all the letters between my parents from that period, and must, therefore, contain details of my birth and first 3 years of life.

However, I have never actually felt able to open any of its contents, considering them private between my parents. I feel it would be prying at the least, voyeurism at the worst.

One day I, or my descendants, might actually open this window into the life of a young husband and wife forced apart by World War II.

Subsequently I had a sister and, though never financially secure, we enjoyed an idyllic childhood - but I always felt a distance between my father and myself.

John Duffield

September 2010

The Bomb

An incendiary bomb dropped on a shared entry in The Avenue, Acocks Green, Birmingham in 1940. Another bomb dropped next door, this went through the top of the bay window. I remember having to squeeze through next doors privet hedge to obtain access to our house. The camouflaged Rover Factory was at the top of the road and barrage balloons were tethered in the Muddy Lane area approaching Warwick Road.

Our shelter was under the railway bank of the Snow Hill to Paddington line. The lights in the signal box were always extinguished before the air raid siren wailed. So we were ready to move down into the shelter for the night. Our garden pond had to be filled in because my brother used to curl up and go to sleep on the way to the shelter and mum thought he might drown by mistake. Mums Spirella corsets were her most treasured possession and it was rumoured that she  never took them off until the war had ended. Jewellery and important papers were kept in a tin and always carried down with us.

Dad was a G W R driver and drove ammunition trains on double home trips where he stayed away for a night. When there was a raid he'd have to cover the fire hole up and hang tarpaulin sheets over the open side of the engine. When held up at the signals for a few hours his catapult would be put to good use for the contents of a good rabbit stew. He also would buy one piece of fruit cake from the buffet on Leamington Station as a treat to be shared.

On my fourth birthday November 14th 1940 I remember watching the glow in the sky 15 miles away as Coventry was bombed in the blitz.

World War I Wallet And Its Contents -
The Property Of 038366 Private Frank Ainge
Of The Gloucestershire Regiment1917

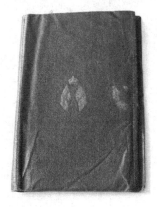

Frank Ainge was my grandfather on my mother's side of the family. Frank married Elsie Johnson in 1917 at Sambourne in Warwickshire. He was an engine driver with the Great Western Railway Company and he was called up for military service on three separate occasions. Each time he was rejected on the grounds that 'he was medically unfit to serve'. Then, due to the huge losses of men on the Western Front, he was finally accepted and enrolled in the army. By this time Elsie was pregnant with their first child.

Frank received six weeks basic training in England before being shipped to France where he did a further two weeks training. Elsie wrote to him to tell him the news that their baby would be born at the end of November. This was to be the last letter he would receive.

Within a short time of arriving in France the Cambrai tank battles were to start and Frank was moved 'up the line' to the forward trenches. All his personal possessions had to be left behind at the base camp. A letter telling him of the birth of a daughter, to be named Joyce, born on 28th November was never to reach him, being held at the base camp for his return. The first news that Elsie had was that Frank was 'missing' and later 'missing, presumed killed in action' from the War Office. His death was officially recorded on December 3. 1917.

THIS WALLET WAS THE ONLY ITEM RETURNED TO ELSIE.

L.G. Bond

The Jug

This little jug is now one of my favourite possessions and I remember it in the China Cabinet as a child.

My father bought this in Germany. After WW2 he spent time there on a "Control Commission" to make sure factories weren't making any armaments etc. and it was there that I was born. He was in the Home Guard during the war but could not join the regular forces because he worked in a steel foundry. (A reserved occupation).

We returned to England, with the Jug, when I was six months old.

The Walking Stick

My Great Grandfather, having risen from a ten year old "Pit Lad" to the esteemed position of Colliery Manager invited several local notables to his house for dinner one evening. Following the departure of his guests he noticed that someone had left their walking stick in the stand in his hallway.

Wishing to reunite the stick with its rightful owner, Great-Grandfather looked at the engraved collar. The inscription read,

> M HECKELS
> From
> A FRIEND
> 1885

He never did find out who left the stick.

Mr. Matthew Heckels died two years later.

Homemaking
and
Craft

HOMEMAKING AND CRAFT

When I received the email from Joe informing us of our next subject for Living History I began to panic as I wondering if I could write 2 lines not 2 pages. So here goes with my interpretation of Homemaking and Craft and I have been assured by Joe that I cannot be wrong!!!

I was very fortunate that when I was a young girl my Mum taught me how to bake, knit and crochet and the gaps like dressmaking and cooking were provided at school. So I was "equipped" for life, looking back I am not so sure!!!! I distinctly remember taking 2 years to make "baby doll pyjamas" hardly a resounding success

Domestic Science classes were available in school and results were rather mixed, the main disaster was my inability to make pancakes, nothing worked and I ended up eating the fragments much to the annoyance of my mother who commented that you are there to learn and you should have come home with pancakes'!!! She did however write to the school and complained that she wasn't able to afford to waste ingredients so she needed assurance this wouldn't happen again. I did successfully make a Christmas cake so now I thought I had cake making "sussed"!!!!

In my teenage years it was necessary for me learn how to make my own clothes as I wasn't earning much money so "needs must when the devil drives" and with a new sewing machine (expenses shared with Mum), clothes appeared, I was able to face the world with what I thought at the time was a trendy wardrobe. Many pictures of the time may contradict this!!!!

When I got married in 1970 we were fortunate enough to be able to get a mortgage to buy our house, so with funds rather tight we certainly had to 'make do and mend' and many people were kind to help us out with lounge furniture etc. We certainly were not able to buy new, so second-hand sheets were converted into duvet covers, pillowcases and cot sheets when the children arrived. For a short period of time I was able to buy inexpensive material to make curtains but this was short lived as shops were selling goods that never made it worth the effort. I was never keen on DIY and gardening so I was lucky that my husband was sufficiently interested in DIY to make the house presentable, but gardening was his "forte" so we always had plenty of flowers and vegetables.

Evening classes were much more accessible than they are now, budgetary constraints now means fewer or no classes for cookery and dressmaking, these were great fun and we did come away with a dish or a garment. I was able to make myself a coat which I was very proud of. I also dabbled in basket making until the craze died out, and these types of crafts became more freely available to buy cheaply on the high street.

Lucky for me knitting has made a comeback and it is now 'fashionable' to be seen in handmade knitwear, I have found it very therapeutic and with the cold weather all my sweaters have come into their own. The recent programme "The great British Sewing Bee" has rekindled my interest in sewing, but with it seemingly being very technical now I am not sure I could make anything other than a skirt that would give me the result I crave. This is where Evening Classes are needed. Lastly I am still making Christmas and birthday cards through my introduction to classes in U3A and with the computer being a great resource there are plenty of ideas and designs.

Such happy memories of easier times, I certainly learned a lot that has stayed with me today.

Margaret Jones

Crafts and Homemaking

We moved into our new house in 1960 burdened with a mortgage of £2545. The cement path ran up the drive to the back door and stopped. Our first homemaking job was to extend the path around the side and rear of the house. An acquaintance cleared out his giant cement mixer on the drive and we put down shuttering and spread out the mixture before it set hard in the hot sun.

We had a coffee table made out of a piano lid, a second hand bed and two deck chairs borrowed from next door. The lounge floor boards were sanded down and stained and we proudly constructed a three tiered bookcase out of bricks and planks and placed our plastic radio on the top. We wove lampshades out of raffene to place on top of our hand thrown pottery lamp bases. With an old single divan installed in the corner, we placed a guitar on top, hired a Van Gogh picture from the library and painted the wall behind it in bright orange emulsion.

Crafts were experienced all through childhood and these all helped towards our homemaking. Coats had been unpicked, turned inside out and remade into short jackets. Dads Harris Tweed plus fours were transformed into two pencil skirts one from each leg. Mums old summer skirts were unpicked and sewed together on the Singer treadle machine and transformed into volumous circular skirts on elastic waist bands. We twirled and danced and imitated the film stars beautifully.

The earliest craft I can recall was sticking cards and pictures into scrap books with an adhesive made from flour and water .Mum was always unravelling jumpers and knitting scarves etc. from the recycled wool. White parcel string was crocheted into two kitchen curtains. We made kites out of canes and thin paper and sewed dolls clothes out of scraps of material and cotton reels with nails hammered into the top were used for corking and the cord was then twisted round to make a table mat.

New woven dishcloths were turned into cushion covers by using various coloured darning wools woven under and over the squares. My aunt made me a bright yellow bathing costume held together with shirring elastic out of a silk parachute.

The linen tablecloths we embroidered are still in use after 60 years. My fitted bedspread I made to match the bedroom curtains was the pride of my teenage life and was piped and had a pleated valance. It was cut up to make an historical costume for Mrs Laurence Sheriff in the school play.

In the 1940s we arduously cut up white cotton sheets and remade them by hand into pillow cases with our initials embroidered on them. My brother was producing wall plaques out of plaster of paris moulded on to brass wall plates as an impression. They were then removed and hand painted and given as presents. He also melted coloured wax sticks and moulded wax flowers on to pictures.

Seasonal celebrations were always accompanied by a craft display on the sideboard. We made painted eggs and Pom Pom chickens together with tissue flowers. At Christmas we made fir cone people, wreaths and paper chains. Puppets were made out of old socks together with moving eyes, felt noses and whiskers and then we entertained the family from behind the settee.

I had to produce art homework for college and I thought I was no good at all. My brother did all my homework for me as he meticulously made the water coloured pictures look like the subject. Now I know why I prefer to paint on silk as you never know what the final result will be.

Pam Wilson May 1913.

Homemaking and Crafts

I was four at the outbreak of war and during my memorable years there was very little choice and it was cheaper to make clothes. So my mother made all of her own and mine, for which I was not grateful, and longed for a shop dress. Everyone and their mother knitted, including children. I recall at one time our local wool shop stocked only skeins of a rather strongly coloured lilac wool – absolutely nothing else. The shopkeepers simply had to take what they were given during the war. There was no choice. Most garments were knitted in 3ply I think double knitting appeared in the mid-1950s. We knitted on bone needles (I still have a pair of my mother's) there were advantages and disadvantages. Sufferers from arthritis said that metal needles troubled their hands when they first appeared, also the bone ones had the habit of snapping in the middle of a row – I can remember that quite clearly. At this time we only knitted clothes which were needed maybe just a few woollies each.

My mother made the curtains and cushions, but rarely as everything was used until it wore out – however bored you might be with the article.

My father was a painter and decorator so our house always looked well cared for – within the limits of the time. After the war I remember new wallpapers came on the market and there was a choice of two designs. We had two large handmade rugs which my father made but for the most part spare time was spent in the garden Digging for Victory.

I cannot recall any other crafts practised at home or in my friends' houses. I am sure such classes did not run at Adult Education Centres during the war. If anything it would have been helping the war effort not for the joy of creating something. Craft classes, anyhow were for the middle classes, and that I was not. Make Do and Mend was the motto.

When I married in 1955 things were changing. A much greater selection of fabrics, wool and everything connected with sewing. When the children were in bed (always early) the sewing machine came out. I have always made my curtains, cushions were much more interesting and I tried many different forms of embroidery. I longed to do patchwork but did not know where to start. Come the late '60s this changed and I have never stopped. I am currently making a quilt for the youngest great granddaughter. Every member of the family has their own quilt, and babies usually have a cushion with their name and date of birth. I have also made family samplers – all sewing, with the exception of darning and mending, gives me infinite pleasure. There is a Tudor style christening gown and bonnet, made for the eldest grandson who is 30 next year, which has been worn by every grand and great grandchild. The family treasure it.

Sylvia Edwards

Homemaking and Craft

My father was lucky (or unlucky – dependant on your point of view). . One of his uncles was an undertaker who died at about the same time we moved into a house that had a good sized shed. My father inherited all his uncle's tools, saws, chisels hammers glue pots etc. All the tools necessary to make coffins. As a 5 year old boy I was allowed to play with these tools and I soon discovered the ability to make things.

By the time I was seven or eight I had developed something of a reputation and one of the teachers at my school asked me to make a cot for her daughter's doll. It wasn't a good idea. Although I could nail some bits of wood together to make a boat that would actually float the right way up in the bath, a cot – one that rocked from side to side and had slotted sides - was completely beyond my skills. My mother thought the teacher was mad to have asked me to do it and my dad refused to help with this "exploitation". Needless to say the teacher was not impressed with my attempt to meet her requirement.

Undeterred I continued to play in the shed and moved on through the balsa wood gliders, elastic band propelled aeroplanes, marquetry pictures, toy rifles until at the age of about fourteen I made my first guitar. (It would be 45 years later before I made my second).

I got married at the age of nineteen and living in a caravan, well away from Father's tools and the shed, we started to turn our caravan into a home. There isn't a lot you can do with a caravan but we managed to paper one of the walls and make it "ours". I didn't enjoy papering walls and Pam was much better at it than me but she would never feel confident enough to put the first piece up. That was my job and then she would take over. My job, throughout our married life was to do the gloss painting. Pam was happy enough to do the emulsion but hated doing gloss paint.

Living in Army houses, fully equipped, there was little I could do and of course the absence of Dad's tools and shed was limiting, but I did make a couple of bookcases. These were just glued and nailed then painted white but they served a purpose. Made in about 1968, one of these is still in use today. Having moved from our Army house to mother-in-law and then inherited by sister-in-law it still sits in her flat in Newcastle.

My Dad died not long before we moved into our first house (before then we had lived in Army houses), and so, with Mother's permission I took most of his tools to a new home. They are still here today and in fairly constant use.

So what do we mean by Homemaking? I'm sure Pam would have written about how we bought our first Spin Dryer (just a spin dryer, not a washing machine) after we had been married for four years. This was used for helping to dry the terry-toweling nappies because our first child was using quite a few of these each day. And maybe six months later we bought a second hand twin tub washing machine. But what makes it a home? Difficult to say. Everywhere we lived in those early days felt like home even though we weren't allowed to do anything much to put our mark on it. Thinking carefully about what we did do, I think we developed an artistic eye for lighting and to this day we dislike bright lights around the house, relying almost solely on strategically placed table lights. That reminds me of the table lamp I made at school when I was thirteen. This was at my bedside until I met Pam and she told me that she didn't have one. I gave it to her and it followed us round throughout our married life. I don't know where it is now but I'm sure no-one has thrown it out. It will be making someone's home somewhere.

Homemaking

My maternal Grandfather, (in his 80's), had been a House Painter & Decorator (as had his father). Also a historic house restorer, sign-writer, etc.

My Dad, on the other hand, "couldn't even hammer a screw in straight". However, he became a skilled paperhanger. My early memories are of him trimming the boarders off the sides of rolls of wallpaper with a giant pair of paperhanger's scissors. My younger sister and I used to help scrape the old paper off the walls. Once cleared, we wrote our names and the date on the bare plaster. I particularly remember Dad using border strip to create 'Art Deco' angular decoration at the top of the walls.

My mother was a skilled home-dressmaker and made many of her own and our clothes. This was not uncommon in the days of war and post-war austerity without the distractions of television or the finances to go out for more than a weekly trip to the 'pictures'.

My first experience of 'Homemaking' was making clothes horse tents – putting a sheet over the clothes horse behind the sofa and furnishing it with cushions.

As a young teacher in London I got a room in a shared house, and brightened up the drab old brown furniture by painting red, orange and yellow diamonds all over it – harlequin style. I often wonder how whoever succeeded me reacted!

In my 2nd house in Nuneaton I placed a large dark piano against the wall, and camouflaged it by painting both white and adding a red line – down the wall continuing down the piano.

I moved into my 4 bedroom 1790's cottage in 1972 with my wife, son and 2 daughters and set about restoring it. When the children became teenagers they needed their own rooms, so I tried to buy the adjacent cottage, but found it was condemned!

So I decided to double the size of my house by building a 2 floor extension and garage/workshop on the side and back. (I learned to brick-lay by joining the air raid shelter to the old outside loo). I drew up the required plans, and eventually got planning permission. My philosophy is "It can't look worse than it is".

At Easter in 1978 I started digging the foundation trenches, and over the next 2 years built it, plumbed, wired, carpentered and plastered it with just the aid of my 9 year old son.

I managed to recycle lots of material, including the old cottage doors from the now demolished 3 adjacent cottages. When I needed windows I looked out for someone fitting double glazing, and bought their old ones. All the electrical cable came from demolished workshops in Kilsby, the roof slates from another demolished cottage in the College grounds.

This new structure included a kitchen, so there was a problem – how to manage without one until the new one was complete? Solution, as with mediaeval stonemasons enlarging church aisles, build around the existing structure, and demolish the old from the inside. We had a period of a week or so when there was just a sink balanced on loose bricks, supplied by a hosepipe! Fortunately, it was a good summer.

Another problem was how to lift and install a heavy 12' metal beam over the dining room window and backdoor floor with just my 12 year old son to help me? The solution I came up with was to peg it up two ladders, rung by rung, end by end.

It still serves its purpose, though I have since had a new roof and double-glazing fitted by professionals.

John Duffield May 2013

Crafts

As an artist, teacher and lecturer in Art Schools, my experience of 'Crafts' is very broad. As an Art Student I studied painting, drawing, sculpture, design, colour, collage, etc. before specialising in Graphics which included Printmaking, (relief: wood & lino, intaglio: etching, drypoint, engraving, aquatint, lithography, etc.) Plus Photography, Calligraphy, Typography, 3D Design etc.

In my post-graduate year at London University I explored basic animation and light shows, and was introduced to ceramics, screen printing and book-binding.

In my first teaching post I learned to weld from a colleague and made metal assemblage sculptures. I also taught life drawing at evening classes. During a Sabbatical Year at Birmingham Polytechnic in 1976 I was introduction to Computers and developed my interest in Digital Art, which I reinforced by a year at Coventry University 15 years later. At Rugby Theatre I designed publicity and stage sets.

The arrival of grandchildren stimulated me to design and make wooden toys, rocking horses, etc. but I could not compete with the highly colourful all singing and whistling plastic toys that are now the norm.

After damaging my eyes I was sent for rehabilitation at the RNIB Manor House Torquay where I learned Wood Turning.

Later I studied for a year at Queen Alexandra College for the Blind in Birmingham, learning glass engraving and teaching myself to design and make Shaker-style rocking chairs. I made rocking chairs for all 4 of my grandchildren, starting with a plank and cutting and shaping each part. I do not employ any metal, (screws or nails), but use the traditional method of wooden peg jointing.

I spent 6 months Teaching English in Hungary where I became friendly with a group of local professional artists who introduced me to enamelling.

John Duffield May 2013

Homemaking and Crafts

I am not an "arty" or "crafty" person and would always describe myself as more mathematical or logical. However I realise that I did pick up some skills along life's path which could be described as crafts and contributed to homemaking, all of which I have to thank my mother for, as do most women.

My mother was a war bride and so adhered to the 'make do and mend', 'waste not want not' way of life. She already showed skills in needlework by making clothes for herself and her sisters before she married which she had picked up from her first job as a seamstress. During the war and afterwards she lived in an isolated area of Burton on Trent caring for two young daughters and an elderly aunt while my father was away in the RAF and then later working for the Civil Aviation in numerous postings around the country. She had to cook with basic ingredients, grow all her own vegetables, make all of her family's clothes, care for the elderly aunt and really do everything around the house.

I was one of those two young girls and when we moved to Rugby, when I was four, I started to take an interest in some of my mother's tasks. I admired her imaginative baking when she made wonderful cakes for Xmas, birthdays and other occasions and remember fondly her little domino and fairy cakes she made for parties but at that early age all I did was admire and request these goodies. I also benefited from the wonderful sewing she did, making almost all mine and my elder sister's dresses and my baby brother's little smocked tops and matching trousers. Remembering proudly the new summer dresses she made for my sister and I to wear each Sunday School Anniversary, made to match but in different colours, as my sister hated to be the same as her young sister.

Brother Antony wears an outfit made by mother.

Mother with us girls, in our new outfits for the Sunday School Anniversary.

The first skill she passed on to me was knitting. She taught me that very early on and I was making my own sweaters from a young girl and then my husband's jumpers, later baby clothes. Even when I was working full time with children, I was never without some garment on the go. It has been some years since I stopped knitting and I am not sure why. Maybe handmade sweaters became unfashionable and my boys stopped appreciating items made by mum. Others admired the things I knitted, some were quite complex so I think I was reasonably good at it. I also crocheted items as well, although I never pursued that craft with quite the same enthusiasm.

At junior school we were taught simple handicrafts, including knitting, but also sewing, tapestry and embroidery. Not many girls seem to take to it but I enjoyed those lessons and took to sewing and by the time I was 11 I had made my first dress. I admit that although it was a school project, my mother helped. I continued these interests by doing Domestic Science at senior school but it was not encouraged at Rugby High School where they were much more focussed on academic subjects, so together with the fact that I had the most awful teacher who was hated by everyone, I chose to stop the subjects after O level.

By the time I met my husband to be, I was quite proficient at knitting and sewing and I had also started to take an interest in cooking and helped mum with the ironing and cleaning, which she was never keen on, thinking the dust could wait preferring the more interesting things in life. I started making things for my bottom drawer, pegged a rug and made all my own curtains for my new home. My dress making still continued a little, but before the children came along I enjoyed shopping for modern readymade clothes and was fortunate enough to have enough money to do so in the early 70's.

Being a new wife I had to start cooking more and although mum had taught me some basics I needed more than that now, not only for my new husband but for cooking a meal for my colleagues at Coventry City Council where I worked shifts in the computer room, when we took turns in cooking a hot meal during the night shift. Mum had bought me a cookery book for a wedding present, this was followed shortly by a food processor. I still use that cookery book to this day and although I feel I am a reasonably good cook, I can do nothing without a recipe, although I do amend them somewhat nowadays. I never reached the heights that my mother did. Her cake making was legendry and she eventually found herself making wedding cakes and other special occasion cakes for friends and family and others. She made my wedding cake and my bridesmaid's dress and only now do I realise what a lot of work I landed her with for my wedding, as well as her working as a school cook, running a home and looking after her family.

My cake making skills are not quite as good. It was supposed to be a canal barge and tender.

Mum made my wedding cake and the bridesmaid dress.

The arrival of children brought me opportunities to make their clothes, knit their sweaters and make their birthday cakes etc. I made fancy dress outfits for them, Easter bonnets and more things than I can remember, always finding time to whip up things like a pink panther outfit. I even knocked up a few outfits for myself when we had Xmas office parties.

No 1 son dressed as
the Pink Panther

No 2 son dressed as
Robin Hood

Me dressed as
Mummy Xmas

However, I never reached the standards set by my mother. I never learnt how to play the piano, another skill she had. I was the only one in the family that took to these homemaking skills with enthusiasm. My siblings and cousins do run successful and lovely homes, but will not venture into home baking, catering for large events, hosting dinner parties, making their own clothes and curtains etc. as I do. I can only thank my mother for any skills I have brought to my home. I know I am not special, others are more skilled but I do try to have a go when some of my contemporaries and the younger generation don't want to bother. I have passed on tips to my sons but I don't think they are as receptive as girls but they do a lot of cooking in their homes. The eldest son has acquired DIY skills from his father, the youngest not quite so, as he lives in London in a rented property so the opportunities are not quite the same for him. However they have acquired skills of their own, as shown here when my 16 year old son painted a box for his younger brother, for a fancy dress competition, as the knave of hearts with his tarts.

I think the homemaking skills and crafts are sadly declining but I am grateful I acquired some and hope my family have benefitted from them, I certainly appreciate the help my mother gave me when she had plenty of other things she could have been doing.

Homemaking and Crafts

Homemaking and crafts to me means many things.

Homemaking can be everything from decorating and DIY to making cushions and curtains etc. Homemaking to me also means making the home comfortable and pleasant to live in. Somewhere you are pleased to get back to when you've been away.

We have lived in several homes over the years, each one being different so each one had different requirements. In a couple Trevor built in wardrobes and he made bunk beds. We also seem to have gone backwards in that we do not always put carpets all over the house these days. The flooring options are better now than the awful thin lino when I was a child.

Also as time moves on the home has different requirements. My mother tells me that our first home was in one room with an open fire to cook on, bathing was in a tin bath and washing clothes was a nightmare and drying them in wet weather was even worse. These days a utility is common with washing machines and tumble driers etc. As for not having at least one bathroom, that would be unthinkable now.

Crafts can be things such as knitting, crochet, dressmaking, card making, jewellery making. I suppose anything that you start from bits and pieces and end up with something useful or decorative can be considered as craft.

When I was young I was given a French knitting kit. I can remember making a bag but cannot recall whether I made anything else. I was also given moulds and plaster to make things but I always managed to chop the heads off when I tried to make figures. As for the fuzzy felt things I never did work out what I was supposed to make with that.

Over time I have taken up knitting, crochet and dressmaking. If I make cards it is on a computer and I use photos of the person the card is for – the funnier the better. Fortunately my family do not embarrass easily. I have never tried making cards any other way mainly because I have no confidence in my artistic ability.

I did consider trying patchwork but that looked like hard work. I also considered jewellery making but as I don't wear much jewellery it is difficult to work up much of an interest in it. I have thought I should take it up just to make presents. Listening to other people talking about making things does get me thinking about trying something new.

Some things overlap as crafts can be for homemaking such as making cushions and patchwork throws.

Linda Peplow

Home-making and Craft

My earliest memories of home-making revolve round my Maternal Grandmother, who passed on her love of home-making and craft to me. It was she who made me beautiful dolls' clothes, a little dressing gown for my teddy, so that he could get ready for bed when I did, when staying at her house. I was allowed to practice my sewing on her old hand sewing machine – which I now have in my sewing room, complete with instruction book, dated 1916! She showed me how to thread it and use it to practise making clothes for my dolls, this led easily into making my own clothes when I reached my teens! She would go to the market and buy bits of "stuff" to make my dresses – new ones each year for the Sunday School Anniversary. I don't ever recall her making things for herself. Her wardrobe was so small that I don't think she can have had many clothes.

My Grandma taught me how to knit. How often, when I am knitting now, I remember sitting close up to her in a chair while she repeated "in, over, through and out". Her patience was endless as I dropped stitches, made stitches where they shouldn't be and got cross with myself!! She and my Mother knitted all my jumpers and cardigans. I was the first child at Northlands to have the school uniform, which was introduced when I was about 6. I well remember the Headmistress (the lovely Miss Cook) coming into our classroom and pointing me out, saying "Doesn't she look nice in her school uniform".

Grandma was a country lady, her sisters were all married to farmers or lived in the country. I have often wondered how she came to live in Rugby, when they were all in Gloucester. She could turn her hand to most things, she knitted and sewed, painted and decorated, gardened and cooked. How I wish I'd asked her how she cooked her runner beans – I've never tasted any like hers. She had remedies for all ailments. I used to have a little bit of camphor sewn into my liberty bodice to stop me getting a cold (it didn't work!!!), she rubbed my chest with goose grease, I can't remember what that was supposed to do and made us drink raspberry vinegar which she made to cure sore throats. When I had an abscess in my ear I stayed with her as my parents were in the middle of moving house. My eyes used to be stuck together in the mornings and she bathed them with cold tea until I could open them.

She would walk along a road and help herself to a cutting from an overhanging bush and it would flourish in her garden. On a visit to Sandringham she took a fancy to the rhododendrons and her tiny cutting secreted away in her pocket became a huge bush by the time I took over her house. Her rockery was splendid with huge begonias. She and my Granddad had clearly defined roles – she grew flowers and he provided vegetables.

Her bed-linen was embroidered with patterns, monograms and flowers. The edges of her pillow cases were so beautifully sewn that when the pillowcases themselves wore out I cut off the borders and still have them sewn onto my towels! Tablecloths were also handmade, with drawn thread-work decorations.

My Grandma liked to paint everything – gloss, not watercolours! She transformed a piece of Parianware (white) with a tin of green paint. A brass fender was given the same treatment! Years later it took me ages to soak this paint off and to this day that particular piece of Parianware has green bits, where the paint refused to budge. She did all the decorating and kept her house spotless.

She had no modern gadgets, cakes were beaten by hand and I still have the fork, worn down on one side, which she used to mix her lighter than light cakes. Her kitchen consisted of a gas cooker, a sink and a dresser, with a little space to work between the cooker and sink. She kept things cool in the pantry which had a stone floor.

When my Grandfather retired they decided to fill the gap left in his life by making a rug!!! They sat one on each side of the fire with the rug between them. I think it had a pattern marked on the canvas and they pulled bits of wool through the holes with a special tool. I was enlisted to help with the rug when I visited and it took ages to complete, but lasted for years and years. In fact it is still rolled up in the top of my Mother's wardrobe at Bilton House. When I cleared my parents' house I couldn't bear to throw that rug away!

Nowadays I love to try any new craft and I think my early days with my Grandma had a great bearing on this. I wonder if I will ever have a grand-daughter to pass on the skills which I have learned to her!

Homemaking and Craft

My first thought was horror of horrors how can I write anything about this subject when I haven't an ounce of artistic skill in me but wait a moment I have a home so yes I must have been a home maker both individually and in partnership with my husband, Frank.

I still live today in the house we bought when we married in 1969. It was a new build so it was a completely clean canvas with which to work. How was it transformed from a house into a home? After leaving the family home and spending several years in student accommodation, cramped bedsits or grubby rented flats in salubrious parts of Leicester and Bristol I remember clearly the sheer joy of stepping into a place that was truly our own.

Having put all our financial resources into the house deposit and mortgage repayments there was little left for furniture and furnishings. We benefited from some generous wedding presents but we also received very gratefully second hand items – a cooker, a stair carpet and some curtains from various family members.

From these basics our home evolved. As funds permitted we gradually replaced the second hand items, taking pleasure in choosing what we liked and ensuring that we were getting good value for money. Over time the home becomes a reflection of the characters of those who live in it which in our case can probably be summed up as careful and traditional. It was quite a day when we felt we could launch into the purchase of something non-functional and buy our first watercolour painting.

Of course, homemaking is not all about possessions. It is about creating an environment in which one feels safe, at ease and contented. It is about the relationships between the occupants of the home; living together, allowing frank and open discussion but respecting others' opinions and individual space. The way we achieve this will be to a large degree moulded by our own upbringings – a wish to recreate the good parts of it but sometimes a need to avoid experiences such as disharmony or repression.

The environments in which both my husband and I grew up would be regarded now as old fashioned with stereotypical roles for our parents as breadwinners and stay at home mothers. Clearly, I have had a much easier life than either my mother or mother-in- law both of whom had the daily chores of tending and clearing open fires and washing and cleaning without the aid of modern equipment. From both of them, though, I learnt about home cooking which has stood me in good stead and from my mother in particular the pleasure that comes from being able to entertain people to meals and to offer the essence of a home - a welcoming atmosphere.

I can't say that craft featured much in my childhood and yet in a way it did. I was the only girl and the youngest by far, with four older brothers who were all good with their hands. My step-father could 'make something out of nothing' and was always working with either wood or metal. He and the boys would carry out all the maintenance work on the house and car so I don't remember tradesmen ever being employed. They also built an Enterprise sailing dinghy which was finished to a high standard and used successfully.

My own ventures into craft were less successful: I can sew and knit but having never been patient or neat enough to persevere, I have left behind me a trail of unfinished items over the years. Perhaps now that sewing and knitting are very much back in vogue I should have another go - or perhaps not!

J.Chappell - 29.05.13

Education
and
Those Who Taught Us

School and Those Who Taught Us

I remember very little about my early school years except that no books were offered for prizes. My early reports stated 3p.- 1st;;   2p. - 2nd; 1p.- 3rd

We moved house when I was seven or eight and I went to The Henry Gotch Junior School in Kettering. This was a new and modern school with verandas all-round the outside. It was reached by a subway underneath the busy road which was a first in those days. The verandas came in very handy when the evacuees started to arrive from London. All our facilities had to be shared.

We sat the exam for High or Grammar Schools but only about six special places were offered to all the schools in the town as in those days they were fee paying schools. Another exam was taken for the central School which was a mixed boys and girls taking the East Midlands school certificate on completion at 15 or 16. Then it was all schools leaving at 14.

I went to the Central school about 2 miles away. No transport so off I went on my bicycle carrying my satchel, hockey stick, tennis racket and anything else I needed and my gas mask. This was a must and if forgotten a return journey was necessary. Games were good hockey in winter and tennis in summer.

Homework was new. And all information needed meant a trip to the reference library as encyclopedias were expensive. A bonus was that the boys also had to revise!

New subjects were introduced. Lovely science labs where lots of experiments were tried out. French which seemed to be all verbs translation and dictation. Open the window, stand up, sit down, or close the door. Saying your name and age did little for making good conversation.

The geography teacher was very stern and forceful and to this day I bet most of us could recite the first page of our geography book on contour lines.

A very nice kitchen and small flat was there to teach us the basics of cooking and cleaning. Old time dancing was taught accompanied by gramophone records and the boys were supposed to say Please may I have the pleasure? But this was only heard if the teacher was nearby otherwise social graces went out of the window. End of term dances were great for an excuse to dress up (as far as coupons would allow) There was a Girl Guide Troop for after school which was very good.

In the fourth year shorthand typing book keeping were added for the girls to help them if office work was to be their choice.

Through all my school years Air Raid shelter practice was a must and sitting in the dark dingy shelter was not nice. Luckily I never had to use one for real!!

Doreen Taffs

Education And Those Who Taught Us

I went to Woodend Infant and Junior school, generally speaking I loved school   didn't have any problems that I remember. I know the class rooms were cold   in the winter and I hated the school milk which I did everything to get out of   drinking.

In junior school that was when I became interested in sport and represented   the school on several occasions at sports days with other schools. At the time I   thought this was great as I used to get out of lessons to practice on the sports   field particularly if there was a county match coming up, I realise now of   course that this was not such a good idea.

I didn't pass the 11+ so moved on to a secondary modern school which was on   the same site as the other schools, so it was a very large complex that doesn't   seem to happen now.

Once again I enjoyed my time at school still always taking part in lots of   activities and of course the sport took up much of my time. While I was at this   school my father died, and I asked to be let off playing in a netball match after   school on the day of my father's funeral and was refused by my form teacher   saying I couldn't let everyone down, but the sports mistress who I was very   fond of overruled her and I didn't play.

This sports mistress became a very good friend as would take me to different   venues to compete in her car, understanding that my mother didn't have the   money to get me to sports meetings.

Leaving sport aside secondary education seems to give you a good education which enabled you to get a job on leaving. I had shorthand and typing, bookkeeping and office procedures certificates when I left, whereas my best   friend who went to a grammar school only had the basic subjects.   I left school at 16 went straight to work in the city of London just off the   embankment as an office junior with a very highly respected firm of chartered   accountants and got paid more than my friend who went to grammar school.   Secondary modern school also taught, needlework, cooking, health and hygiene   all of which gave you a good grounding to things in the real world, I think if   schools today prepared people for the skills they need in everyday life people   would manage their budgets etc. better, I think I received a good basic education and just remember it being a safe place to go with no trouble that I   can remember.

..

School and Those Who Taught Us

The first teachers I encountered were nuns at the Catholic convent where I started my school life; shapeless figures of indeterminate age, dressed in billowing black garments and stiff white bonnet-like head-dresses. In the main they were kindly individuals and they must have succeeded in imparting some knowledge to me as I generally seemed to be near the top of the class and by the time of the 11plus and my move to the Grammar School, I was already way ahead in subjects like French and Algebra.

This position did not last. What I wasn't taught was the danger of complacency when amongst a class of equally bright pupils. The result of this was a school career which should definitely be summed up as 'could do better'.

The staff at Ware Girl's Grammar School were predominately female. There were two men - Mr. Laski (Polish, I believe) who taught Physics but both his accent and the subject itself caused me constant difficulties. Then there was Mr. Jones, a tall rangy man with a droopy moustache who taught Latin but managed to speak without opening his mouth so he too was rather difficult to follow.

Girls between the ages of eleven and fifteen are, or at least were then, silly but merciless creatures always ready to pick up on mannerisms or idiosyncrasies of teachers so that a word or a particular stance could trigger fits of uncontrollable giggles, disrupting the class and often resulting in being sent to stand outside the classroom. The ultimate threat that of being sent to the Headmistress. During my first year Miss Woodhouse was still the Headmistress, an elderly, stern individual who certainly instilled respect within the school. When she retired and Miss

Robinson was appointed the atmosphere in the school did seem a little more relaxed.

Some teachers were disliked or even feared because of their strictness; others were worshipped as was the case of the Games Mistress, Sheila (I can't even remember her surname) on whom I had a crush for at least two years. The other Games Mistress, Diana, also had a following. I don't know whether they found this idolatry embarrassing but they seemed to take it in good part and it certainly meant that we put a lot of effort into sport which in my case might have been more usefully directed elsewhere.

Each form had its own form mistress who had a pastoral as well as a teaching role and as one progressed up the school one began to appreciate them as human beings who might even have something interesting to say rather than regarding them as remote, authoritarian adults.

Some staff never lost that aura of authority. One such was Miss Clarke, the English mistress, ramrod upright, strict and at times scathing who took the Lower Sixth and of whom I think I would still be wary if I met her today.

Janet Chappell - 24.09.13

School and memorable Teachers

My memories of school and the teachers that stood out are still quite vivid in my thoughts. When I started school in Ireland in 1952 it was quite a stressful time for me but more so for my long suffering mother. Having been the only child for over 4 years I found it very difficult to accept my sister into the household and when it was time for me to go to school I rebelled, Elaine would be dressed and ready in her pram and I was marched to my school nearly a mile away. After milk break I decided I had had enough so donned my coat and marched home, life was so much more sedate then not many cars or buses and Health and Safety not even a blot on the Landscape. Needless to say Mum was very exasperated as she was tending to Elaine, but dropped everything and together with Elaine in the pram I was marched back to school with the clear message that school was on the agenda for the foreseeable future. I did eventually accept school and began to enjoy all the 'adventures' that learning brought. We only had 3 teachers, Mrs Leach, Miss Skuse and Mrs Bell, in this very small village school, I learned to read and write, I don't recall the books that we learned from but a great emphasis was made on enjoying play and communicating with my classmates and behaving in an appropriate manner. I still believe to this day that when I painted a bird the wrong colour and was reprimanded for it, this dulled my enthusiasm for any form of Art and this was to blame.

When we left Ireland we went to live with my grandparents in Wales and I attended a local school, I believe that as I was there for a short time the teachers didn't make much of an impression on me. I vividly remember my classmates taking the mickey out of my accent, which was heavy Northern Irish, and I seemed to spend all my time talking to them and not able to speak like them which was a constant source of amusement to them. My next school was in Swindon, where I attended many schools, as the influx of people from London necessitated the rapid building of schools to accommodate the rapid rise in population. I clearly remember my Junior School being enjoyable as far as it was obvious to me that with streaming' in place I was never going to pass my 11 plus and go to a grammar school, so Penhill Secondary School was where I would complete my education.

I spent five years there, and looking back was quite eventful, none more than one of my classmates Terry Reynolds coming into school assembly 'sporting' a Mohican haircut, utter shock and horror was experienced by the Headmaster and staff and he was suspended for such time that his hair style was more appropriate for the school. He returned quite soon and all was forgotten but perhaps not forgiven.

The school was remembered for many of the staff with the name Jones, the head, deputy head, trench teacher, and PE teacher were all referred to by their first initial and surname, confusing to start with but commonplace to us all quite soon. Strict discipline was the norm and it seemed to be accepted without question. Any behaviour problems were dealt with by the headmaster who gave us the slap with the cane on our hands or the PE teacher Mr T Jones giving the dap' on the boys backside. This is certainly frowned upon today as it would be construed as Child cruelty. The deputy head Mr E Jones seemed to have eyes in the back of his head, we never seemed to get away with bad behaviour, as even when he was writing on the board he called out our names if we weren't paying attention, very eerie we thought but we all respected him. Mr Coombs our History teacher was always throwing chalk at me as I was never paying attention, I really hated the subject and was learning this subject under duress. Mr Suter our Maths Teacher was the teacher we all were very scared of, we never dared step out of line and all the class learned in silence, not really sure we all enjoyed Maths but this was what we had to do. Not too sure if this would happen today, but we accepted this as the norm without rebelling. On reflection my school days were enjoyable, if only I had questioned why certain things happened, it would have equipped me for life outside school as it took me a long time to accept that I was responsible for everything that would happen in my working life. The word naive springs to mind and not sure if it is any different today for the majority of school leavers today.

With hindsight, how things would have been different then, but I appreciate that my parents did what they could for me and left me to make mistakes so I only had myself to blame.

My Grandmother's Education

In 1873 my grandmother was 2 years old and left in the charge of the lady next door whilst her mother went out to work. Eliza played together with other small children in the neighbourhood, running in the fields and woods surrounding the cottage where she lived in Olton Solihull.

Eliza's first impressions of any school education were extremely grim to say the least. Her elder brother and sister would come home from school and report of the sour character of their school mistress and all the punishments they had had to undergo.

Her school education began in 1876 when she was 5 years old. She remembers her first visit to the place of learning quite be clearly. Dressed for the occasion in her clean pinafore black stockings and buttoned up boots and accompanied by her elder brother and sister she was helped over the fields and stiles to the school house situated at the bottom of a hill approximately three miles from the row of cottages where she lived.

Her first impression whilst entering the school where she was to attend daily for the next six years was very frightening. Even now she remembers the forbidding school marm sitting at a table, the register in front of her and her gaze grimly set on rows and rows of children's faces turned towards her. Teacher took her name and gave her a registration number and wrote in the book before her. Tightly clenched in her hand was two pennies to pay for her education for the week. She was then taken to sit on the front row.

School was held daily in a dingy room which served as the congregational chapel on Sundays. The windows were tiny and high up on the walls. It was cold in winter, but cool in summer and throughout the day shafts of light pierced the chalk filled atmosphere.

Thinking back Eliza said she was sure the room must have smelt appallingly as the ventilation was so limited and lots of the pupils were dirty. A large pulpit stood in the centre at one end of the room and two smaller rooms opened off on either side of it. These were filled with odd chairs and discarded school equipment and they were the punishment rooms. If you failed to know your lesson or sum you were considered to be bad and thus shut in one of these rooms for the morning. All the wooden desks and forms were arranged horizontally across the room

Eight children sat at a desk and there must have been twelve rows to accommodate the ninety pupils .The desks were all one size and when she sat down her feet did not reach the floor. The room was heated by a single stove which the teacher had to refuel at various intervals during the day .The lighting consisted of oil lamps hung at intervals from the ceiling.

Lower standards were seated at the front gradually increasing in status to the 4th standard at the back. Several chairs were placed down one side of the room for brothers and sisters who were under age.

Eliza came every morning at ten to nine carrying her sandwiches wrapped in newspaper. The majority of children brought their lunch with them. At half past twelve they sat at their desks and ate the food without a drink. Water had to be carried from a tap in the lane. The teachers ate with the children at the top of the room.

School began with a short service a hymn a prayer and a passage read from the bible by the pupil teacher. Then they divided into two and the t two, standards would be taken by the head for reading and arithmetic. The rest would be the responsibility of the pupil teacher who taught the three r's .Teacher used the blackboard and sums were graded in difficulty according to the standard. Eliza used a pencil and slate to write with and to copy from the board. If the sum was correct you were good but if wrong you were classed as bad and in disgrace. Reading lessons were very noisy as everyone read out loud. After lunch they had sewing or knitting. She remembered making a scarf, stockings and a pinafore in sewing.

The children hardly moved from their desks for the whole morning, but if a child in the centre had to move they all had to stand up. They had a play time in the morning but as there was no playground they stood around the outside of the church building. They had no object lessons and learned very little geography or history in fact it was all three r's. In spite of this her two brother s left school unable to read or write. There was no nature study or painting but scripture was taught from the bible every morning.

Eliza passed the various standards not by written tests but by the inspector's scrutinisation of her work. She entered the third standard when she was ten and this was the year for pen and ink. Eliza was now allowed to sew chemises and boys shirt s and for this work she received praise.

The Christmas tea was a happy occasion as a large paint firm nearby supplied tea and presents for the school. After tea the children in best clothes would take their presents to the director's wife an invalid who lived nearby. Eliza had to curtsy and then receive the value in money for her present

Eliza remembers making fun of her cousins who went to a six penny school in London this was considered to be quite classy. Her mum had to pay eight pence per week for her four off springs to attend. Arthur who was two when Eliza was seven was carried to school by Amy the eldest. The teacher put him to sleep on two chairs at the side with several other siblings. Quite often the lessons were interrupted by the screams as they awoke. If for any reason they did not attend school on a Monday they were kept off for the week as it was considered a waste of money to pay for only four days schooling. The school inspector's visit was a dreaded time as quite a heavy fine was administered for absence

When Eliza was 11 in 1882 she passed the 4th standard and therefore her parents could take her away from school. She started in domestic service in August of the same year and assumed adult duties and brought in a weekly wage. Since leaving school she went on to marry and rear ten children and at 85 years of age was the enthusiastic secretary of an old peoples club.

School and Those Who Taught Us

About 1940 in the middle of the blitz of Midland cities our little used front room was cleared out, small tables and chairs were delivered from our local primary school. The pupils were unable to attend because of the danger of air raids and fire risk as it was a wooden building. The class was split into two and the children attended either morning or afternoon sessions. The teacher was a man who came from Shrewsbury and went home on Fridays. Mum told tales of him arriving early Monday morning absolutely covered in white hoar frost after riding his motor bike from home!

Apart from the convenience of having a school room handy for play and using the desks for birthday parties together with chalk and blackboards I have no memories of organised per school activity .

We met other young children at the clinics whilst collecting orange juice, rose hip syrup and cod liver oil and malt. I do remember my first visit to Yardley Road School .The austere heads room had a glass fronted cupboard in the corner containing brand new toys and a large glass jar of sweets. Whilst being allowed to play with the large spinning top mum was interviewed and then I was given a sweet from the jar. Evidently the Americans had donated toys and sweets to schools in the area.

The reception class had flat wide wooden steps leading to classrooms on either side. There was a toy shop in one corner and a Wendy house in the other. We had to take a mug for morning drinks of hot cocoa. Mine had a cat with Puss in Boots how fine he looks on the side.

The head was nicknamed old Pritchbags her hair was scraped back in a tight bun and her glasses were on the end of her nose. Woe betide anyone who fidgeted coughed or spoke as she announced The Lord's Prayer. The order to, STAND IN THE CORNER BY THE DUSTER BAG rang out. Besides being terrified by her I was always intrigued when she often pulled up, the hem of her skirt and polished her glasses on her petticoat.

I attended primary school until I was 10 years old but memories of lessons are vague I was good at English but not at maths. Once I hid in the toilets and then ran home because I did not understand long multiplication. Spelling tests were regularly given and hand sewing lessons were done in the afternoons when one class member would read a story aloud whilst we sewed a pillowcase with French seams. Knitting was a pleasant pastime and on Fridays our desks were inspected tidied polished and the inkwells were cleaned with Brasso. Oral music sight reading was performed from huge charts strung from the easel. Times tables were called out every morning until we knew them by heart.

The high light of the school year came in July when the whole school had a week of festivities including fancy dress parades, decorated bicycles and competitions with sports days. I did win a prize for dressing up as a potato, they were under threat from the Colorado Beatle at the time. I had a tin hat with potato flowers around the rim and dressed in a hessian sack with new potatoes as a necklace I strode forth.

I passed for the local co-ed Grammar School and moved to Yardley Grammar in September. We caught the bus from The Dolphin Pub or cycled or walked the two and a half miles each day. I enjoyed school, always did my homework but looking back at my text books I certainly did not tax myself. I loved biology and English geography and history but never did understand physics and chemistry. Mr Mac had a wooden leg but was an enthusiastic teacher of English Literature. We studied Shakespeare, Eothen and Paradise Lost. I loved sport rounders netball and hockey and joined the school YHA walking group. We borrowed books from the local library regularly. I can recall the smell of polish and the quiet atmosphere and the creak of the metal turnstile within the building.

The school owned a hut on Wellesbourne aerodrome and various groups spent weekends there on field trips. The maths teacher said he would buy me a bottle of cider if I passed my O level maths (he was extremely knowledgeable about my capabilities.) Music lessons were obligatory and took place in a room with elevated large wooden rows of desks. You could manage to play pencil and paper games under these Oxo's or hang the man without being seen. Miss Wilkinson was a brilliant musician and played the grand piano well but her choice of songs from the English National Song Book left a lot to be desired. David the Bard on his death bed lies always sends shivers down my spine!

I came within a new law passed by parliament that I came within the age group to stay on an extra year before taking my G C E exams. So in a new class we coasted along repeating the same old curriculum.

I had already decided I wanted to be a nurse before my brother had his accident with a deck chair so now I changed my career path and I was going to be a primary teacher. My parents agreed but stated that if I wanted to further my education I would have to go out to work first to establish myself independent .and pay for my own course. This I did and after two years of repetitive office work I applied and was accepted at Coventry Training College. At this point my true interest in education took off and I worked very hard and thoroughly enjoyed my college life and a career in teaching afterwards.

Pam Wilson.

My Education and Teachers

Early Days

I don't remember much about my first school or if I attended a playschool or nursery school which probably didn't exist in those days. I have just a few memories of Newbold Infant School which are:-

Being put on a bus by my mother at the Crown in the village and going one stop to the Glebe Estate. I am sure I didn't go by bus every day and maybe that is why I remember it particularly.

I was the register monitor and one of the registers went missing, I wasn't register monitor again.

I was milk monitor and fell over with my face falling onto the glass. I can still see the blood in the milk. Fortunately at the moment of my distress my mother arrived at school to bring my library books which I had forgotten and was able to comfort me and take me to hospital where I had stiches. I asked if I would have a scar and told no, but I still have that scar to this day.

I recall being in class talking about China and China Tea. I put up may hand and said we had China Tea on Sundays. The teacher said I wouldn't have had it because it wasn't very nice. I didn't argue but I knew we did and I also knew it wasn't very nice. I am sure that is why I became withdrawn in class environments and reluctant to speak out for fear of ridicule.

I don't recall anything more about the school or the teachers although I can picture the building which is no longer there.

Penny at Infant School about 1956

Junior School

I recall more of my time at the Junior School in Newbold and being in several different buildings. My first year was in the old building, now the village hall and I remember playing in the playground and my sister being there as she was in the top class when I was in the bottom. I don't remember the teacher that year but my report tells me his or her name was G Martin.

My next year was spent in the school room of the local Methodist Church, a few hundred yards along the road. The pupil numbers had exceeded the capacity at the old school and some of us needed to be sited elsewhere. I can picture the class room and the teacher who was young and probably naïve. Mr Jenkins argued with the class once that the Sabbath was Saturday but came in the next day admitting he was wrong, it was indeed Sunday. Was he an atheist or Jewish, who knows. My only other memory of that year was running the tuck shop and benefitting from being able to eat the broken biscuits.

For my next two years we were in the new building, not brand new, the senior school had vacated it for a new building next door and we settled into their old one. It seemed very modern and I can picture my class rooms, the hall and the dining room where we had chips! We never had chips at my senior school. We had the same teacher, Mrs Stephens, for two years, to bring continuity to our studies leading up to the 11 plus, an exam that meant very little to me and never bothered me. I felt no pressure to pass it. I just remember the head telling us to have a good night's sleep the night before we took it. Mrs Stephens was a good teacher but may have been politically incorrect as she once said she could tell which children lived over the bridge, meaning Parkfield and Meadow Roads and she inferred they were inferior. She taught us everything from maths to sewing, English to PE. My reports suggest I excelled at Maths, English and PE and not too bad at the other subjects. The head teacher, Mr Butler, gave us one lesson a week in current affairs and I remember the lesson when we talked about the opening of the new M1 which was very near Rugby. Being indifferent to success in those days I was surprised to be told one day on arriving home from school, that my parents had received a letter telling them that I would be going to Rugby High School. I was surprised, partly pleased with myself but sad not to be going to the same school as my friends. Only five of us went to Rugby High and a few boys went to Lawrence Sherriff. Mum took me to see the school for what is now called an induction day before the term ended and the summer was spent kitting me out in the new school uniform.

Education and Those Who Taught Us

Mrs Stephens's class of 1960/61 before we moved to different senior schools. I am third from the right, second row. The stout boy in the blazer at the back was the headmaster's son Timothy Butler.

Rugby High School

September 1961 I started a new experience to last five years. I was keen and determined to do well but things didn't go quite as well as I thought. I went from a big fish in a small pool to a small fish in a big pool.

We weren't supposed to know which class was the top one, each of the three classes was labelled with the initial of the form teacher. I was in 1C but we soon became aware that this was the top as we were being groomed to take GCEs one year early. I had some stiff competition and soon felt the underdog. I was still good at maths and sport but everything else only mediocre and felt inferior to others and also felt a class divide, thinking all the other girls were of a better class than I was.

Ready for my first day at Rugby High

Each subject had a different   teacher and I had differing success with them. My first form teacher taught Religious Education and she observed that I was shy and didn't take part in oral work. I blame that teacher who ridiculed me over the China Tea. There were lots of elderly spinsters who taught there who didn't seem to like me, including the Headmistress Miss Linsley who in the first year taught us for one lesson a week although I cannot remember what she taught. At the end of the first year my marks were mostly A's and B's so that wasn't so bad.

Miss Herrington, my maths teacher was our form teacher for year two where my standards in some subjects were slipping. Miss Herrington was a good maths teacher and I had her for maths all the time I was at that school. She was younger than some teachers, a Methodist who I sometimes bumped into out of school as we were Methodists at that time. Most of my marks were getting lower but still not too bad, weakest at Latin and French. I had no aptitude for languages.

Year three and the geography teacher, Mr Edwards, was the form teacher that year. My geography wasn't too great, the teacher was a bit weak and we could manipulate him easily but a nice man generally. I began suffering from lack of commitment as my interests out of school in pop music and boys were distracting me considerably. This was beginning to show in my work. The daunting Miss Bailey and I were at loggerheads in French due to my poor work and lack of effort. She was old, little but plump with beady eyes, I feared and hated every lesson.

With Mr Edwards on my last day at Rugby High in 1966

By year four we were no longer working towards taking GCEs early. It had been decided the drawbacks of doing them early outweighed the benefits, mainly to do with university entrance. My form teacher that year, and the next, was the English teacher, Miss Crawley. We had her for that year and the fifth year also. She proudly announced in front of the class that I would never pass either my English Language or Literature GCEs. That was a red rag to a bull and I got both. However it was decided by Miss Bailey that although French was a compulsory subject I and another girl would not take it as neither of us would achieve a pass. I was not bothered about that due to our mutual dislike for each other.

I still took the required eight subjects and passed 6, failing only Art and General Science. I passed Maths, History, Religious Education, English Lit, English Lang. and Needlework.

Some of the most memorable teachers at that school were Mrs Rettie (formally Miss Jack), who taught History and brought the subject alive for me. I wanted to take it at A level but in those days you could not mix arts with sciences and my other subjects were to be Maths and Further Maths. She was also involved with Rugby Theatre and known to my father. Miss Oral taught Cookery and Needlework and was known as 'orrible Oral' and she really was horrible. I don't know what her problem was but she could not be nice to anyone. Luckily I had a nice Miss Austin for Needlework for my GCE year and she helped me achieve a pass. Mr Roberts taught Latin, he was a young Bohemian

type, handsome in a way with a goatee beard, everyone 'fancied' him but I was soon out of Latin due to my poor language skills. I can't recall the teacher's name we had for some Science but recall her being very sick one morning and only later did we realise she had morning sickness and left for a while, coming back married.

1968   East   Warks. College   with   fellow students. I am bottom right.

Education and Those Who Taught Us

As I could not take my chosen subjects to A level, I reluctantly left Rugby High after O levels and went to the East Warwickshire College of Further Education where I took an Ordinary National Diploma in Business Studies together with A level Maths, but I dropped the Maths as I found it difficult at A level and preferred the OND subjects. The syllabus mirrored those for O and A levels in most subjects and so as well as the OND that I achieved with Merit, I obtained A Levels in Accounts, Economics and Law, a few more O Levels and passes in Exams for Shorthand and Typing. I was a big fish in a small pool again and received a student prize in the last year at age eighteen.

None of my teachers there left me with lasting impressions and I can't remember their names although I can picture some of them.

By this time I had had enough of full time education and working part time on Saturdays and Sundays, so I sort a job working nine to five Monday to Friday, firstly in Accountancy. One of only a few jobs I had in my working life.

I enjoyed school mainly, with peaks and troughs but I regret I did not try harder, especially at French which I came to need later in life. I regret not going on to University, but in those days you did not need a degree to get on in life and only later did I go on to improve my qualifications as an adult student. I firmly believe it is never too late to progress in education and its value should never be under estimated.

Penny Woodford 18/09/2013

School and those who taught us

My first school was Kilsby infants' school. I do not remember any of that as I was only there for 1 year when we moved to Rugby.

I then went to St. Maries. I can remember the nuns teaching us in the younger classes. I can remember the final year with a male teacher, Mr Watson I think. I remember we were graded in the class. Those in the top grade were given the cane on the hand for each sum wrong. He was also very handy with the blackboard ruler, throwing it at pupils. Funnily enough I remember him as a good teacher though.

I then went to Dunsmore. Some of the teachers were good and could control a class, others were useless and the pupils took control. Two of my maths teachers were the ones I remember most and they were very good. I took needlework at one time and I upset that teacher because I would not put lace round the neck and sleeves of the nightdress I had made. It would have been a complete waste of money as I would have ripped the lace off when I took it home as I wouldn't have worn it with the lace. She suggested I transfer to art which I did. I do not think I have an artistic bone in my body. The art teacher did not appreciate my drawing of a bicycle which I had done with a ruler and compass. She wasn't able to suggest another class as dressmaking and art were the only options, she did try to help me learn to paint and stuff but she was flogging a dead horse. I took up dressmaking when I was older and was very good at it, still no good at art though.

The music teacher wouldn't let me sing in the choir, she said I was almost tone deaf. Still don't really know what that means as some music sounds ok to me but some is just noise.

I liked science but I don't remember any of the teachers. The domestic science teacher was a bit posh. She expected us to cut the crusts off sandwiches and make things look pretty. I also annoyed her because I told her that my mum would not be happy if I threw half the bread away.

That's it really as I think those years are best forgotten.

Linda Peplow

Schools, Teachers and Education.

Most of us probably remember being told that "school days were the happiest days of our lives". My wife, Sue, who taught infants and juniors for over 40 years, tells me she is still reminded by ex-pupils she meets in town that" those were the magic years". Magic for both parties, the children and for those who taught them

I began my schooling in 1946 at Crabbs Cross County Primary School at Redditch. This was a typical, small village, Victorian school built in 1877 and is still in use today. The infants were taught in one half of the school and the juniors in the other, and played on separate playgrounds. Our family has a long association with the school, my grandmother, mother, my brother John and I, John's four children and for a short while my daughter all have attended the school. We sat in our classrooms in pairs, in a row of desks and the classrooms were heated by a large open fireplace. We were most grateful for this, particularly in the very harsh winter of 1947. Schools were not allowed to close and we would struggle through deep snowdrifts to get to school. Here we would strip off and sit around the fire wrapped in a blanket whilst our clothes were dried off ready for the trudge home.

I had always loved books and I could read quite fluently before I started school and knew my tables up to 10 so I was quite ready for school. We learnt our tables by rote and our spellings. The school had its own garden plot next to the Headmaster's House and we all had to take our turn in weeding and planting it. I guess this was a throwback to" digging for Britain". I loved school and became top of my class. The school did not perform very well in the 11 plus being able to only get one or two pupils through to the High School, and that was in a good year. As a result my father was asked by the Head if he could put my name forward to take the exam at aged 10. The Head was not able to promise a re-sit if I failed so it was quite a gamble. In the event I was the only one to get through that year. Other schools in the area would readily get at least a dozen through. This turned out to be a problem later as I lacked the necessary maturity to take full advantage of it, but more on this later.

We learnt our early lessons using an individual blackboard and chalk .moving on to pencil and paper before we were able to use a dip-in pen and ink. Fountain pens and later ballpoint came in senior school.

One of our teachers, Mrs Bradbury, one of the few married teachers on the staff, spent her entire career at this school. She would often remind us that she had taught all our parents so look out if you got into trouble. We knew if we stepped out of line our parents would soon get to know and our parents would be on her side. How unlike today! The older boys could get up to six strokes usually delivered with a ruler for offences such as fighting or poor work. You would not mention this at home!

At the age of seven or eight we would take part in a music festival at the local grammar school and the whole class had to take part. The teacher would walk round the class listening intently to us and would then tell those of us who couldn't sing in tune to mime the words. This nearly put me off singing for life. I still feel sorry for anyone standing next to me in church.

I don't recall the names of other members of staff at the school but do remember a male teacher who had the same Christian name as me who I had in my last year at the school. He gave me a parting gift of a history book for passing the II-plus and L still have it somewhere in the Loft.

Among the many skills we learnt early on was to knit. I was still able to knit two plain two purl when we had our first child, and to sew. I made a lovely little embroidered purse using daisy stitching and blanket stitching. Papier-Mache puppets were another thing we did ready for our puppet shows.

I also recall a Mr Wright, our Head, who was involved in a tragic accident. He found some broken glass in the playground and was on his way to the dustbin with it when a young girl ran round the corner straight into him. She lost the sight in one of her eyes. He was so devastated he resigned his post.

September 1951 I started at The Redditch County High School. The school had a three form entry and was co-educational. We had a school uniform, navy blazers, grey trousers for the boys together with a cap and the girls wore white blouses, navy skirts, and ties. We had a badge on the pockets with the school motto NIHII. QUAM OPTIME which we were told meant "Nothing but the Best". Several years later we had a new Latin master who pointed out that this was incorrect and the motto had to be re written. It's now NIL NISI OPTIME which doesn't fit into the school hymn the Head had written! We were delighted, we didn't like the hymn anyway but the Head persisted.

The school had been opened in the mid-1930s with 300 pupils which had risen to 500 by the 1950s and following further building to 900 some years later. We were split up into groups Angles, Saxons and Jutes and were awarded house points for good work or sports prowess. The school was co-educational and the staff pretty' evenly divided between the sexes although most of the females I recall were unmarried. This was because of losses of male partners caused by the war

In the first two years we took all subjects, but were in sets based on ability. I was lucky being in A set for all subjects except English (B). In the third year in preparation for the O level exams we had to make our choice of subjects. As I had opted to do the three sciences I had to take Latin as opposed to Geography and also drop History which was my favourite subject. Art and woodwork also went- not that I mourned either. Three hours of homework each night was the order of the day and of course no help from computers. We had to rely on the local library.

The school arranged holiday trips at home and abroad and at 13 years old I spent a week staying in a hoarding school just south of Paris. Discipline was strict, we had to travel in school uniform including those much hated caps, and with one member of staff to five pupils it was all very regimented. The only freedom we had was a couple of hours in the grounds after tea, girls only in one area and boys in a separate one. We slept in dormitories with one bed screened off for the teacher on duty. Together with other Midland schools we numbered about two hundred travelling there on a special train. When I got into the sixth form we went to stay with families in Cologne and only took two staff with us and had loads of freedom but I'm jumping ahead.

As in all schools we had our special names for our teachers some more respectful than others. Walter Stranz the head of history was "goofy", the head of physics "Bisto" Bailey, and they had theirs. The three first years became "grublets" developing over the years to "grubs" or "worms".

The important day of our school year was Speech Day when we all assembled in the hail for the presentation of the subject prizes given out by a visitor of note and "colours" for sporting achievements. We all sat there usually seeing the same handful of names receiving all the honours. The high-light of the day was when the visitor announced an extra day's holiday. It brought the loudest cheer. For me the lowest point was the annual cross-country run. No-one was excused without a doctor's note, three miles for the first three forms and six for the others. I was never keen on sport, football was okay but I was never to make the first or second eleven.

The Spring term of 1956 we all took our mock G.C.E. exams and on receiving my Latin result I was told I would not be entered for the actual exam. The teacher was unimpressed when I said I never did see why we had to learn a dead language! As I was only 15 at the time of the exams I needed each teacher's permission to sit the exam. All the other teachers gave their consent Five G.C.E passes was the passport into the sixth form and as 1 had seven all was well.

Redditch had been lucky for those failing the 11-plus for at the age of 13 it was possible to take a second exam where those successful could go to the local technical college. Here they could learn woodwork, metal work, technical drawing, basic engineering skills, secretarial work- shorthand and typing. All the skills the many engineering factories were crying out for. Unfortunately while I was in the sixth form there was a change of policy by the government of the day and the 1 3plus was phased out. An extension was built onto The High School to take some of the subjects previously done at The Technical School but the engineering was not included. A rather short sighted policy change.

In the sixth form I continued with the sciences but needed to add German as this was considered an important "scientific language". I didn't mind this as I had always had an interest in the second world war. We could also put our names down for a week's holiday in Germany staying as guests of a German family. Only two members of staff could accompany us and we had as a result we had a high degree of freedom. School uniform was compulsory but generally ignored and as we were all over 16 a blind eye was turned on smoking and drinking! The Head would have had a dicky fit as anyone found smoking at school could be expelled! Two of friends were banned from school outings for getting caught on school premises.

The Head, Alan Dalton - Murray, took holy orders and left the school shortly after I left to take up a parish in Yorkshire. He had never been very popular. Some years later after another change of government policy the school became a secondary school after the ending of the 11 plus exam.

In 2001 two ex-High School girls met up in Redditch and over a cup of coffee talked of the good old days when the suggestion was made to try to trace the 1951 intake. Of the 90 who started that year they managed to trace the whereabouts of over seventy and a get together at the old school was suggested. A positive response was received from over 90% including 10 former teachers. The current Head offered to open up the school and to show us round. We were all a little dubious but as things turned out we had a meal together and compared our careers. It was surprising the range jobs people had finished up doing, one had been awarded a knighthood. Several people had thought it worthwhile to fly in from the States and we finished the afternoon off by singing the old school hymn.

THE FRANCIS FRITH COLLECTION
REDDITCH, COUNTY HIGH SCHOOL AND PLAYING FIELDS c1950

The Technical Department   Built in 1950

Austerity
And
Childhood Poverty

The Effect of Childhood Poverty and Austerity.

Life in my parents' childhood must have seen mega poverty and austerity. The Hunts from Percy Street in Oxford with father as a printer and a mother who produced twelve children starting in the late 1890s.

Whilst my mother was outcast from the family in Warwickshire and reared by a widowed aunt who also had a young son at the austere Barracks cottages in Lyndon Road, Olton, with outside shared privies, no electricity and a shared cold tap in the middle of the cobbled yard. Mum went on to have twelve step brothers and sisters.

She told tales of scrumping apples and hiding them in her long school knickers until the elastic broke and they all rolled out on to the classroom floor. This action was not because she was hungry it was more of a question of being daring. Her most coveted possession was a silk parasol given to her on her very first day at school by the teacher. She remembered about getting a good hiding for eating the burnt crust from the parish loaf which she had walked 2 miles to get from St Bernard's Road Olton. So it certainly would appear to be a step up from poverty when she met and married Frederick Roberts Hunt and they lived in The Avenue Acocks Green Birmingham. It had a proper bathroom plus an inside toilet. Because they had hardly ever received anything of monetary value, dad had a postcard of the Oxford Colleges for his 21st present, his austere attitude was passed on to his offspring .When they had saved up enough money for a deposit on a house prior to the war in 1937 they purchased a terraced ex council property for £450 in the same road. It was not until 1957 they had servo warm central hearing and mum had the kitchen brick walls plastered over. She was the very proud owner of a free standing unit in bright yellow Formica .She was so proud of this and never stopped talking about it.

Life was very simple as a child we never went hungry and just accepted our surroundings thinking that everyone lived exactly like we did. We used to make fun of the neighbours particularly if they showed off or became uppity about possessions they had acquired.

During the war the large garden and allotment and duck pen under the railway bank became the basis of our existence. We were well fed even if food was plain and home grown. Rabbits chickens ducks eggs together with potatoes cabbages carrots parsnips etc. and fruits in season lots of rhubarb raspberries for bottling and jam.

With clothes on coupons we hardly ever had any new. It was always hand me downs from relatives or neighbours. Skirts and dresses were turned up and down and let out and in. Cardigans were undone skeins of wool washed and knitted up to your size. Zips and buttons were taken from old clothes and sewn into others.

Mr Fenackupan was a saviour. He was the black market salesman who you could not speak about. He visited after dark when curtains were drawn gave three knocks on the door held a case in his arms and trusted. Neighbours knew the time and came to meet him in our front room. The luxuries he sold were white socks silk stockings and enamel butterfly brooches.

It was always instilled into us the importance of your coop number and life was not worth living if you had shopped without it.

Austerity in childhood must lay firm foundations for imaginative play. There was not a sign of a push button devise no phones or I pads or even an electric vacuum cleaner. The old chicken pen on the railway bank became a genuine play house. It was cleaned painted prepared and played in for many hours. It was a library, shop, hospital, house or ship. We spent all the daylight hours ensconced in imaginative play worlds.

The only luxurious toys I received were two huge teddy bears one blue one brown given by my two aunts from Oxford. I adored the blue one but tortured the brown one. One small rag doll with removable clothes was exceptionally receptive to any vaccinations or medicines we administered. My pride and joy was Angela a black crock doll the one who fell apart around the middle because it was bottle-fed consistently. She lasted throughout the war years held together by a wide Elastoplast bandage.

On Saturdays we walked to the Olton cinema for the 5 p m film and enjoyed a bag of chips on the way home. This was sure luxury.

So we did have very little money but we were not poor. We never felt deficient or inferior but I was treated with sternness not severity and we did live without luxuries.

When we were young a luxury was getting what you wanted very soon. It did not have to be expensive or fanciful but may be a hair slide or perhaps a banana because you had never seen one before.

Pam Wilson   26th August

AUSTERITY - WAR YEARS AND ITS IMMEDIATE AFTERMATH.

Austerity. My dictionary defines austerity as" The trait of self-denial especially from worldly pleasures, harsh or severe restrictions"

At the out-break of World War 2 my mother was in South Kensington Hospital in London giving birth to my brother, John. The family was evacuated to the Midlands almost immediately due to the possibility of bombing, and we were lucky to be given a three-bed roomed house with a sizeable back garden. I was born some eighteen months later and so being so young knew nothing of the realities of living with all the restrictions that war inevitably brought about. I had nothing to compare it with, and only by reading about it much later in life was T able to understand how lucky I had been.

Father was at home doing "essential war work" and we were living in the country with the facilities for supplementing war time rationing. We grew our own vegetables, kept chickens and rabbits, father had as a child been brought up on a small holding. The local farmers would also help out with pigeons and wild rabbits which they had shot.

We had no car so when the first commodity to be controlled in 1939 was petrol it did not really affect us. Rationing began on 8th January 1940 with bacon, butter and sugar, to be fairly quickly followed by cheese, eggs, lard, milk and canned and dried fruit. Fresh vegetables and fruit were not rationed but supplies were always limited, things like lemons and bananas being unobtainable for most of the war and for some time afterwards. Oranges were available but greengrocers usually reserved these for young children and pregnant women. Bread was not rationed until after the war, but "the national loaf "of wholemeal bread was introduced to replace white bread An order was passed that bread was not to be sold until the day after it had been baked because (1) it was difficult to slice just-baked bread thinly and (2) the tastiness of just-baked was likely to encourage people to eat it immediately. Customers also found it mushy, grey and blamed it for digestion problems.

Rationing had not been introduced in the First World War until very late on and as a consequence by the end of 1917 the country was down to its last six weeks of supply! One good thing to come out of rationing was that in 1938 when the government started to draw up its recommendations for the various categories of foods to be included, it found that the working classes could not afford to purchase the basic ration. A cost of living allowance had to be introduced. This at least ensured everyone would get a fair share.

Food and petrol were not the only things to be rationed and on June 1' 1941 clothing was added to the points list. Initially the allowance was for approximately one new outfit per year but as the war went on the points system was reduced until buying a new coat could take almost a year's clothing coupons, It was to stimulate a growth of "make do or mend" and" hand me downs" which I do remember. John was not only 18 months older than me but a good deal bigger and I well remember having to adjust bracers until my trousers came up to my arm-pits. The cold winds fair whistled up the trouser legs! Neither my mother nor Gran with whom we lived were needlewomen so all alterations had to be made by a friendly neighbour, their forte were the knitting needles. Sweaters were made and remade although sizing was not all it might have been. Gran seemed obsessed with bed-socks which came in one size, large enough to get both feet in one, but as we had no central heating we were probably grateful for. Old dresses were cut up and for years we produced rugs from them through something I think was called "pegging"

When we moved to the Midlands the family had little furniture and what they had was bought second-hand from the market in 1939 and so any bits of furniture that we required either had to come from similar sources or bought as "utility furniture". This was of poor quality but was all that was available in the shops. Father did not believe in buying "on tick" - credit - so we had to learn to save up for everything, or go without Buying on tick was definitely frowned upon, there was a social stigma attached to it. Buying a house with a mortgage was on the other hand respectable.

As a child the one restriction which did directly affect us was sweet rationing, we had to exist on 2 ounces of sweets a week1. The answer was "dolly mixtures", you could get a lot for 2 ounces and I also remember Id bars of chocolate. Two nibbles and you had eaten it. Toys were also in short supply and I remember my favourite toy was a fort I received one Christmas that a friend of father's had made at work from an old packing case. I was very proud of it and it made a great home for my lead soldiers. My older friends would scrounge old pram wheels and apple boxes to use to make their go-carts. Nothing was allowed to be wasted.

The end of hostilities in Europe did not bring an end to restrictions millions of people in Europe were starving and somehow or other had to be fed. Rationing had to continue in order to produce a surplus that could be sent to assist.

Bread rationing ended in mid-1946 but had to be restored when the wheat crop failed following weeks of continuous rain. It was 1948 before bread rationing finally ceased. In the period January to March 1947 potato rationing had to be introduced following the long, hard frosts which destroyed stored potatoes. May 1949 saw the end of clothing coupons. In 1946 Eileen Wilkinson, the then Minister of Education, persuaded Parliament to bring in "the School Milk Act" under which all pupils under 18 would receive a third of a pint of milk free. This was part of her campaign against poverty. I remember well that we all had to undergo a medical at school where we were weighed and measured and the results compared to a national scale. If either fell below a certain figure we were obliged to see our family doctor with a view to being referred to a special school where we would have to stay until we had reached the recommended levels. I was one of those who should have gone but our family doctor would not sign the necessary papers.

February 1953 saw the end of sweet rationing followed in September by sugar" According to "Jam Tomorrow" (Readers digest) when sweets came back. . .there was a bit of a stampede. People got so excited about it - adults more than children, because they remembered what it was like to be able to buy a packet of sweets before the war.

All food rationing came to an end on 4th July 1954. Food rationing in World War 11 improved the health of the population, infant mortality declined and life expectancy rose - discounting deaths caused by hostilities. This was because it ensured that everyone had access to a varied diet with enough vitamins.

My wife reminds me she had a different experience from me. Her father worked on the railway and her family lived in a small back to back house in the town. There was no garden so it was not possible to supplement war time rations with a policy of Digging for Britain and no farmers to supplement rations either. Feeding Sue and her brother was always a problem and often, even after the war was over, a meal could consist of diced up potatoes cooked in OXO or cheese and potato pie – potatoes layered with thin strips of cheese, when it was available - very little cheese, mostly potato.

She remembers her mother producing dresses from parachutes - three pink dresses all the same style.

L. 0. Bond

Child Poverty

I started school, aged 5, in September 1949 but I have no recollection of meeting and playing with any children before that time, apart from my younger cousin and companion who lived in the same house. There's child poverty for you. We moved house a year later and I formed a close friendship with the children next door but one.

We were not poor - I was privately educated until the age of 11 but at the same time we didn't seem to have any money. My mother had to manage the household expenses very carefully and was always concerned that bills might not get paid on time.

In the post war years whilst rationing was still in force there was a general state of austerity and everybody existed on less food and, by today's standards, a far less varied diet but where we lived and the way we lived shielded me form any contact with real child poverty. Life in the East end of London as depicted in 'Call the Midwife' would have been contemporaneous but I never witnessed anything of the kind.

My first introduction to poverty was when I entered the world of social work, training to be a Probation Officer. Initially in Leicester and then in my first job in Bristol I was confronted by the squalor and impoverished lives of so many of my clients which quickly put into perspective any hardships that I might have considered I had previously endured.

J.Chappell

27.08.13

Poverty and Austerity in my Life

I have never considered myself poor or felt I needed to practise austerity in my life, but I have always considered myself not well off and surrounded by people who are better off, better educated and of a better social class than me. This was probably not true and whether it is true or not now, it no longer bothers me.

When I was young we always seemed to have everything we needed but were always late in obtaining new technology. We ate well, dressed well and had a holiday every year. My father was buying his own house and would be classed as a white collar worker, yet there were some struggles and differences to my friends that confused me. My parents practised the 'waste not want not policy' in life so nothing was discarded lightly or wasted from food to furniture etc. but there always seemed to be a shortage of money. We didn't go short of things but the money always seemed to run out before the month did. Unlike our neighbours my fathers, mine was monthly paid and mum received her housekeeping monthly. She always had to borrow from the Sunday School funds (she was the treasurer) until pay day when she put the money back and the vicious circle began again.

Money was the most common cause of arguments between my parents. Dad probably thought mum wasted money on material for new clothes for us, as mum liked nice clothes and making them, Dad was more cautious and would like to save, yet we could never afford the latest things. The weekly paid factory workers in the street could afford a television etc. and we were last one to have one. Then the last one to have ITV, a washing machine, a phone, a car, a record player, you name it we were the last in the street to have one. Even after I left home they didn't get central heating, double glazing, colour television and holidays abroad until very late on. As a youngster I never did understand why we couldn't have everything the neighbours had. I realise now that some of it had to do with choices of how we spend our disposable income and whether we want to use credit. My parents rarely had credit and then it was usually my mum when she had a part time job later on and could use her own money as she wished.

We were taught, not so much austerity, more how to be careful with money. We all had pocket money and when young I used to spend mine on Milky Way bars. Two every day, I bought them after tea when I went to the out sales of the Crown Inn, Newbold to buy them. They then lasted until the next evening when off I went again. We never had sweets or chocolates other than for birthdays or Christmas and the same applied to toys. There had to be an occasion to have treats. I can remember my Dad getting his pen knife out and cutting a Mars bar into 5 pieces to share between us and that was probably when on holiday or some special occasion.

As a teenager eager to grow up, I couldn't wait to wear nylon stockings and when I was eventually allowed I had to buy them with my pocket money and I remember how upset I was if they laddered and I hadn't got any money to replace them. Of course it always seemed to me that other girls had plenty of money for fashion items and we were 'poor' but it really wasn't that bad. Life only became bearable for a fashion conscious teenager, with little money, when at 15 I could get a part time Saturday job which I did, working first in a cake shop, then Woolworth's until I reached the dizzy heights of Marks and Spencers before leaving school at 18 to take up my first job. Those part time jobs gave me the money to dress how I wanted.

Although my parents seemed less well off than others, they were always very fair to us children. A popular practice in the 60's was to buy a bicycle when your child passed their 11 plus. My parents would have none of that. So each summer when we were 11 we all had a bike whether we passed our 11 plus or not. I was the only one of us who did go to a grammar school and people looked at my shiny new bike and said ' I bet I know why you got that' and I would tell them, no we all had a bike when we were 11. Equally my parents wanted us to have a holiday abroad with the school, another popular thing in those days. So my sister went off to Paris with Newbold Grange School, I went ski-ing with the High School and my brother went on an educational cruise to Spain , I can't remember whether that was with his junior or senior school. I know they had to scrape to afford those holidays and sacrificed a lot to give them to us.

Equally my parents never went out socially, only with us to church events or to see my Dad in his plays at the theatre. They didn't drink or smoke or have holidays abroad. It was a very special treat when we all walked along the canal on a summer evening to have a bottle of pop and a packet of crisps with a blue bag of salt in, in the garden of the Barley Mow at Newbold. We never had a baby sitter for them to go out without us.

I earlier commented on being of a low social class. This happened when I went to the High School when I really felt an underdog and was sure all the other girls had rich families in large posh houses, in better areas of Rugby that we lived. It simply wasn't true but it was years before I realised that. Not knowing the other areas of Rugby that well I didn't know whether their areas were better than mine or not and had no idea if their families were better off than mine. It just felt like that. The headmistress was quite snooty and always called me Penelope and was never very pleasant to me until she met my father and realised that he was involved in the theatre and suddenly she was more polite to me. When they were trying to fund an outside swimming pool at the High School, another popular fashion for schools at that time, I was annoyed when my parents were asked to loan or donate money to fund it. My parents donated money which I knew they could not afford. I thought it was a waste of money to build an outdoor pool in a country that rarely saw the sun and I vowed never to go in it and I never did for the short period after it was finished I was still at the school. I doubt it is even still there.

No I was never poor, nor was I ever well off and that seems to be the way my life has gone. I didn't engage in austerity measures to any great extent but I did hear of the lengths my parents went to to cope during rationing. Drawing lines on my mums legs when nylons couldn't be bought. Making food stretch and using substitutes for meat. Growing their own vegetables. Recycling clothes from my sister to me (I hated that). But by enlarge I know I had an easy life and have been very lucky. My father was never out of work, neither was I or my husband, brother or sister or their families. I have a reasonable pension, as did my father and I am a lot better off than many. However I would like to think that I did learn to value things and am still reluctant to throw away anything, especially food, ignoring sell by dates preferring to use my judgement before giving in to wasting things. I wish I could feel that my children will be as lucky in this world where there is no safe job or a job for life. Neither of them have private pension provision, only one of my two sons is buying his own house, the other won't buy in London, where he works as he could only afford a cupboard. So I know how lucky I am **to have been to be a baby boomer!**

RUGBY
U3A

Our Living History

234

Holidays Remembered

Holidays.

It would appear that childhood experiences of so called holidays during and after the war formed the pattern of future vacations in my life.

During the war we would visit my brother Trevor who was evacuated to the depths of The Forest of Dean in Lydney. We went by train all the stations were blacked out after dark and the names were removed because of the threat of invasion and I remember being terrified of getting lost at the wrong station. We would count the stops but were often confused by halts at signals. We stayed overnight at the village pub but I do not remember any other details.

We always had lodgers in the war, the rule being if you had an empty bed you needed to fill it to aid the war effort. We had girls from rural Ireland who worked in local factories, crossed themselves when they thought the crucifix from the local church was in view and called my father Mr Gun and slurped their tea without using the handle of the cup. Mum said they did this because their hands were so cold from working in the potato fields at home and no way were we to copy them.

Fred came because dad found he only had lard and jam sandwiches in his packing up box on the engine. So he had to be rescued. He came from Ellesmere and I think he was quite a lad because one night he was found trying to hang himself up in the wardrobe and put his clothes in the bed. We had many happy days spent with his parents in rural Shropshire and I remember I saw my first black man down the garden and ran screaming in to their house. It was explained that as there were no pit head baths he had to come home for a wash. So apart from a day out on the train to Leamington Spa to see the lights in Jephson Gardens excursions were few and far between.

The first time I saw the sea was at Tal y Bont near Barmouth where we had gone by G>W>R for a week's holiday in 1945. We stayed in a boarding house with my aunt and uncle. Uncle Connie worked in the goods sheds on Moor Street station, where our new kitten came from. It was said that the spiders were as big as your hands there. This very first break since the war broke out caused lots of laughter fear and trepidation as to whether we should have stayed in dirty digs with dubious food. One exemption was the creamy milk puddings cooked in the range in the hot kitchen. I remember the sandy beach was boarded up with long rolls of barbed wire and my woollen swimming costume drooped with sand and salty water and my dad's even had moth holes in it.

The next year and many after that was spent in Cornwall at the coxswain of the St Ives lifeboats tiny cottage at The Old Arch in the Digey St Ives. The journey was exciting as we travelled overnight on The Cornishman from Snow Hill to St Austell. We took cases and bags loaded with bananas fruit a large fruit cake bread pudding and a cooked chicken from the duck pen. We used to hang clothes from the luggage racks and make beds for the night and try to sleep but we were that excited and often got so over tired we were delirious by the morning. The best part of the journey was from St Austell to St Ives on the SLOW stopper as it ran alongside the sea and rocks. Awaiting at the station would be the dray wagon our cases etc. would all be piled up on top and delivered to the Digey.

Miss Hodge was our housekeeper and she would cook our evening meal. The bakehouse was directly opposite the house with the cobblers adjoining it. Every morning the baker would give a shout and produce the warm loaves through the kitchen window. The house had open drains alongside the narrow paths and with low beamed ceilings and twisty stairs it was like dwelling in the past. It was only 5 minutes from the harbour. We walked to the beach always Porthminster and we always tried to find a new way of getting there over the rocks down new alley ways whenever the tide allowed us to We picnicked every day, swam, made sand castles, unloaded the sea into our moats, buried one another, played cricket and rounders, sun bathed and went wearily back to the smell of a proper dinner at tea time.

One day was reserved for our annual treck to Zennor a walk over the cliffs to see where the choir boy in love with the mermaid and to tickle the trout in the clear water under the bridge. Walking back we always wearily asked how much further we had to go and the reply was always the same it was the last mile home. We sang all the way thoroughly enjoying the fantastic scenery.

Uncle Connie refused to take more than one pair of trousers with him so if they got wet he had to go to bed whilst they dried in the gas oven. The men always had a day mackerel fishing and the ladies went by train to Newquay to have time away from us kids. One day we found a huge fish with an ugly face and lots of teeth washed up on the shore I honestly believed it to be a whale and I remember running up the beach hot footed to get dad before it came after us. The men quietly killed and beheaded the monk fish skewered it and carried it home to have with a pile of chips next day.

On Sundays the Salvation Army always held a service on the slipway opposite the Sloop inn in the harbour and we would go and sing in the open air. Auntie Connie was a tailoress and one year she found a roll of cellanese material in a haberdashery shop and as clothes were in short supply they bought the whole roll of cloth to take home and produce nighties, petticoats etc. from their rare find. What a contrast from the expensive gifts we buy now a days.

The two wonderful weeks flew by and soon we were travelling back to the city to save up for next year. I was still worried when dad got off the train at a station with his billy can and was nowhere to be seen when the guard waved his flag and blew his whistle. He always turned up when the train chugged out having got a fresh can of tea and having leapt in the guards van and walked up the corridor from the rear of the train.

In 1952 we decided that as it was my last year at -school we should spread our wings and venture to Holland for our holidays. Dad's free travel included the ferry to the Dutch coast, but unfortunately it was the year of the coastal flooding and as well as Lynton and Lynmouth and the East coast the dykes of Holland suffered as well. So we took off for the West coast of Scotland to a Workers Travel association Hotel called Cowal House Dunoon. This was a huge house overlooking the Clyde. It was early May but we were able to swim in the water warmed by the Gulf Stream. The holiday was very different with organised events throughout the fortnight and dances at night. We so enjoyed all these new activities that I took a friend the next year when we made a return visit. We went on Mcbane ferry trips and took the coach up into the Trossachs and Oban where I bought my parents an original oil painting of Loch Awe for their silver wedding.

In 1954 my free tickets on the railway came to an end so as I had started work 1 went to lend a Hand on the Land and went to Lincoln to pick potatoes. We lived on a disused aerodrome and slept in corrugated huts and our early morning wakeup call was by a stick being dragged along the sides. It was a back breaking occupation from early morning to late afternoon and you got sunburnt in unlikely places. We prayed for the spinner to break down and then we could have a rest. However it was good fun hard work but healthy and we looked forward to our day off when we went into Lincoln to enjoy ourselves.

In 1955 I saved enough to join a party from the local evening class and travel to lgls and Saltsburg for an Austrian holiday. The scenery was great and the mountains and passes through the countryside were mind blowing. We had rides in cable cars, coach tours foreign food arid fun shopping in the Austrian shops. We travelled by train across Europe and I enclose the bill from Transglobe for the total cost of the holiday

During my teacher training I cycled down to Treyarnon Bay on the North coast of Cornwall. 1 went with two friends on a sit up and beg bicycle borrowed from my mother and we youth hostelled all the way down. via Stow on the Wold, Holford, Barnstable and Bodmin Moor via the Quantocks. We hitched a lift in a biscuit lorry around Porlock and managed to rotate the rear wheel so that the milometer would record our journey. Apart from wind burn and sunburn we thoroughly enjoyed our adventure.

In 1956 1 was invited to go to Northern Ireland with a college friend to stay in Portrush and then go south to County Antrirm to stay with her relations for a week. One of her cousins had just returned from Australia with pockets full of pound notes and a naked lady on his tie. We dined on Brack water which was brown in colour and Jacket potatoes placed on the wooden table top next to the dinner plate, but the hospitality was faultless. we watched the Orange Order marches in Omagh we drove the cousins car without a license and went over the border at the place where Lord Mountbatten was assassinated and then dared to miss our boat back to Liverpool and had to stay for another week. Oh dear my dad was furious and insisted that if I had not completed my college work I had wasted public tax payers money.

After I had completed my course I went .straight to Eastbourne to work at the Barrington Hotel on the sea front. My cousin and her friend were just going up to Oxford and I was just going down from Coventry. My wasn't this holiday an eye opener when the honeymoon bed collapsed and we had to sweep up the woodworm dust every day and tip it into the Ming vases on the landings. The kitchen was the worst with the exact amount of food served on to plates if you dropped one the food was carefully placed back on a clean plate. Days off were precious and we would wend our way into the lovely shops and spend the weeks wages, We ended the day at Fortes ice cream parlour for a Knicker booker glory and then sit under the breakwaters on the hot stones to read a book. We paddled home in the sea to our digs. I stayed with a Miss Pether in a tiny room just off the front and she had a parrot who shouted < no bats please> incessantly. I had no idea that the parrot existed and was quite relieved when she showed me.

In 1958 1 was off to San Rerno on the Italian Riviera with two college friends and it was sea sun and sand and dancing the night away to Marina Marinio on a postage stamp. 1 remember swimming in the dark with the tour guide swimming with a torch strapped to his head in case we got lost in the sea. The worst and most scary part of the visit was that my passport went missing on a day's excursion and I was all set to go to Genoa to get a replacement when it reappeared.

1959 was the year when we spent a long weekend in North Devon at Combe Martin and Lee Bay where the fuchsias were magnificent. We walked along the cliffs ate fish and chips and sampled cream teas in beautiful locations.

After suffering from mumps three weeks before our wedding in 1960 we had a one night honeymoon at The Lamb inn, Burford and then motored down to Lyme Regis in a hired van for three days to stay bed and breakfast in mediocre accommodation. We could not wait to get back to our new house together with our second hand bed and a deck chair.

The next year my husband and I cycled to Dorset via Youth Hostels where we stayed at Lyton Cheney in a watermill attached to a cheese factory. We liked the area and visited Dorchester Swanage and Weymouth on our bicycles.

We really went to town in 1962 and borrowed a two man tent, bought a 1936 Ford 10 car which we called Pooh because it smelt stale and off we went to Morthoe in North Devon, Unfortunately the first night we arrived at the camp site on the cliffs it was very foggy and we were not sure where the edge of the cliffs were and so despite all our good intentions we had to stay in a b and b. We had good weather and cooked in the back of the car and made friends with the countryside. We crossed down from north to south and stayed next to the sea in Mevagissey for the rest of the fortnight.

Holidays continued from 1964

At this time we discovered some new neighbours who we befriended and then spent many years going on holiday together. We decided to rent a cottage in Cornwall it was on the waterside at Restronguet Creek near to Falmouth 200 yards from the old smugglers Pandora Inn. We had a super holiday with our two toddlers visiting deserted Cornish coves on the North and South coast. The weather was super and we really enjoyed the experience that we decided to rent a similar venue the following year. This was to be a caravan and cottage in its own grounds in mid Wales at a place called Solva It was idyllic and the views fantastic but garden ended on the cliffs and the staircase in the cottage disappeared through a hole in the floor. It was highly unsuitable for our young family of three. It rained every day and as it was so remote we had to make our own fun. It was warmer in the caravan and at least you could dry the nappies in the chimney area. We vowed never to go to Wales for a holiday again after 14 days of continuous rain.

So with this in mind we booked in at the rectory Llangwnadle on the Llynn peninsula where the sheep lay against the front door and the weather and beaches were superb. .We picnicked every day swam, played tennis dipped in rock pools climbed small mountains and loved every minute of it. We even spent the day at Butlins Pwllheli to see how the other half lived. We all decided that it was not for us and formed an escape committee to get us out quick.

The following year we heard of a farm house to rent near Aberdaron further down the peninsula I have enclosed the initial letter received before we booked note that it was £13 rent for the accommodation to sleep 9 for the week. This was the introduction to the happiest holidays we ever spent. The farmer welcomed us like old friends and we stayed at Nyffryn Bella for many years after. We rented half of the old stone farm which was built on rock. The farmyard was unkempt with old chest of drawers, old disused farm implements and derelict tractors left abandoned. The children loved all of it they fed the animals collected the eggs cleaned out the cow sheds and learned how to swear loudly when they were annoyed. The farm dogs killed the stray ducks and they always raced up to visitors cars to bite the tyres. They saw calves born

Letter From Farmer re Rent

chickens killed they collected hay and then rode on top of gigantic wagons bringing it back. We organised treasure hunts around the farm yard which became an annual event and even rode on huge Leicester sheep in the barn. One of the many hi lights was taking a chosen Iamb to the death house and then watching it cut up by farmer Willy in the huge kitchen by the Aga. before we packed it up to bring it home. We fished from a blow up boat had beach barbeques and danced in the sea in the moonlight. After dinner every night we had a lucky dip bag with chocolate bars and lollipops. We ran out of shampoo one year and decided to all walk about three miles along the beautiful secluded lanes to the nearest shop only to be told no sorry it is coming in a week on Monday." The Woodlands Hall Hotel was an annual extravagance when we all went for one evening meal. Every one dressed up the boys in bow ties and the girls in pretty dresses. This was a unique occasion as we never could have afforded to all go out together. I found the bill for this and 8 coffees were 1 pound 20

After several years Mr. Willy bought an isolated farm on the coast and we holidayed there under the Rivals together with harebells and blue butterflies around our feet. We even visited at Easter in deep snow helped with the lambing and played snowballs on the way up.

By 1973 we were short of cash and had just saved enough to buy a freezer and have a holiday on a tight budget. It was the season for high winds and gales and after a day out at the hydroelectric power station in the mountains our two cars were parked under three old elm trees by the orchard. We all went to bed and were woken in the night to hear Farmer Willy swearing and shouting "Oh my God" What shall we tell him. Torches flashed swearing continued and the grownups assembled to find that one tree had fallen down across our car and completely squashed it in two. That very morning we had heard that Dave had won 700 hundred pounds on Vernons pools and now" what no car we took the children

Creamery Label Off Milk Churn Collected Every Day

horse riding on the cliffs whilst the car was towed away and Dave mourned its death. The tree s were sawn up and found to be completely hollow inside. We loaned the pig van from the farm for the rest of the holiday. It smelt terrible so we had to have the windows down but it was all part of the unusual events. Mr. Willy drove us home minus safety belts what were they? He exchanged the car for a lovely fat cockerel for Sunday lunch. Every year after that a barby was held in honour of the car and we burned the tree on a huge bonfire and the whole peninsula learned of our fate.

By 1975 our friends were travelling abroad so we decided to buy a 5
berth Norwegian tent with a trailer. It was a great success in spite of all
the bad language whilst being erected. We have written extensive camp
logs for our tent and caravan holidays but there lies another story.

*Milk Bill given at end of
fortnight*

Bill for Annual Night Out

Holidays Remembered

EARLY HOLIDAYS.

In 1946 I was five years old and my brother John six and a half when my father was demobbed from the R.A.F., the war having finished the previous year. We had not seen him for about two years as he had been serving in India for most of that time. Before returning to his old civilian job, the position having been kept open for him, it was decided we should all go on holiday together to get to know one another. Money was tight but mother knew of a lady with whom she and her mother had stayed before the war and she wrote to her explaining their situation. We were offered a double-bedded room at a special price on the understanding that we would all have to share the one bed. Off we set by train to Weston Super Mare, a real adventure for John and I. Yes we did sleep four in one bed, Mum and Dad at one end, John and I at the other. Fortunately we had all had a bath before setting out as of course we got our parents feet right by our noses!

For anyone who knows Weston, and we didn't, it would hardly come as a surprise to find that for most of our holiday the tide was out. Plenty of room for donkey rides and building sandcastles but a long walk to have a paddle. In fact it was a walk almost to the end of the pier and then across the mud flats. If only the weather had been kinder, it rained I am told, for most of the time. Dad vowed we would never return and we have not.

Before the outbreak of the War my folks had lived in London and only moved out as my mother had just given birth to John and it was considered safer to return to mother's old roots in Redditch. They continued however to write to some old friends, Norah and Len Down, during the war with perhaps the idea of returning to London after hostilities had ceased. As things turned out they were nicely settled in at

Redditch with a house and garden and a reasonable job for dad and decided to stay put. While father had been away mother had formed a very close friendship with a neighbour, Violet Goldring, whose husband was ill with "chest problems". After the war ceased his G.P. advised them that perhaps it would be wiser to move to the coast where the air would be fresher. This they indeed, did do but not long afterwards unfortunately he died.

"Aunt" Violet offered to exchange houses with us for our annual holiday as she was living at Brighton so we would have the beach and she could maintain her war time friendships with her old neighbours at Redditch. At the same time we received a similar offer from Norah and Len, and the decision was made that we would take up both offers on alternate years, a week in a flat in Shepherds Bush, London, and then the following year a sea-side break. This arrangement was kept up for many years.

John and I loved it, a chance to see all the museums of the great city and all the famous sights. Dad having lived in London made an excellent guide, something he had done to get beer money and to pay for his "smokes" when he lived down there. I well remember his notorious walks, "you see nothing and learn nothing on the underground" he always told us, so we walked everywhere. Starting at Hyde Park Corner, down Park Lane to Buckingham Palace to see the Changing of the Guard. Count the number of buttons on the soldiers jackets and whether they were single, or in twos, threes or fours so you could tell which regiments were involved in the Change. Across the road to Clarence House, home to the Queen Mother, to watch the Change there, and through St. James' Park to Horse Guards Parade to view the Change there. Two regiments, was it going to be the "Blues" or "Royals" on duty?

We soon learnt the names of all the government offices, the statues in Whitehall, stood on the steps at 10 Downing Street (you could in those

days, the street was open to the public, fencing only came much later.).
Onwards to Westminster Abbey, the Houses of Parliament and of
course Big Ben. If the weather was okay we took a trip on the boat up to
The Tower London naming everything on the way, or walked it. Up
"The Minories" to the banking area and towards St. Paul's Cathedral,
no time allowed on this trip for visiting, on down to Fleet Street, the
then home of all the newspapers. The Strand beckons us on and into
Trafalgar Square with its pigeons - sorry no time for feeding them got to
press on. Through theatre land and the statue to Eros, into Regent Street
and possibly if Dad was in a good mood a quick stop at Hamleys for a
cheap souvenir. Swing left into Oxford Street and back to our starting
point at Hyde Park. It is quite a trek and one I have repeated over and
over again with my kids and their friends, always insisting on going by
foot.

Not only did we do the museums-The Natural History was always my
favourite closely followed by The Imperial War Museum but never the
art galleries, but the theatres. We would always try to take in one of the
big shows and saw many of the big names of those times.

That was the hectic year Brighton was more relaxed. John unlike me
was a real water baby and spent most of his time swimming in the sea
or getting sun-burnt. I was just as happy curled up on the beach reading
one of my war stories. Dad would sit in his deckchair, always with his
hat on or on rare occasions a knotted handkerchief, reading his
newspaper whilst mother either knitted or dozed. One day would be
spent at Brighton Races where I only remember one year where mother
astounded us by going straight through the race card and backed all the
winners! Well Gordon Richards was riding.

As I've said this routine went on for many years and was only broken
when I had the chance to go to Paris with the school. A train had been
booked as we were going to be staying in a boarding school in the south
of the city. Nearly 200 of us went from a number of schools in the

Holidays Remembered

RUGBY
U3A

Birmingham area and were very closely supervised by, in our case one teacher to every five pupils. We had to travel in school uniform which the French found rather odd. The accommodation was in dormitories, each taking about 30 children and around a couple of beds were screens behind which the members of staff on duty slept - if they could. The school was designed for boys only and we were in mixed groups so it created a number of possible problems. The most important one was toilets. Being a boys' school in the grounds of the school the urinals were open to the elements, and the cabins only had a small door just about covering your dignity. The areas of the grounds were heavily "policed" by the staff ensuring all was as it should be! One thing they failed to spot at first was that the shower block had a transparent roof and for the first 24 hours all was revealed.

We would travel into the city by tube each day and were taken to see all the sights and apart from the constant presence of teachers I really found the city to be a magic place. We didn't get much chance to try out our French, but collected all sorts of useless "souvenirs" such as bus tickets etc. which we were supposed to stick in our holiday diaries. Versailles Palace and the chateau at Fontainebleau were the highlight of our trip where we could at least explore the grounds on our own.

The truly magic holidays of my youth were the two years when I spent in Germany. We were fortunate to have a German Jew who had escaped in 1938 from Cologne but managed to keep a friendship going with a colleague from the school he had taught in the city. After the war finished they managed to get back in touch and started one of the first school exchange schemes in the country. It started by a party from my school staying in a youth hostel in the Eifel forest near to Cologne with a group of German children. The range of activities apparently available to them was a little limited and so it was agreed in subsequent years to house the children with families in the city or in Redditch. Joy of joys we were to be trusted and the two years I went only one member of staff and the father of one of party went with us. No school uniform- the

251

question was never asked- and a blind eye was turned to the older students having the odd cigarette.

We travelled by train, the journey taking nearly all day as we were constantly changing engines just to the destruction of the railway systems caused by war-time damage- this was 1957 - Europe was changing from steam to diesel electric rolling stock. We were met at the railway station by the families we were to stay with and quickly dispersed around the city. Free tram passes were supplied so we could travel freely around the city. The family I stayed with were Jehovah Witnesses, the father was German and the wife Belgian, and they had one son called Rheinhold and he was about my age. No-one spoke English and as my German was virtually non-existent most of the time we spoke in French, backed up by a sprinkling of bad German. We got on very well together and although I did not attend church at that time I was touched by their genuine and well-meaning attempts to get me involved in their meetings even going to the trouble to get translations of "Awake" and other leaflets in English for me. I was excused those meetings but Rheinhold wasn't and no objection was made by my going into the city at night to meet up with friends. Excursions were laid on every day and the German families encouraged to come along as well. I even saw the German Grand Prix at the Nurburgring. Holidays were arranged for us to go during August and the return trip for them was at the following Easter. We certainly had the better deal the German Education Authority pulled out all the stops for us but that was not true for Worcestershire Education Authority. I corresponded with the German family for many years and was sorry I let things slip when I left college a few years later.

HOLIDAYS

When I was young foreign holidays were available to the rich and adventurous, generally people holidayed nearer to home. Being in the Midlands it was a really exciting time when we went to the seaside. I can remember the train journey starting at Rugby Station and my Dad carrying our cases (why didn't they think of wheels earlier?>, the smell of the steam train and the whistle as we started

slowly at first chugging out of the station and then gathering speed, so that we rushed past houses and trees and then eventually being the first to say "There's the sea!".

We went away for a week each year and my first memory is of a boarding house (not hotel!) in Bournemouth. We went to the beach every day and dug in the sand and paddled. During the day magnificent castle were built all over the beach, decorated with pebbles, shells and little paper flags. It was a race to get bucketsful of water to fill the moat before the water disappeared into the sand. Then as the tide came in we watched as it demolished the carefully built structures.

The men seemed to always wear suits and they rolled up their trouser legs to paddle. Paddling seemed more popular than swimming — maybe because people were modest about getting changed. Deck chairs were on hire. They were incredibly difficult to put up and uncomfortable to sit on. I always  had to wear a sun bonnet, but noticed men wearing their handkerchiefs knotted in each corner to keep the sun off their heads!

One holiday which I always remember was at Hunstanton. There had been floods earlier in the year — 1952 I think — and a distant relative had a converted bus, used as a caravan, which we borrowed for a week.

Holidays Remembered

The flood water had nearly reached the caravan park and there were derelict houses all the way to the beach. I can remember looking at one half demolished house and seeing a book lying on the floor, its pages flapping in the breeze and wondering about its owner.

We saw lovely sunsets at night and I only have top hear the song "Now is the hour" to be transported back to sitting watching the sunset and hearing it playing nearby. There was a row of shops with a model of a policeman in a plastic case. When you put a penny in he would laugh as the music played "The Laughing Policemen". Before going on holiday generous family members would give me money to "buy an ice cream"

— bother the ice cream — my money went on the laughing policemen! It was customary to buy a present to take back to those who might not have a holiday and I chose April Violet scent for my Grandma — how she loved it! One of our neighbours collected shells for her garden and we always took a few back for her. Collecting shells and pebbles were reminders, once we got home, of our holiday, especially when we put the shell to our ear and "heard the sea". We also took a piece of seaweed home — it was supposed to be a weather forecaster when it was hung outside.

Eating out in Hotels was not the usual thing to do — we took picnics onto the beach. The sand in the sandwiches gave them a taste of their own.

Along the promenade there were photographers who would take souvenir photographs. We had our photos taken early in the week and had to collect them before we went home. Sometimes the photographer put a little dressed monkey or a parrot in our hands.

All too soon the holiday would be over and we "waved goodbye to the sea until next year" as the train set off for Rugby again.

Family Holidays

Family holidays brought back many happy memories for me. When we moved to Swindon in the late 1950's this was when we started to regularly take holidays. Dad was always keen for us to take an annual break to the seaside when at the beginning of July, the Railways always had 2 weeks called Trip fortnight when the whole of Swindon went away. I clearly remember Dad commenting on many of our neighbours who never went on holiday, so we felt rather fortunate. I can only imagine that in his childhood Dad being one of 13 children and being raised in Ireland was never fortunate enough to go on any type of holiday. So for him he had his priorities right, they both worked very hard so this was their present to us.

Most of our holidays were by the sea in either Weymouth or Weston-Super-Mare, and we travelled there by train, Swindon being a major railway junction and going to most popular destinations. We always stayed in Guest houses as Mum wanted to be waited on, as she worked hard throughout the year and didn't want to do the same in a caravan or any self-catering establishment. Weymouth back then had a lovely beach were we spent much of our holiday and generally there was plenty to do. We would play golf on the pitch and putt course several times in the fortnight along with spending much of our time on the beach. Mum and Dad never ventured into the sea so they hired deckchairs and read their newspapers while we built sandcastles and went for a swim if the water was remotely warm.

We also went to Weston-Super-Mare, this was very close to Swindon and notorious for its tide that was rarely in, we remember walking it seemed for miles to find the sea. So there was plenty to do and see, like Punch and Judy shows and donkeys rides on the beach, also there was The Marine Lake an enclosed man made beach where it was safe to swim. Like many seaside resorts there were many amusement parks and slot machine

emporiums. I always remember there being many people and the beaches were very crowded, this didn't seem to bother us, but you wouldn't get me on any crowded beaches now!!! As holidays to us were the 'norm', perhaps we took them for granted and no particular holiday stood out.

Perhaps the most memorable family holiday was in 1961 when after we celebrated my grandparents Golden Wedding the previous Christmas.

Holidays Remembered

Uncle Chris, Grampy and Nanny Gough, Uncle Frank. Left back, Auntie Audrey my mother, Auntie Ivy, cousin Billy, my sister Elaine, back right, Auntie Edie, me, cousin Irene, fiancé Derek and cousin Sallie

Taken December 1960

We all decided to have a holiday together and hired 2 bungalows on the seafront at Jaywick Sands just outside Clacton-on-Sea in Essex. There were 15 of us, my grandparents, my Mum's 3 sisters and their families pictured above. With our accommodation being virtually on the beach we spent much time swimming and playing beach games and hiring a bicycle for 6.

Like many families not everything went smoothly, my uncle was taken ill and went to hospital where he spent a few days but soon recovered. Nearby Clacton-on-Sea was a rather busy resort with a large funfair and in particular a very large big dipper where I spent many a happy hour. My Dad also had some good fortune and won some money backing horses, when he brought his winnings home this caused an atmosphere as not everyone shared his joy at a large win!!!! I wonder why.

We had a very enjoyable time with many happy memories of the family holiday for the last time. However my sister, my cousin and I were bridesmaids at Irene's wedding in 1963. Distance did not permit any other holidays as we all went our separate ways and priorities changed when we all married and children came along. Looking back I realise now that my parents made many sacrifices for us, it is only now that I appreciate what they very happily did for us despite resources not being very plentiful. Oh happy days, I hope I am not looking at my past life through rose coloured spectacles!!

HOLIDAY MEMORIES

One of my earliest memories of holidays was of when I was about five years old and all the family went to London. Dad had relatives in Hertfordshire so we combined the London trip with a visit to them. We didn't see them very often even though they were quite a close family. He was one of five children and born in Ulverston, so I guess they'd left their roots and headed down south – probably for work.

The journey to London was on the overnight sleeper train from Newcastle to Kings Cross. We were all very excited at the prospect of going to London, where the streets were paved with gold! I remember being rather disappointed to find they weren't! The train arrived about 5.30am, and Dad had suggested we all go to Lyons Corner House for breakfast. I seem to recall that it wasn't open when we arrived but there was plenty to look at close by to fill in time. We children had never seen such big grand buildings and such wide pavements. London was just waking up so the traffic was light and few people around. Lyons opened, we had a super breakfast served by waitresses called 'nippies', all dressed in the uniform of black skirts and white starched aprons and caps. Suitably fed, we again headed for the station and on yet another train to Hitchin in Hertfordshire, to be met by some of our relations. All I remember of the Aunts, Uncles and cousins was happy times and lots of laughter and fun playing with all my cousins that I'd never met before. We must have spent a few days with them plus a couple of away days in London to do all the usual sightseeing. London Zoo, Houses of Parliament with Big Ben, Buckingham Palace with the guards standing in their sentry boxes guarding the entrance. It was all so splendid and very grand! We had thought Newcastle was a large and impressive city but London was so special!

The holiday camp featured in childhood – at Clayton Bay, near Scarborough. It was perfect rain or shine. Always lots to do for everyone in the family. Kids clubs run by the 'redcoats' were always popular with varied activities – if sunny they involved the swimming pool where various games were hilarious. Mum and Dad had the coaching in ballroom dancing. Knobbly knees competition, talent contents, glamorous granny competition (my mum won this one year). The variety shows in the evenings were first class. Bikes to hire would seat two side by side and could be taken all over the camp. We went there a few times – sometimes in a chalet and later on a caravan. All very basic, but it didn't matter as we only seemed to use it for sleeping!

I remember spending a few holidays in caravans. We ended up buying a small caravan which we kept on a farm on the Duke of Northumberland's Estates near Alnwick. Many good weekends were spent there. Very Spartan – outside loo tent with chemical loo, gas mantle lighting, no heating, water to be collected on a trolley from a tap at the farm. The farm had a few dairy cows and we always had warm milk bottled or jugged straight from the cow! Delicious! Dad and I would go mushroom picking before breakfast so we had a feast with our bacon and eggs. I did quite a bit of fishing in the nearby River Aln – bought the rod and line with savings – cost 12s.6d.! Don't recall catching anything worth eating but enjoyed the experience. At harvest time we helped stack the bales of hay. It was amazing to see it gradually cut down and all the wildlife escaping as the farmer got closer to the centre of the crop.

All summer holidays I remember in childhood had wall to wall sunshine! I'm sure they weren't but they were always full of activities and certainly not boredom!

In future years, when we had our own children, we repeated the experience of the holiday camp and caravan holidays. For years we went camping in France which was the only way we could afford to go abroad but things have now changed!!! We lived in Iran for a while and have now become well-travelled to far flung places. China, America,

Thailand, Turkey, Greece, Spain and many more! Now travelling seems so much easier than in the past when I remember that long, long journey overnight to London when I was 5!!!

HOLIDAYS

There are not a lot of memories of childhood holidays. For several years we had a week in London, looking at the sites. On reflection this was a very expensive holiday for my father's wages. I recall that every Friday, pay day, the money would be divided into various envelopes: gas, electricity, water and holidays. We always stayed at The Regent Palace Hotel which was not cheap. I suppose one could visit many places for free then, that we pay for now, and there was a lot to see. Just wandering round the large department stores was exciting. We usually had a meal at Lyons Corner House and I always had pancake with apricot jam. One theatre visit was imperative — usually the London Palladium. On one occasion we visited Broadcasting House and hoped to see a live radio programme. The Commissionaire said only children over 12, at which I piped up "Oh, I'm 11" so we couldn't go in. I was in trouble. My parents frequently went out in the evenings and I was left quite safely in the hotel bedroom.

One year we went to the Isle of Wight for a change and to visit my father's mother and sister. It rained every day and we went to the cinema every afternoon. My parents had no idea of going for walks or generally exploring the countryside. It was vowed never again, but I still have happy memories of digging on Ventnor beach. We revisited it about 12 years ago and poor Ventnor is very run down.

When I was 18 and engaged to David, we went on holiday on the Broads with two other engaged couples and a spare brother. It was the best holiday I had eve r experienced. In those days the girls were strictly in one cabin and boys in the other. That poor brother it can't have been much fun for him.

Once we were married with a small family, holidays were difficult. We had a few staying in guest houses, and then David heard about friends who had camping holidays. That was that. We camped for years, long after the children had left home. It meant that we could afford a couple of weeks away every year, freedom for the children — and the usual work for me. The children still remember the first holiday abroad and the excitement of just being there. We set our tent directly opposite some old RAE friends — it is amazing how these coincidences happen throughout life.

In 1969 David was on a course at Lossiemouth, Morayshire converting on to Buccaneers. I have to confess that it was my own idea, but I said I would drive myself and the 4 children up to him and we would then have a holiday in Scotland. This journey of over 500 miles was for years the record in the family for the longest solo journey. We lived in Suffolk and really I just had to point the car's nose north and keep going until I fell off the edge at the other end. Fortunately Christopher has all his father's navigational skills — but it was a long way. We stopped over at Dalkeith and then drove through Edinburgh early on Sunday morning — I was amazed at what I was doing — and the children were so well behaved. Somewhere during the second day in a very mountainous region, I pulled in to have a drink and collect myself. As I sat there a caravan pulled in front of us, and I watched with envy while a women made a pot of real tea and she and her husband sat on comfortable, civilised seats and enjoyed it. That was it — by the time I arrived at our destination — it was decided we were going to caravan in future. And we did. The Scottish holiday was reasonably successful we did a lot of walking and exploring, then the rain set in and we left a couple of days early, and I was driven back to Suffolk.

All of our children have such happy memories of those camping holidays and the eldest three have had many themselves with their children.

After they had all left home, we were still caravanning then decided to have walking holidays. We went with Waymark, where David was a leader, for several years. The holidays were graded and you chose the appropriate trip for your capabilities — we were always of mixed abilities and I found the distances a bit gruelling. Rambling friends had told me about Holiday Fellowship (now HF), most of the holidays are in the UK and there are three grades of walk each day. Once again David became a walking leader and we had some of the best holidays of our lives with HF. And only stopped when I developed foot problems. We took two granddaughters to Freshwater, Isle of Wight when they were 7 and 8, and they still have wonderful memories of this. This continued for several years. We also had an annual holiday with David's church at Prestwood. They would book a complex of holiday cottages and we would self-cater. These were either in Cornwall, Devon, Dorset or Pembrokeshire

I think we walked nearly all the coastal footpaths and had again wonderful, companionable holidays in some of the most beautiful parts of the British Isles. Once again, granddaughters came with us.

Then things changed, and we tried cruising — having no idea if it would really appeal to us. We go with Discovery which is an old boat, which takes about 600 passengers, and we love it. I enjoy the days at sea with all that space around me. We have met pleasant passengers and seen countries I didn't expect to visit. This can only be every other year.

A couple of weeks ago we had four days back in Portsmouth, our home town, which we left 56 years ago. Obviously we have been back in the past to visit parents, but they are all long dead. It was a fantastic success we tootled around using our bus passes and had a good look around the whole city. David stood in the playground of Portsmouth Grammar School which he had attended. When we visited the cathedral a woman came up to speak to us. She was an Asst. Chaplain, on talking we discovered that she and I had been at the Northern Grammar School in the same year, but in different classes. We remembered all the teachers — it was amazing. Portsmouth had changed a lot but there was still so much that remained unchanged — another incredibly successful holiday.

I can't believe what I have left out. Our son emigrated to Australia about 14 years ago and we have had three holidays out there. The first time we stayed in Queensland with Christopher and Cherie for about 10 days and then flew on to Sydney for another 10 days. Sydney is, I think, still my favourite overseas city. It has such a buzz, and there is a lot to see. We bought a week's travel pass and moved around by ferry or bus and visited every corner. There was a lot of good walking and lovely weather. A city that looked forward and not back — like Europe. On the second occasion we had a couple of weeks in New Zealand, and finally a couple of years ago visited Melbourne. The 26hr journey to Australia is horrific and we had decided to hang the cost and travel business class. However, we asked our middle girl to come with us so we were back to economy, once more.

On re-reading these notes I am struck by the change that has taken place in our expectations. To my parents, visiting London was just as exciting as me flying to Australia — during these trips we visited Singapore and Dubai en route. Unbelievable a mere 60 years ago. Now, we are all conscious of the need to fly less — we were lucky to make these visits when we did.

Our Living History

Holidays in the' 30s

by John Hobson

Much as I loved school from when I entered the infants' class in 1933, I valued the freedom of our farm fields even more. Holidays to us village boys just meant no school. No-one went away. It was a grand opportunity to scour the Easter-time hedgerows for birds' nests.

Actually, there *were* day trips to the seaside. Len Stevens' charabanc would set off for Southsea early on a Saturday morning in midsummer.

From Charney Bassett in what was then West Berkshire – since shamefully given to Oxfordshire – was only about 60 miles away. To a six year old farm boy in 1934 it was a major adventure. After all these years I can still recall the excitement of smelling the sea as we approached through Portsmouth.

I suppose it was a slight disappointment not to be able to use the new bucket and spade on the pebbly beach but it was a great thrill to swim in the sea after our little River Ock, a sluggish tributary of the Thames on its meandering way to Abingdon.

A year later the charabanc outing was to Weston Super Mare. There was plenty of sand *there* when the tide was out. The beach stretched for miles.

Those outings and the annual visit to my maternal grandparents in North Wales were the main holiday events.

Less distant but equally memorable were the Sunday afternoon picnics on White Horse Hill, only six miles away near the ancient Ridgeway that runs from near Swindon to Goring. (That was the route of a walking holiday several years later). The high-light of the White Horse Hill picnics was tobogganing on an old tin tray down the steep grassy slope into the hollow called The Manger. It was below Dragon Hill where we believed the chalky lines from the crest were where the beast's blood had trickled after St. George had done the deed.

Little did I know in those carefree pre-war years that I would return to Southsea as a games master, to Weston hospital to comfort my son in intensive care after he fell off his bike and to White Horse Hill to picnic with our own children and grandchildren long before it became a recent murder scene.

Holidays Remembered

The first thing to remember is that my dad only got two weeks holiday each year. He also worked five and a half days each week but got Saturday off once every four weeks. That's the bad news. The good news was my Dad had a car which came with his job as a representative in the building trade. So when he did have a holiday we could go anywhere - by car.

I'm told that my first holiday was in Whitby when I was just four months old. Looking at the photos Mum and Dad looked pleased to have me along. A year later it was Silloth, a seaside town on the Solway Firth not too far from Carlisle. This was the first of two holidays there. Why we went there I don't know. Seaside however was always part of our life. Living only eight miles from the sea we would go there every fine day when Dad was not working.

Looking back on photographs from my early childhood we seemed to have a lot of holidays with relatives. My Mum's sister lived some thirty miles away and it seems that we spent quite a bit of time on holiday with them and my cousins in those early years.

I remember one year my Aunt, Uncle and cousins being on holiday. They had rented a caravan on the Cumberland coast and we travelled from Newcastle to see them one weekend. Now these were the days before anyone had a telephone and even with the super-fast postal system that was in place at that time it was traditional that the postcards arrived on the day you returned. (letters would arrive next day but not postcards). Well, after my cousins and family had been there a week, as arranged, we went off to see them. The weather was not too good, no rain but overcast. Not the sort of day you wanted to spend at the seaside really but we had said we would be there and we always did what we said.

We found the caravan from the address we had been given but it was all closed up and there was no sign of my cousins. The whole site was deserted so there was no one to ask where they were. The site was really grotty. One or two caravans in a yard. The ground was just cinders and everywhere looked really dirty. We waited about for almost an hour before we went off to find a café for a cup of tea. We stooged around for a couple more hours then went back to the caravan site to see if they had returned. Still no sign. So back to Newcastle with Mum and Dad really worried. A bit like the Mary Celeste. Whatever had happened to them?

Well, the next weekend, when their holiday should have been over we travelled to their home in Bishop Auckland for our usual Sunday visit. They were home and had been for a couple of days. We asked them what had happened the previous weekend.

"Oh! Well we didn't think you would come. The site was absolutely terrible and we knew you wouldn't like it. The weather wasn't very good either. We spent most of our time trying to avoid spending any time there. We went off each morning and didn't come back until bed time. We never thought that you would actually come to such a terrible place."

"But how were we to know that it was so terrible unless we went there?" my Mum asked.

"Oh! Yes – I see. Well we just thought you would know."

(Not a bad thought process for my Aunt who was to become a school teacher when her children were a little older!)

Many of our "Holidays" were spent visiting relations. My father's sister had a pub in Somerset and I remember holidaying with her while my Dad spent much of his time fishing.

As I grew older the holidays became more adventurous. When I was about 10 we went off to Scotland staying in a small hotel in the middle of nowhere. There was a small Loch in the grounds

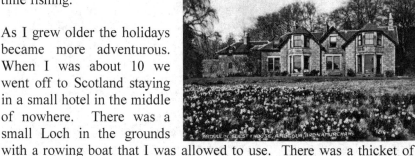

with a rowing boat that I was allowed to use. There was a thicket of

Bamboo in the grounds and I remember enjoying myself hiding in there with my new friend Angela who was about my age. We were the only children there and we were allowed to amuse ourselves out of sight of our parents. She found a Slow Worm and allowed me to keep it in a tin in my room until next morning. I didn't get much sleep. Was the tin quite secure? We let it go next morning. That was a good holiday. We went to a highland games and I went to see the film "Geordie" staring Bill Traverse that was showing in a village hall.

The next holiday I remember was when I was about 12 or 13 and we had a week on the Norfolk Broads in a cabin cruiser. That was so good we repeated it the following year. I think that was the end of my holidays with my parents. By this time I was in the Scouts and each

Holidays Remembered

year I would go off for a week's Scout Camp. As I got even older the Scout Camp became a week long trek across Denmark.

Once married, and in the army, holidays stopped. Being away from home it was almost a duty to go and visit our parents whenever I got leave. We didn't have much money either so the idea of paying for a room in a hotel or even renting a caravan by the sea was out of the question. That policy stayed with us for many years and when our children were old enough we bought a tent and spent a couple of weeks each summer on the west coast of France, lazing about on the beach and visiting local towns. As a result of this our kids seemed quite happy making their own fun on the beach or around the campsite. Very few amusement parks, roundabouts or the like.

Things move on of course and now we are avid package holiday takers. Our Children however seem to be following in our earlier footsteps and take themselves off with their children on holidays very similar to those we used to enjoy with them.

Joe
April 2011

HOLIDAY CHANGES OVER THE YEARS.

My father was demobbed in 1946 and we had our first family holiday at Weston Super Ware. It was a case of a "getting to know one another" as father had been away with the Royal Air Force. We travelled there by train, quite a new and exciting experience for my brother and I, he was seven and I was six. We stayed in a boarding house, sharing one room and all four of us sharing one bed, two at the top and two at the bottom. My brother and I slept between the feet. It was all father could afford. The weather we recall was dreadful, plenty of rain. It was to have been a traditional bucket and spade holiday on the beach with donkey rides. The tide always seemed to be out and we trekked over miles of sand and mud to reach the sea. We have never been back!

Our holidays then alternated between Brighton and London. One of mother's war-time neighbours and friend had moved to Brighton after the war on the advice of her doctor. He told her the sea-air would be good for her chest and breathing problems. Unfortunately he died not long after they had moved into a bungalow there. My" Aunt" got in touch and suggested we could do a holiday house exchange, giving her a chance to meet her old friends and for us, the beach. Before the war my parents had lived in London and had friends and relations there. They had a fiat in Shepherds Bush and so an agreement was made for an exchange with them. It all worked out very well.

Aunt's bungalow was on the outskirts of Brighton on a main bus route, perfect. We always believed that the summers then were always sunny and our days were spent on the beach. We have photos of father in a deckchair, always with either his trilby hat on, or a knotted handkerchief protecting his balding head. Invariably mother would be knitting whilst my brother and I threw stones into the sea, the sand only being available late in the day when the tide was out. One year my brother got badly sunburnt after sleeping on the beach and we had to take him to the hospital for treatment. One day was always reserved for a day at Brighton Races for a flutter. I remember one year when mother backed the winner in every race. It was the year Gordon Richards, always a favourite with the ladies, rode there for the last time. It was ice-creams all round.

Thanks to our holidays in London we got to know the city very wall and knew all the museums and sights of London. Every Sunday we would start at Marble Arch and set off down Park Lane to see The Changing of the Guard at Buckingham Palace. From there through Hyde Park for the Change of the Horse Guards at Whitehall. Onwards past The Cenotaph, 10 Downing Street, the old New Scotland Yard to Westminster Abbey and The Houses of Parliament. From here it was a question of following the Thames up to The Tower and Tower Bridge and back through the City to Trafalgar Square. If you've never tried it, it's quite a walk. "It's the only way you'll ever get to know the real London on your feet" father would say. Many, many years later our own children would learn to appreciate the city in the same way.

The only changes made to this routine were when I started at the grammar school and had the chance to visit Paris and Cologne. On the Paris trip we stayed in a boy's boarding school in the south of the city. Our school was part of a bigger group from schools all around Birmingham and we travelled on a special train and ferry. It was a mixed group of boys and girls. Our group was of about twenty to thirty of us and six members of staff accompanied us. We had to wear school uniform at all times and had little freedom. However we did see not only the major sites but also visited Versailles and Fontainebleau. We slept in dormitories; the girls were in a dormitory on the floor below us. The shower area and toilets had a glass roof and after our evening meal we boys had to go out into the grounds while they got changed for bed.

The Cologne trip was completely different; we stayed with German families around the city. As with most families our knowledge of each

275

other's language was very limited, if at all, we had only studied German in school for a year. The family ¡ stayed with did not know any English but the wife was Belgian, she had married a German airman during the war, and we could get by in French. They were a very friendly lot and gave me a key to the flat and a free tram pass so l could go in to the city to meet up with my friends when I wanted to. Their son, Reinhold, was not allowed out in the evenings as they were Jehovah Witnesses and had religious meetings in the fiat most evenings that he had to attend. I tried not to abuse their trust but we would often meet up at an open-air dance place in The Rheine Park where I have to confess we met the girls and smoked and drank beer. ¡ was only 16 at the time. It was perhaps lucky for us that Reinhold was not allowed to accompany us as his mother would have had a fit. Only one member of staff and one parent accompanied us and we only saw them when we went out on coach trips. We were there for a fortnight and saw a great deal of the Rhine and Mosel valleys as well as a trip to the Grand Prix at the Nürburgring. We were there when the British driver Peter Collins was killed not far from where we were standing at Karusel. The following year we were hoping that Reinhold would come and stay with us but his parents would not let him come. I did have a different boy come instead.

The 1950s saw the growth of Holiday Camps (Hi-Dl-Hi) led by companies like "Butlins" and "Warners". They had all the facilities families were looking for, indoor/outdoor swimming pools, theatres, dance floors, on-site catering, and bars. Any children were well taken care of by a group of dedicated helpers. My girlfriend Sue - now my wife - together with two good friends decided to try them out. We were surprised when all sets of parents readily agreed but we were going off to college/university on our return! We went to Puckpool, one of Warners' camps on the Isle of Wight. It even had its own small private beach. We soon learnt to be "happy campers" and even joined in all crazy activities.

Holidays Remembered

RUGBY
U3A

The following year we opted for a camp at Douglas on the Isle of Man travelling there by ferry. The crossings were dreadful! The camp had been an internment camp during World War li and was well past its best. All the facilities needed updating and were very limited, even the pool had tiles missing. While we were there over half the camp went down with sickness and diarrhoea. It was a holiday from hell! Our two friends left early and went home but we moved into a Bed and Breakfast at Ramsay further up the coast. The weather was pretty good and it really is a lovely island as we found out.

Sue and I were married soon after leaving our colleges in 1963 and honeymooned at Betwys-y-Coed. The wedding day at the end of October was blessed with a lovely warm sunny day. On the contrary the next day when we set off for Wales it was pouring with rain. After two days of heavy rain and low mist making it impossible to see Snowdon we gave up and came home to our flat in Walsall. We lit a fire and snuggled up on the rug.

When our daughter was born two years later we had our first family holiday at Butlins Holiday Camp at Minehead, it was several steps up from our earlier camping experiences and had for us, the luxury of a baby-sitting service in the evenings.

Eighteen months later our son was born and our holiday this time would be in a hotel at Ventnor right on the sea-front a few yards from a perfect beach. The weather we remember as being idyllic and we have great memories of the two little ones digging in the sand, and playing in the paddling pool or rock pools. It was magic, a real seaside holiday.

As the children grew up they joined the cubs and scouts and the brownies and guides and enjoyed going off to annual camp. They both asked why we as a family had never been camping. I had to be honest and said it had never appealed to us to sleep on mother earth sleeping under canvas. They persisted and in the end we agreed to give it a try.

We bought a six berth tent and our first weekend we spent at Stratford on Avon, close enough to home in case the weather was inclement, or things did not turn out to our liking. On the contrary we pronounced it a success. We got used to sleeping in sleeping bags and cooking on a small stove. We would often take the tent down to the Cotswolds at weekends in the fruit picking season. We had quite a few holidays under canvas before graduating to a trailer tent. When the kids left home we swapped the trailer tent with one of our neighbours for a dishwasher!

Our first flight on an aeroplane was to The Isle of Man with our children and my parents who came with us, or more correctly, they booked onto the same flight and hotel as we did without telling us. A bit sneaky. One the way from the airport on the coach we stopped at "The Fairy Bridge" near Douglas. Tradition requires that you get out of your transport and walk to the centre of the bridge where the gentlemen have to raise or remove their hats and the ladies curtsey whilst saying "good morning "to the fairies. Fifty of us complied feeling like a right lot of plonkers. Our first morning on the beach my father disappeared and we thought he perhaps gone to get a paper. Imagine our surprise when off came his trilby, jacket and tie and he struggled to take off his trousers and appeared from behind his towel wearing a pair of trunks! He said he was determined to go in the sea with the kids. A real one off! It really made all our holiday. The island has many quirky types of transport including the "toast rack", a horse-drawn tram which goes along the front at Douglas and a number of little railways

We discovered the fantastic idea of Gites in France. There are about 23.000 converted farm cottages which serve as holiday lets either self-catering or as Gite d'ilote a sort of guest house. They are mostly in the countryside near small villages but there are some near the sea. We have stayed in a number of them with the children as they tend to be on farms. On our first occasion at a place called St. Pierre des Ifs we were taken out into the fields to meet the cows and asked which one we would like to milk. Being "townies" we declined the kind offer, it all looked a little too technical and too near the rear end. It was easier to send my son on a borrowed bike into the village for milk and our daily bread. We were amazed at his ability to come back with the goods, his French was obviously better than we gave him credit for. A visit into the village one day revealed a small supermarket!

Only when the children finally left home did we start looking at package holidays and the luxury of being looked after. We have since taken in most of Europe, Canada, gone on Safari in Kenya. China, Cyprus and Crete. This year we are even changing our form of transport and travelling to Provence by train. Next year we have already booked our first cruise- we have decided to catch up with the rest of U3A. It's to the Eastern Mediterranean. Not quite sure if it's really us but it seems to be "the in thing".

First Jobs

JOBS

In the last year of School, shorthand typing and book keeping were added to the curriculum to prepare the girls for office jobs where the money was good and prospects greater. But I was not interested I wanted to work in a chemist shop. On hearing this a lady from our church took me to see her father who owned a well-known chemist shop in the town centre and that was IT!.

Chemist's shops were different in those days. Medicine was not so sophisticated and as doctors visits had to be paid for people had to get their own remedies or seek the advice of the chemist. Mr Silver was a very clever man with his own made up linctuses and remedies much sort after. We were very busy serving customers, dressing the windows and cheering up the poorly people bringing in their prescriptions. We were very happy for those who got better but sad for the ones who did not make it. We each had to do a turn in the dispensary learning how to mix the medicines, dish out the tablets etc. all very serious occupations.

The war had just ended and toiletries were in short supply but we three girls always looked smart and smelled nice as we had the first choice of all the current perfumes i.e. Yardley Californian Poppy, Evening in Paris to name but a few. Jockey Club came from the Indians who worked at the market just across the road from our shop at the weekends. I stayed in this job until I left to have my first baby.

I did not work again until we had moved to Rugby and the children were older. Televisions were being rented out to save repair expenses and I was asked if I would run the one at Bosworth and Carvells, I stayed there for a few years and quite enjoyed the routine but when an advert was in the paper for an opening at the Co-op Bank in Chapel

First Jobs

Street I applied for the job and once more I was dealing with the public again.

There were only two of us on the counter and once again we were very busy. Monday was manic as the Workers Club paid in their weekend takings. Ryton Gardens had just opened and we dealt with their finances too. We had to balance completely and stay over until we did. Mistakes were frowned upon, I got on well with the general office girls and they still keep in touch today and take me out for a meal at Christmas although I am old enough to be their mothers. I was very fortunate but I shudder to think how vulnerable we were at the top of the building just two of us out front with loads of cash in our tills. We would have provided easy pickings for the clever thieves of today. Just a counter in front of us and no protective screens like today. Then I took early retirement to put my feet up. WRONG!

A friend and neighbour asked me if I would cover as a classroom helper for six weeks at a special school. Here I was to discover an entirely new outlook on life and at the end of six weeks I was asked if I would be a helper with a boy with autistic tendencies. I said yes and then filled in the application form, an inside job I think it is called.

Now my education had begun. My vocabulary improved and when a pompous lady once asked me if I was disgusted at the language in the stage musical Billy Elliot I could truthfully say no as I had an A level in bad language. That shut her up. It was hard work but the teachers were excellent. Trying to teach a class of children with such a variety of learning difficulties was quite eventful especially not knowing when a chair was going to be thrown across the room or throw a tantrum over a minor event but they managed with excellent results and we even had fun!

The boy I supported was not expected to read but with patience he achieved it and a few months ago I was in a restaurant and a tall good looking young man came over to me a menu in his hand ready to order his meal. He told me he was with a group of friends. That really had been worth all the effort.

When I think how bad it was when one of my boys brought his school report home and it said: not in immediate danger of over work: compared to what these children were going through and just how their parents were handling difficult situations. We have a lot to be grateful for. I stayed here until my proper retirement age.

Mrs Wilson refused to let me rest and age graciously. When she started up an after school art club at a local Primary school she roped me in. This was a very happy hour the children loved it and some interesting work was produced I even surpassed myself by making craft models.

What a happy way to complete my working life!

JOBS Full Time

I worked at a special school running the lower classes with 5 to 7 year olds all with specific learning disorders, some were autistic, deaf or most difficult of all the emotional behavioural disorders. We were given a skeleton curriculum to build on but were able to follow a flexible approach. I discovered we were able to use diverse learning situations all to be recorded on individual educational programmes. The children had all failed and were often too frightened to try again in case they slipped down the slippery slope. Progress was slow and my motto was "You cannot teach a child until you have reached that child" Social training was a must and happened every day Circle times were important when you took your turn to speak and everyone else had to listen. This was achieved by passing an object around the group and only the holder could speak. Rewards were given often for the recipient to just sit in the circle without interrupting and then they graduated to giving a short piece of news. The teachers and assistants all joined in and eyebrows were never raised even if the news was a bit hairy e.g. Me bruvver was on the repro on the motor way, there were two bodies in the crash and an ear on the seat". Another instance was the whole of a tough local family had bought electrical goods from a car boot and found that some did not work and the tough guys had gone back to the stall to do them over! We actually found out that these news items were true. The most confusing piece of news I ever had to deal with was when a whole family had been to hospital to have their tonsils removed and related the operation and the aftercare including ice creams. We rang the hospital only to find the appointment had not been kept. The same family reported mum was pregnant again and we all rallied round collecting useful clothes etc. only to find she was unable to produce any more off springs any way. One little boy who was extremely violent sat in the group steaming one day we thought he was on fire but he had put on the only jumper from the pile of washing and it was very damp.

Bearaerobics was great fun and worked well, it soon got the circulation going and it was exercise to music in the wet weather but when it was dry we used to jog around the playground each day with the staff and head joining in. Some children needed breakfast before work or even a cuddle or reassurance. The nit nurse was not a favourite character especially when she told us that the lice could not live off a hair strand and we took great delight in keeping one in a coffee jar to show her next day. The head gave us no sympathy until we combed one child's hair and kept the offending mites on a piece of kitchen roll and counted up to eighty. The joke was that if anything moved in my class you stamped on it.

We had a farm at the back of the school with two milking goats and a few hens. The older pupils cared for them and the children related to the animals kindly. The individual learning programmes ran alongside the behavioural ones so that teachers' helpers parents and advisors were able to obtain an all-round view of the child's progress. Behaviour was monitored in detail and reports had to be handed in to the head of department regularly. We concentrated on a reward system and The Gold Award Charts were visible in most classrooms. Targets were written at the top and then rewards given if these were reached. The Nasty Curriculum was certainly not relevant in many cases but these rewards were.

Once a year in June often the wettest week of the Summer we took the whole class over to Napton on a campsite. We travelled daily and the tent and caravan were used for the children. This was such a success that eventually we kept the children overnight only a few at a time. The days were planned carefully and the time table included walks diaries outdoor games and sing songs in the wet tents. It was hard work but great fun and many parents and grandparents joined in.

In the early 90's Special Schools in Warwickshire were reduced and eventually many were closed in order that the children might be contained in Mainstream education, together with their statement of needs and support. I wished them all the best and took early retirement and went to work in a local primary school as a teacher's assistant looking after a statemented pupil. I worked for two years and enjoyed the contact with a caring school and then when my husband retired I ran an art club after school for an hour every week. This was very messy but many fine art was produced and we exhibited our work in the entrance hall. Sadly this came to an end but I regard working with the children a most rewarding occupation and never regret all the diverse experiences.

JOBS

I can't remember having to do jobs as a child, mum never worked full time until I was a teenager and so we helped one another to tend the garden livestock, rabbits hens and ducks and necessary housework at the same time. I enjoyed collecting waste paper and jam jars for the war effort but only the beer bottles were taken back to the pub for reward. A favourite job was gutting the mackerel and preparing it for sousing, but in the back of my young unsuspecting mind I longed to be a nurse, just like Googie Withers in White Corridors. That was all before my brother trapped his finger in a deck chair and I had hysterics at the sight of all the blood.

My first paid job was to look after two little girls prepare their dinner and entertain them whilst their mother worked in the mornings. Then I had a short employment with a neighbours golden retriever feeding and dog walking it for two weeks. After leaving school at 16 I was quite content to start work straight away and caught the outer circle bus to Bourneville to work in the post department of Cadburys. It took an hour to travel around Birmingham and I had to leave home early to arrive by 8 30 am, if I was a minute late you lost a quarter of an hours pay. The only reason I had gone there was that they operated a day release so that you could continue your education on one day per week. I attended Bourneville day Continuation College together with all sorts of students and I remember swapping miss shaped chocolates with Ever Ready batteries. I even travelled back on Saturdays to play in the hockey team, sorted post in a huge flap sortograph machine which moved forward and backwards in alphabetical order of the departments. We had maggots sent in match boxes together with descriptive examples of how the customer was in the dark picture house enjoying his fruit and nut chocolate when he got a nasty shock. Next door was the art studio where Christmas boxes and Easter eggs were designed many months before they were needed. In the basement was the C Cub department where a large lady pretended to be Colin one of the Cadbury Cubs and she was replying to all the fans who had joined the Club. I found the journey arduous and the work repetitive so I looked around for alternative employment.

An enterprising neighbour had just started a small business recovering pram hoods and aprons and reconditioning coach built prams. He acquired a large Victorian house and set up stripping rooms coach painting reupholstery and machinery departments employing local women. The packing department was over the garage where the newly covered hoods were dispatched in purpose built bags to pram shops all over the country. I worked in the office and was sent to typing lessons one afternoon a week. My job was to work out the wages invoice the goods work out the tax find new customers and answer the telephone. The job was local with no bus fares and the pay was the same. I enjoyed the responsibility but I had decided to go to train as a primary teacher as soon as I was able .So my holiday that year was potato picking in Lincoln at Lend a Hand on the Land.

In September 1955 I departed to train as a teacher and so apart from my studies I was a lady of leisure until 1957 when I finished my course and went to Eastbourne to work in a Hotel for the summer. The pay was poor and the hours long but we had lots of fun in the back ground. In the Christmas vacations I worked on the post delivering the mail, carrying heavy bags in the freezing temperatures being attacked by dogs and trapping fingers in letter boxes all added to the fun and by Yuletide you were dead in your feet. My very first real career job was in a new school on the outskirts of Birmingham. I rode my first bicycle the three miles there in all weathers and really enjoyed my time there. It all ended in 1960 when I caught mumps off the little girl in the front desk only three weeks before my wedding day.

After getting married I worked full time in a very old church school it was quite a shock after the modern conditions I had been used to. There was no hail and all the iron desks were immovable some of the children had no footwear but they used to run up and down the piles of coke in the playground. I left to have my first child three years later.

So three children and 15 years elapsed and in 1978 I worked in the home tuition department caring for children who for various reasons could not attend school. The children ranged from 5 years old to teenagers. There was such a wide range of disabilities ranging from social deprivation, broken legs, epilepsy, truancy, court orders, emotional disorders. They were all allowed two hours tuition per day either in their homes or in mine. They taught me so much. How to pinch lead off church roofs, How to lie and keep a perfectly straight face. There were several dyslexic pupils and as Warwickshire did not recognise this learning disability we had to find ways around this problem. Several had had very bad experiences at school and at home, but we had to get on with the job of teaching regardless. One pupil said he could not read unless he was standing on his head. This he executed with ease and proceeded to read quite fluently. Others hated books so much that we went up the garden and buried the reading books in a hole. We then proceeded to read anything in sight posters, cereal boxes, recipes. We had great fun and as soon as there was a need to find relative information they mastered the text. One boy brought his motor bike parts together with the manual and this helped him sort them out. Several children were awaiting their final assessment for statements of their individual needs, but most pupils responded to individual attention and diverse learning methods. Sometimes I had two pupils and had to travel in between but all these experiences provided me with a solid foundation for work with special needs children which was to be my next full time job.

MY EARLY EXPERIENCES OF WORK.

L.G. BOND

1 was 10 years old when I started at the local grammar school. We were told that in the second or third year we would have the opportunity to go on a school trip to Paris. This would be for a week and we would be living in a boarding school in the south of the city. The cost of the trip would be in the order of £10, which may not seem a great deal of money today, but in the early 1950s was more than a week's pay for my father. I was desperate to go and my father said if I could raise £5 he would meet the balance and include some pocket money. This provided the incentive for me to get a job.

My brother John, who was older than me, had a paper round and I applied for a job. The newsagent described me as "too young" and "too puny" to carry the heavy bags and so I was rejected. My father's reaction was that I would not have lasted a week! I hated the cold weather but I was determined to prove them wrong- the thought of money being the driving force.

Several months slipped by and John was offered a job by the local bakery delivering bread door to door. I asked him to try and get me a job too as a Saturday boy. It would mean an early start as the vans had to be on the road by 7.30 a.m. and I would have to be at the depot by 6.30 to assist with loading the van. I had a book of my own customers, a cash book and cash bag and was responsible to see all bills were paid promptly and the cash receipts balanced. I was out in all weathers and don't recall ever having time off for illness. The round was the largest on the company and some weeks it would be 5.30 p.m. or later before we finished.

In those days before you could be employed you had to take a "medical" test set by the local health authority. The working hours were laid down as 9:00 am to 12:00 noon and 4:00 pm to 6:00 pm. This may have been okay for paper boys but not for us, we needed to be able to deliver all day. We were briefed by the foreman as to the answers we were to give and although I doubt the local authority was fooled we all signed on the dotted line.

The pay was 5p (a shilling) an hour with a small extra amount for selling biscuits and cakes. I soon learnt that with a little cheek and a smile you could persuade some families to buy a treat for the weekend. I found I enjoyed the challenge.

Stan Warren, the driver, had a reputation at the depot of being hard on his boys but I found him easy to work for. He was a wizard at figures he could add up three columns of figures at once, pounds, shillings and pence in a second. Writing however was not his forte and I had to enter all the customers' names in our collection books. He loved to back horses and my first job on the round was to "borrow" a newspaper from someone's letter box and write out his betting slips and return the newspaper to the right customer. My last job of the day was to repeat the exercise so he could check up on how his horses had fared. If he had had a good day I could look forward to a bonus. Soon learnt all about "doubles, trebles, Yankees, roll-ups, each way betting" but was never tempted to indulge in gambling. I always remembered those weeks when I didn't get any bonus!

During school holidays I would go down to the yard every morning .even though I didn't get paid. I enjoyed the job and knew that if Stan had a good week with the horses he could be generous. I loved driving the van (strictly illegally of course), it was so easy, there were only three very basic controls. A switch which had three positions forward, reverse and neutral, a foot pedal that acted as an accelerator, a brake, and a neutral position. The van had a top speed of only 10 m.p.h. when the batteries were fully charged up (it was an electric van). This was done at night. Over the driver's seat was a notice which read" under no circumstances should this vehicle exceed 20 m.p.h." That would require a miracle, you would be hard pressed to achieve that down the side of Mt. Everest! A fully charged set of batteries would give a life of about 12 hours which made things a little difficult during the winter. We would often return to the depot at the end of the day without lights and at walking pace to conserve the battery.

After about three years I realised I was one of the older boys and was still on the same basic rate of pay as when I started. I plucked up courage and asked for a rise. I was told that the company had a list of lads looking for employment so no rise was forthcoming. I felt I ought to make a stand and went on a one man strike and took Saturday off. I knew I was risking losing my job which over the years had paid for my school trips abroad and my bike, but I thought it was a risk worth taking. About 7.30 a.m. the foreman turned up at our house and told my father that Stan had refused to accept any other lad and wouldn't take the van out. A promise was made to increase my pay to a pound provided I agreed not to tell the other lads. I naturally accepted the offer and Stan still went on adding his little bonuses to it.

I was 15/16 when Stan decided to retire and I thought I would have a break as well. With the loss of Stan's perks the job was becoming less attractive. The break only lasted for a few weeks and I returned to be working with a different driver, George Grimmett, and a new round. The round was shorter than my old one because we largely serviced shops and clubs but also had a fair number of door to door deliveries. We didn't seem to stop eating all day. Our first call was to a working men's owned by the B.S.A. and 7:30 a.m. saw us eating toast and drinking tea. This was breakfast No I. Half an hour later we were at Studley Agricultural College where the kitchen staff had prepared a full breakfast for us. Breakfast No2.This was followed by a busy hour of door to door selling before arriving at our first café in Studley. Here we were given a nice sausage sandwich and a cup coffee. Breakfast No3. At midday we stopped at a local pub and had a ploughman's lunch washed down with a pint of beer. Yes I know I wasn't old enough! This was dinner No.1.

An hour or so later we were back in the village at another café where we had a fry-up. This was dinner No2. The afternoon was broken up by a visit to the home of my brother's girlfriend where we were to drink more tea and eat cakes. What a job!

I left school and was all set to go to Brighton Technical College to study Pharmacy and had two months to kill. Father decided I was not going to hang around the house all that time and I should get a decent job to help meet some of my forthcoming college expenses. He worked at The Royal Enfield Cycle Company as an electroplater but said he could get me a job in one of the offices. Saturday I was sent into town to buy a new sports jacket and a white shirt ready to start work on the Monday. Father handed me over at the gatehouse of the factory to a security chap and said he would see me at 1 o'clock with my sandwiches. I looked very smart in my new clothes and was surprised when I was asked if I had brought any overalls. I didn't think I would need any for office work I said. Office no. I was to start in the Milling and Drilling Department

The work was to take a head lock nut that had been rough drilled, place it in a vice and lower the drill to smooth the inside of the nut. The foreman showed me how it was done and watched me do a few. I was told that behind the wall near the machine was another machine that produced several thousands of the nuts and dropped a thousand at a time into a tin on a conveyor belt which brought them to my machine. No walking was involved and all I had to do was to keep pace with the other machine! I was covered in oil and swarf from the drilling machine and my lovely new clothes ruined. I was also on something called piece-work. I had to keep asking for the other machine to be stopped as the number of tins piled up on the conveyor belt. That did not endear me to the foreman! By lunchtime I was knackered and had had enough of the inside of a factory! I met father who was shocked by the state my clothes were in but not very sympathetic about the job. I told him once I had eaten my sandwiches I was going home. He said I would get used to it and went back to work, made for the factory gates and left vowing never to go back! Father was furious when he got home and said he had worked at the factory for over 20 years and I had let him down.

The next day I got up early and went back to the bakery. One day in industry had been enough! I was surprised on the Friday night when father arrived home from work with my pay-packet for half a day's work!

That summer saw me at college where I was to qualify as a pharmacist and spent the next 47 years working in retail pharmacy. I count myself as lucky. I had always enjoyed meeting and helping people .Counting pills can become a bit of a bore after a while, people never!

MEMORIES OF MY FIRST JOB

I left school in December 1962. In 1963 I started my first job! I had ideas of wanting to be trained as a hairdresser, but apprenticeships were extremely difficult to come by. My parents were prepared to pay for an indenture but it wasn't to be.

I soon got a job as a junior clerk in the Central Electricity Generating Board – the Power Station side of the electricity service. The offices were located on the 4th floor of Carliol House, in the centre in Newcastle. A distance of about 3 miles from home into town. I used to travel in by trolley bus. We had a good overall training in many departments, but first of all duties was in the mailing office – all juniors started there, as it was thought we would get to know the layout and departmental functions of the various offices in our capacity of 'postmen'. The hours were very good. 8:30 – 5:30 with an hour and a half lunchtime – time enough for a good browse around the shops as well as having lunch! Even time for visiting the hairdressers!

Our duties in the morning were taken up by sorting and delivering mail. Then came the task of scanning all the daily newspapers for articles on the Generating Board then circulating them to the relevant department heads. We had a large typing pool – all the staff seemed to be trained in shorthand and typing to a high standard – it always seemed a hive of activity. We juniors were phoned constantly to deliver work back for signing etc. The typing room also contained a Telex Machine and Gestetner machines. I remember the tickertape of the telex messages – rather like old fashioned telegrams, and the long foolscap stencils corrected in pink correcting fluid before being put onto the machines. We juniors had typewriters in the Mailing Room for our use.

Thinking back we had a varied training. We were sent to college one day a week for Office Management. This covered learning Pitman shorthand and touch typing as well as various office routines. In house we had training in various duties – the filing room and the telephone exchange. We had two GPO type switchboards with plugs on leads and switches which seemed strange to operate until we got used to it. Think my favourite duty was accompanying the Training Officer to the Power Stations to help setting out the exam papers for would- be apprentices, and helping to assess their marks for the exams.

I stayed at the Generating Board until I left to get married and leave Newcastle to head south to Salisbury Plain and begin a new chapter in my life – a soldier's wife!

Employment in early Life
Newcastle upon Tyne – 1960 to 1965

Working started when I was about thirteen. You had to be fourteen to get a morning paper round but evening papers could be delivered by younger people. So that was my first job. Delivering evening papers to one of the more affluent parts of Newcastle. There were several benefits of having an evening round. One was there were no evening papers on a Sunday so I only had to work six days a week. The other perk was that in the evening you were much more likely to meet your customers. That was a benefit a Christmas when you could get some nice "presents" from the customers. It would have been better if I had been pushy and knocked on the doors to wish my customers a "Merry Christmas" like the other paper boys did but I was a bit shy. Still, my round customers were more generous than the others so I did quite well. I got paid 4/6 a week for my pound. It was 7/6 for the morning paper boys. I delivered papers for a couple of years but never progressed to a morning round.

Between the age of 11 until I was almost 17 I was a keen Boy Scout. Each year we would be part of "Bob-a-Job" week. Knocking on doors in full uniform and asking for work for the payment of one shilling. If there were two of you, you could only expect a shilling between you! It is amazing how hard some people make you work for your shilling. I remember being asked to wash a car. It was a hot, sunny, day. The black car dried streaky and the owner made me do it again. Still streaky he refused to pay! As I got older we got wiser and one year four of us landed a job (Bob-a-Job) working at the RAC Offices in Newcastle. We got paid a shilling an hour each! Our job was to define routes for drivers going off on their summer holidays. They would write in and ask for the best route from, say, Newcastle to Norwich. One of the RAC guys would write out the main towns and we would collect papers from the files that defined the roads between one place and the other, eventually, with a sheath of papers that defined the route we would post these to the Member. All free for RAC Members. We would work at this each evening throughout Bob-a-Job week and made quite a few pounds for the Scout Funds.

The summer I reached the age of 15 marked my entry into "real" employment. My mother had been worked in Fenwick's department store in Newcastle before the war and for four weeks I follower her example. I got a Summer Holiday job in the Towel Department selling everything from luxury Bath towels to towelling material, sold by the yard. £4 a week, 9am to 6pm – 5 ½ days a week – Wednesday was early closing so it was all day Saturday. I found this really hard work and I was so tired that I was in bed by 8pm every night. At the end of week one the accounts staff came round to collect all the money from the tills. My till was 6d short and I was chastised for my poor skills in handling change. At the end of week two they came round again and found that my till was 6d UP. "Great" I thought, but I was soon to learn that it was not good. Chastised again for my poor skills it was pointed out that accuracy was important – not being right. There was never a suggestion that they may have missed counting a 6d the first week! After those 4 weeks it was back to school for my "O" Level Studies. Our year group of about 100 students had now reduced to just 15. The rest had started full time work.-

So eventually, at the age of 16 I left school with three 'O' Levels and found myself a real job of work. My mum was very disappointed. The job title was good – "Progress Clerk". That was good – I had an office job. The problem was it was in an Electro-Plating factory and with all the acid lying around the normal footwear was Wellington Boots. Mum was mortified – I would leave the house at 7:15 every morning looking like a Workman and carrying my sandwiches – there was no canteen at work.

I started work at 8:30 and finished at 5:30 with an hour for lunch. I had to work every other Saturday until 1:00. Pay was £6-0-0d a week with two weeks Summer Holiday. My job was to keep track of the work as it went through the processing in the Factory. I had to keep records of where each item was at any time. It was a good job really, I would be the link between the clients and the factory floor but it wasn't really the "Office Job" that my mum thought. I had an office that was really a cupboard. The general office where the secretaries and typists worked was not my domain at all. I was a Shop Floor clerk.

After six months in this role our Storeman went off sick for a week or two. I was put in the stores to look after things until he returned. There was no training given, just "Write down everything that anyone draws out of the stores and get a signature". Well, there was a difficult job going on and on my first morning one of the lads came for a Hacksaw Blade. He told me that these didn't have to be signed for – they were "consumables". (That was true). As I have said, it was a difficult job – they kept breaking these hacksaw blades and at the end of week one we ran out. The job came to a standstill. I found myself summonsed to the General Office where the factory owner grilled me about where all these blades had gone. I explained but he was furious. At one point he asked me if I had a Hacksaw at home. I said "Yes – but what are you suggesting?" "Well it's difficult to believe that you lost all these blades without telling anyone that we were running low!" It was my turn to be furious but I didn't retaliate. I pondered things over the weekend and handed in my one-week's notice first thing on Monday morning. One week later I was jobless and learned the cost of pride. I was out of work for the first (and last) time in my life and spent the next three weeks job searching.

My Mum knew someone who knew someone who (etc) who ran the Central Billing Office of the Northern Gas Board. I wrote in and got an interview. Along with two others I started work on the Monday. This was a real office job. I had to wear a suit and shoes to work and the hours were better. 8:30 to 5:30 with an hour for lunch but no Saturdays. The pay was better as well. £6-9-0d a week. After three months, when I was 17 I could afford a car. It cost £25. The job was so boring though. My job was to search the records to show when people had not paid their Gas Bill prove that they had been sent the Final Notice (Red) and then the Notification of Legal Proceedings (Black) and then send them a Solicitors Letter and after all that, send out the Cut-Off instructions. I lasted a year at that and kept sane by spending weekends and evenings with the Territorial Army. That was great – lots of fresh air and I got to play with Radars and Missiles. After one weekend away with the TA I called in to my fiancés house on my way home. "I really enjoyed that weekend" I said, "The only thing that spoils it is I have to go to work tomorrow". "Why don't you join the regulars then?" she asked. Next day I did. Mum mortified again, "But you're going to be an officer aren't you?" "No Mum, you need 5 "O" levels for that". The pay was £6-9-0d a week. But that's another story.

Joe Heckels

My First and More Memorable Jobs

Thinking back to when I didn't get into the A stream at Junior School, then subsequently failing my 11+ I was told I was never going to get to Grammar School and then onto University. This was a generally accepted fact and it was very rare for anyone to buck the trend. If anyone in the A stream failed it was a disaster and I recall one girl being devastated and reduced to tears.

After leaving junior school I went to my local Secondary School where I was a very average pupil as my school reports clearly state. I don't remember the Careers Officers being much help, but getting a job was never a problem as there were many companies to approach. I was very clear that I didn't want to be a secretary, so no need to learn shorthand or typing, and I didn't want to follow my Mum into nursing. To be quite honest I don't really know what I wanted to do, like many of my school friends we all wanted to get married and have children so a job in the meantime was all that was required.

My first job was in the Co-op Grocery Warehouse where I was a Stock Control Clerk, everyone was very friendly, our boss was more like a friend to us all as most of us had just left school, a good introduction into the world of work and incidentally earning £4.11.6d a week. I did manage to save as well as buy clothes and go out to all the local dancehalls etc. As I hadn't yet met the rich man of my dreams I began to realise I would really need to earn more and find something more challenging, so out came the local papers and scanning the situations vacant columns I applied for anything that I felt I could do. Lo and behold a letter dropped on the doormat inviting me for an interview at Atomic Energy Research Establishment at Harwell, some 30 miles from Swindon. No problem as there was transport laid on, the only drawback was I would have to catch the bus at 7am and get back home at 5pm. The interview was successful, and I started sometime later as I had to be security checked and visited at home to meet my parents. I would also be doubling my salary to £9.4s a week so I really felt like the cat that got the cream, just think how many more clothes I could buy!!!

Harwell being a major player at the time in Atomic Energy Research, employed thousands of people so jobs on the site were many and varied, my first job was in the main library where I felt very privileged to help many eminent scientists in their work. Computers were not in use at the time but some form of automation was being looked into so we still had to look for book titles in the numerous catalogues and the card catalogue in the small drawers, very tedious but we didn't have any choice. I also worked in an engineering library and in a finance department gaining valuable experience in the world of work. I particularly remember being able to view samples of moon dust that was brought back from an American Space trip to the moon, and on display at the site and also watching Concorde's maiden flight, this in the late 60's.

In 1969 I met Laurie and married in October 1970 soon I realised I wouldn't be able to work so far from home so I found a job in the Employment Exchange in Swindon, where I happily worked issuing passports, signing people on for Employment Benefit and placing claimant in jobs, this lasted until I became pregnant and hoped I would be able to fulfil my hope of bringing up my children and generally enjoying being a mother and socialising with my friends. How wrong was I!! Quite soon after Haydn was born the reality of another mouth to feed and lack of money we soon felt that I should return to work, I was able to go back to the Employment Exchange, although there was no Maternity leave I was fortunate as I had been a Civil Servant so there were many vacancies.

In 1971, Laurie's brother announced to us that he was leaving Swindon to live in New Zealand, and very soon after we decided to join him, we bought a house and settled in, life was so very different from the UK and children were very much welcomed into every aspect of life there. After a short period of living there, our second son Kenton was born, and realising family had a great pull so after 18 months we sold up and returned to Swindon and set about job and house hunting. I was fortunate to return to the Employment Exchange to similar duties as in previous times.

When the boys started school I had itchy feet and started to scan the situations vacant columns in the local paper to get a more challenging job with an eye on an increase in salary. I was fortunate to get a job in Hambro Life where I had a variety of rather boring jobs, the working conditions and the many perks made up for this but not for too long. I then had an interview at another insurance company that were in the Marine Insurance business and I worked there for 5 relatively happy years. My great pride was being given the Aristotle Onassis fleet of Ships to maintain the insurance and ensure that they were invoiced correctly. I was occasionally able to go to London to Lloyds' of London to meet some of the people that provided the insurance on my fleet of ships.

It seemed that after 5 years of employment in any company I needed a change, out came the local paper where I spotted a vacancy in the British Computer Society (the Chartered Institute for IT professionals) and started the very next week. I was an Admissions Advisor helping people join the Society by providing information on the qualifications required. The Computers that I operated were not as you would imagine, on the cutting edge of technology but were fine for the word processing that we carried out. Sadly after a couple of years we moved to Rugby in the Midlands with my husband's job so my employment ended.

From here on I really started to enjoy working, no family to worry about as all had flown the nest so soon I secured a job at a government Quango NCET, they provided IT help and advice to all schools and were able to negotiate that computers of some kind were put into schools. I worked on the reception desk and later moved into a post where I helped produce their website posting all the information and keeping the site updated. This was so exciting as it felt like I was learning new technology, as this was in the early 1990's this was very much in its infancy. After a change of government in 1997 the council's work brief changed so they restructured and made people redundant and this is when I departed.

I worked for a temping agency for Rolls Royce in a very large Engineering Department as an Administrator, my work was interesting and varied and nothing like I had experienced before, I really had a free hand to carry out whatever clerical duties I felt was needed to, to support the engineers and my colleagues in the other departments we had dealings with. I was able to use my initiative and solve any problems that came my way; it was pleasing to know that the management had my complete trust without question. After a couple of years Rolls Royce were curtailing their operations in the UK and moving most of my department's work to Canada where a few people relocated but many found employment in what engineering companies remained in the Midlands, so sadly I was looking for employment again.

Through the agency I was working for I was able to secure similar employment at Peugeot Cars for 6 months covering Maternity leave and after that a contract to work in the Research Department in Jaguar Cars in Coventry. This I can truthfully say was my most enjoyable and memorable employment; like in Rolls Royce I was given a free hand to provide clerical support for the department in whatever way I felt was best. I was able to participate in testing all the new innovations that were soon to be used in the new cars, such as reverse parking aids, the automatic gear selector, night vision equipment and the prototype of Satellite Navigation systems that is in most cars now.

My employment lasted for nearly 6 years until Jaguar was bought by Tata Motors and the management team changed so this was my prompt to think about retirement, I had already worked for 2 extra years so I was ready as I had made this decision myself and was very happy now to pursue my sporting hobbies and take the holidays we promised ourselves when we had more time.

On reflection I wish I had had the type of work I undertook in the last 10 years of my working life, but as with age and experience comes confidence to meet these challenges and I cannot believe how I drifted from job to job with no direction, my parents were keen for me to have a job and didn't influence me, letting me make my own mistakes, In the meantime I have attended the University of Life and have acquired valuable experience. So with hindsight would I have done things differently, I don't think so!!!

MY FIRST JOB

My parents withdrew me from Grammar School before I took School Certificate. There was quite a fuss about this, and quite rightly so I think on reflection, however, I am sure this is one of the main reasons I have been studying something for the rest of my life.

Having left I was enrolled at The Underwood Secretarial College, about half an hours walk from where I lived. It had been decided for me that I would be a secretary... I didn't have the slightest idea at 15 as to what I wanted to do with the rest of my life, and raised no objections. This was a year's course, and due I think, to my mother dying during this period I was the first pupil to be sent out to work.

I was to be a junior typist at Hall, Pain & Foster, one of the major estate agents in Portsmouth. In those dim and distant days a young girl did not emerge from training as a fully-fledged Secretary, but as one of the humblest members of an office staff. It probably sounds reactionary but I think this system was excellent, there was so much to learn by simply working with more experienced women – real secretaries – I would have been horrified if I was told to go straight in to a partner's office and take dictation.

I made the tea and coffee for the people on our floor. Hall, Pain & Foster were also auctioneers, and this involved walking through a huge room filled with lots to be auctioned – and the men and boys who worked there. At the very end was a, probably quite unhygienic, corner with a tap and kettle. Strangely for the mid-fifties we used fresh ground coffee, placed into a jug with hot water poured on, I imagine it was strained but can't remember. Then I carried a heavy tray back. This walk proved advantageous over time. I wanted a record player and one was given to me for a ridiculously low sum of money. Please don't picture anything modern – it was a wind up machine. I was also given a pile of heavy old records which my parents would have deemed old-fashioned. But I played them all with gusto – I think our immediate neighbours knew them well.

My work was primarily with the surveying side of the business. I worked for a delightful man called, I think, Pat Tarrant. In his thirties, tall and kindly. Looking back he was a typical example of the society of the day. He was ex-RAF and I don't think he had really settled into post-war life. He and his wife were very hard up. He still wore his old service raincoat, and when I babysat so that they could see Gone with the Wind, it was obvious from their flat that there was very little money. During my working hours I would type up his reports, rang the Borough Council regarding rateable values etc. As if I understood what I was talking about. This work gave me a love for houses which has never faded, in all the future jobs I had I never again worked for estate agents and I can't think why.

There were a lot of young people working there – other girls like me, articled pupils and the boys involved with the auctioneering side. I worked in the same office as the boss's secretary – today she would have been a PA. Gwendoline Rose – known to all as Rosie. Probably mid to late twenties and she took me under her wing and became a confidant. Things click into place with hindsight I am pretty certain she was having an affair with a member of staff, and eventually she left to go to Birmingham I missed her a great deal. I made close friends with girls of my own age and it was I think the very best of first jobs. It made the sharp change I needed in my personal life, increased the social scene and probably rubbed off a lot of corners that required smoothing.

There was a lot of bombing in and around Portsmouth, due to the dockyard, Royal Navy and aircraft factories, and even in the 50s houses were not easy to come by. I was friends with a girl of my age, Thelma, who worked in the front office. Her family had been bombed out, had very little money and were living with relatives – which is never easy.

Somehow, the firm found a house for them on a new housing estate. I can still remember her happiness and radiance, and gratitude. With more knowledge, her mother must have been quite ecstatic. Another friend, Joyce Jarrold, was in the accounts office. Her family were strict Baptists, and I learned later that before she started work her mother called in to say that she did not want her daughter exposed to any bad language. Apparently, her boss was renowned for his colourful expressions, but he was fond of her and nothing unseemly ever reached her ears. Nor mine for that matter. There were a lot of young men around but I never heard swearing. Come the 60s no doubt it would have been very different.

This exercise has brought back so many memories. I can see myself. Right back to my very first day there.

Sylvia Edwards ... 1.7.11

MY FIRST JOB

As I got off the bus I almost stepped on a huge shell, with hundreds of holes in it. I was outside one of the few pearl button factories in the country. It was a tiny little building. I had come to the edge of a large city, to an old village school to which I had been appointed. At that time the city appointed a pool of teachers and asked them the kind of school they would prefer. Inspired by the "Miss Read Books" I had described this school so perfectly that the Inspector who interviewed me accused the head of "putting that girl up to it". When the bus moved away I saw the prettiest little school I had ever seen. The path lead down through the village green and was lined with cherry trees in full blossom and tulips in the borders. The school was very old and pre-dated the 1870 Education Act which saw the large "School Board" schools built. There was a house attached and I had come to meet the head. I was met by a smiling lady who had prepared a wonderful tea. It was to be the start of many parties and gatherings I would attend in the school house.

There were two big classrooms, one with a tiny room adjacent and a small built on kitchen and an office/staffroom. It was an infant school - I was to have the Reception class and the head had the rest. The children moved into the second class when they were ready, There would just be to two teachers, a caretaker and a crossing lady, a part-time lady who doubled as secretary and teaching assistant (then called Infant helper) and a gardener, who seemed to be there all the time!

We had 56 children when I first started. A council estate had been built on the edge of the village to re-house people from the city slums and they had a spanking new school. We tended to have the children from the old village, although some of them had been impressed by the new school and had gone there. The head had only been at the school for a term and quickly began to build the school up.

We often had parties of children from inner city schools visit (and we went to their schools). At the side of the school was a large garden with an orchard. The head would put loads of potatoes in to bake in her kitchen and these children would stare in wonder at our beautiful view over the countryside as they sat on the seats which the gardener had built around the trees, eating baked potatoes or jam sandwiches. One day the gardener and I collected all the old balls from the PE cupboard and he halved them, painted them and made toadstools with different numbers of spots on them for the children to practise their counting!

Each day I did playground duty while the head made her 'phone calls and other jobs which were involved with the running of a school. She would sometimes knock on the window to tell me she needed a bit more time, so keep the children out a bit longer! If it was wet, then the whole school came into my classroom for stories and impromptu concerts!

Fridays were special days. We started the morning with films. The children assembled in my room and with the aid of an ancient projector watched nature or educational films, which we borrowed each week from the county. We also borrowed pictures, books and objects on a monthly basis. Whilst the children were watching the films I totalled the registers and attendances and sent them to the office. After play lessons continued, but after dinner if it was fine we put all the play equipment in the playground and then head and I sat on the steps of my classroom, where we could see all that was going on and made/ mended books and equipment. We designed games to help children over difficulties in learning and made reading books for children with special interests. All these were done by hand – no computers in those days.

Our numbers began to increase and we were able to appoint a part-time teacher. The head decided to use the tiny room for children who needed special attention. This idea was ahead of its time – recently "nurture groups" have been introduced into schools doing the same thing. The part-time teacher had 10 or 12 children who were going through a difficult time for whatever reason. They thrived in this small group and the group was constantly changing.

Assembly was held in my classroom and was after play. The older children went into the tiny room first and sat on the floor to listen to music to calm them, whilst I settled the Reception children. The only problem was the rabbit who shared a cage in the Reception room with a guinea pig. As soon as it heard the music it would start to thump its back legs, because it knew that then someone would sit by it and stroke it to keep it quiet!

Each year around the beginning of the school year we would get a visit from the inspector. A red hymn book sent to me from a child in the head's class was my sign that she'd arrived!! The head greeted her warmly and assured her we were doing alright, gave her a basin and she went for her annual blackberry pick in our garden!! She would put her head round my classroom door and say "Hello, Miss Russell, still enjoying yourself" – or words to that effect and we knew we were safe for another year!

One summer we decided to organise a grand fete. Each day I travelled to school with the deputy head from a nearby school. We had to catch two buses from the city and got to know each other quite well. She asked if we needed help at our fete, so, of course, I said yes and we decided that she would be the fortune teller. It was all meant to be a joke, and each morning she read the horoscopes in the papers to get some idea about what to say. We decorated the gardener's shed with saris (the head had worked in what was then Ceylon) and I painted a sign directing people to the Fortune teller. In the picture I painted a dark haired lady wearing green – my friend was fair. When she arrived she carried a small case and took herself off to the bathroom. Unbeknown to me her family had owned a theatre and she made herself up, donned a black wig and a green gypsy dress. She absolutely looked the part.

First Jobs

RUGBY
U3A

That afternoon the queue from the gardener's shed stretched right across the garden and the playground and the head, on her way to take a drink to my friend was told not to push in! Private bookings were requested and that night we held a barn dance in the playground. My friend, now back to her normal self, sat on a straw bale next to me and another friend sat on my other side. They were both discussing the afternoon, but fortunately neither was listening to the other. One was saying "I couldn't believe that people took what I said seriously" and the other was telling me what a wonderful fortune teller, where did we get her from, could she book her for an event they were having!

I could go on for pages, life at the village school was hard work, long hours, but very rewarding and great fun. Our children were happy and worked well. The school continued to grow, the large classroom was divided into two and we had to get a terrapin hut in the playground and I was appointed Deputy Head. For personal reasons I then decided to return to Rugby and became deputy head of New Bilton Council School. I kept in touch with the head and had news of the school. Then came the news we'd dreaded – closure. The new school on the estate was to be extended and would cater for the whole area.

In 1998 my Dad and I decided to see what had happened to the school. I was devastated. The playground was littered with rubbish, lead had been stolen from the roof, doors had been taken off and incredibly we were able to go in. I stood in my old classroom and looked up at the sky. The wallpaper I had chosen was still on the walls, but the building was a wreck. The following year Barratt houses stood on the site.

Those days at the village school were before National Curriculum, Ofsted and the challenges which teachers face today – it was a different world, but one which I'm glad I saw.

313

Young Farmhand

Universally, I'm sure, farmers' sons are given jobs to do. In Canada, I heard them called "chores". It's expected. We didn't get paid. I don't count the simple jobs of feeding the chickens, collecting the eggs, stone-picking before hay-making and grinding the mangolds in the barn as being a farmhand. They did provide an introduction to the real work though. It's when I was older and strong enough to do men's jobs that I considered that I was a real help to my father.

Pumping the water from the well he had dug in 1925 into the cows' trough in the fields, bringing them in for milking and mucking-out afterwards were not difficult jobs but necessary.

The winter job of loading the manure onto the horse-drawn dung cart was torture. The smelly tendrils of straw would be entwined in the stony floor of the cow-yard and dragging it out was nearly impossible for my undeveloped muscles, especially if I was trying to shift it from under where I was standing! Muck spreading from the little heaps where it had been dumped was a pretty unpopular job too.

On the unforgettable occasion when I was considerably older, about twelve or thirteen I expect, I was taking out a load of manure in the two-wheeled dung-cart. Mary was in the shafts. It must have been a warm spring because the flies were buzzing around her head. As we went through the gap between the two fields, Mary swung her head round to shake off the bothersome flies. The ring in the end of her bit caught in a hook on the shafts. Here she was with her head stuck the wrong way round. It has been a matter of pride to me ever since that I kept a cool enough head to force the bit free in spite of her frightened struggles, unhooked the props from under the shafts so that the cart would remain level with its heavy load, released Mary and led her back to the stable. Although she had broken off a few huge teeth in her bewildered struggles, she was otherwise none the worse and my father assured me she would be alright.

The worst job of all though was at threshing time. If I was put on chaff-bagging at the back of the threshing machine it was pure purgatory, defined in my Shorter English dictionary as a place of torture! The dust got up my nose and I would sneeze uncontrollably. My eyes would run and I would feel absolutely awful. I pleaded not to be put on that job. It was the only time I experienced anything like hay-fever. Haymaking was my favourite time. Still not into my teens, I used to lead old Mary from heap to heap of hay and shout, "HOLD TIGHT" each time I moved on. This was before we had a hay-loader hitched on behind the wagon. The men pitched the hay up with a two-tined hay-fork. I wasn't strong enough to do that or big enough to be up on the wagon, loading. In any case the loading had to be done properly by an expert to ensure the load would travel back to the stack-yard at the farm without falling off. Sometimes the loads were so heavy it took both horses, Mary and Major, to haul it back along the bumpy cart-tracks. Mary was in the shafts and Major ahead in the traces. Small though I was, I could harness the horses. The big collar was pretty heavy but Mary would lower her head for me to make it easier. Sometimes when I was trying to put Major's halter on he would tease me by lifting his head out of my reach but I always won in the end.

Horse-raking after a field had been cleared was my favourite hay-making job in my 'teens. To and fro, Mary and I would go raking up the whispy left-overs. I would be stripped to the waist, soaking up the sun, not knowing that it might be harmful to my skin. That was announced many years later. Not forgetting to 'trip' the rake each time we arrived at the growing line of rakings, I would sing uninhibitedly at the top of my voice all the wartime songs I knew by heart. I never had to repeat a song all afternoon.

315

Quite early on in the war we took delivery of our first tractor. It was a Standard Fordson from America and it came with no spade lugs on its wheel rims. My brother Dick had already joined the R.A.F. so I was the one who helped my father bolt them on one by one. My knuckles were raw at the end because the spanner frequently slipped. When they were all on, the tractor wasn't allowed on the roads because the lugs would have chewed-up the surface so we had to bolt on a huge pair of steel road rims. More grazed knuckles – my only war wounds!

I did quite a lot of the tractor work when I was at home. Starting it was a bit difficult because you had to turn the fuel tap to 'gasoline' first and after it was warm, turn over to 'kerosene' – my first Americanisms, I

suppose. Once, when I had driven the tractor somewhere a bit tricky I managed to knock off the air intake pipe which stuck up vertically beside the exhaust. I thought I had ruined the tractor beyond repair until my father patiently explained to me that it was a very minor mishap, easily rectified by bunging the pipe back in place!

I formed memories of my own of wartime Britain. In a workshop my father and I had built in the orchard I put up a chart of all the aeroplane silhouettes. I became quite an expert at aircraft recognition – British and American ones that is. We only heard the German bombers as they flew overhead at night en route to bomb Coventry. One returning enemy plane jettisoned its two unused bombs onto one of our fields but they didn't explode. The bomb disposal unit came later and blew them up.

When home from teacher training college in Cheltenham, I would eagerly don my old working clothes and do whatever jobs needed the expertise I had accumulated as my first job as an unpaid apprentice farmhand.

Housing

Houses

I was born in 1936 in November in a pea souper fog that lasted 4 days. The birth took place in a rented Corinthian Pillar house in a long terrace situated in a mature tree lined avenue. The road contained Edwardian Victorian three and four storey houses. The Avenue stretched from the Yardley Road Acocks Green Station down to the canal bridge which bordered Olton. There were approximately 300 houses in that area. Soon after we moved four doors away into a council rented property with two bedrooms and a non parlour downstairs. My parents wanted to buy a house in the road that was not overlooked at the rear with a big garden.

In between the older terraced houses the council built some three bedroomed properties some terraced and others semi-detached all with wooden fenced front gardens, My parents proudly bought number 72 The Avenue in 1937 for £450 when my father was earning £4 50 a week on the Great Western Railway. The area where the house was built had been used by the council to grow privet hedges for council estates. Hence we had a bright yellow hedge along the front of the house.

The kitchen was basic with a solid red quarry tiled floor brick walls which were emulsioned green and yellow. The huge table top mangle was folded down for cooking and baking. In the corner stood a gas fired copper and adjacent to that a gas stove with a top grill and three burners. A large ceramic sink stood alongside attached to a wooden draining board.

We had a black iron Triplex grate with an open fire and an oven at the side, It had a hood over the top and a damper controlled the flames. The fire place was tiled with bottle green rectangular tiles with a fender along the front attached to a coal box at each end. These had upholstered tops that lifted off. We used to fight to sit on these to toast our bread on the toasting fork for toast and dripping. After the war this was removed and a Courtier Stove was fitted it was square with glass doors on the front and would burn smokeless fuel. All the houses had built in dressers at the side of the chimney breast. They had two deep drawers and two cupboards underneath made of thick hard wood. The cupboard was always warm so the cat frequently had her kittens in there.

We had fire places in the two double bedrooms. The single room was built over the entry on the front of the house next to a large glory hole which was a walk in storage cupboard over the stairs. The bathroom was ample with a washbasin under the small window, a bath and toilet and an adequate airing cupboard over the bath which enclosed the hot water tank. There was a man sized trap door in the ceiling on the landing which gave access to the loft.

The pantry door was in the dining living room and this contained a large meter cupboard with a settle on the top and plenty of storage shelves for food. The pantry had a window which opened on to the entry between the two houses. Alongside this was a full walk in coal house with a wooden door into the entry for the coalman to tip the coal from his sacks.

Both the bathroom and the kitchen were brick with no tiling present. In 1960 when we were married my uncle who worked at the Bakelite factory gave us a quantity of sheets used in the interior of diesel trains, as we had no need of these dad attached them to the walls of his bathroom in doing so created an easy wipe down surface.

Dad and mum always did the decorating with much argument and laughter. In fact dad papered his bedroom with blue rose wallpaper at the age of 81. He had always been practical and attended carpentry classes when his shifts on the railway would allow. He made a bed head in *oak* with beaded decoration at the top, a waterfall bookcase with a *magazine* rack and an oval table beautifully polished with room for books at the bottom.

About 1.9.60 dad had central heating installed and we all thought we had died and gone to *heaven*. The front room which was hardly ever used except for special occasions had one fire place but now it housed the major radiator for the system and thus Servo Warm was established and most rooms ware heated from there. We had a twin immersion heater in the airing cupboard for the tap water, It was at this time of improvements that dad had *a* lean to conservatory built so the mangle

went out there and Mum was taken to Coles of Bilston to choose here kitchen unit, It was bright yellow drawers and cupboards covered with melamine of the same colour, This was the pride of her life. and. she was always telling people about it. Wash days were never the same as she hired a single tub washer on Wednesdays and the lean to became the washhouse.

Purchased in 1937 for £450

Sold in 1987 for £26,500

Housing Contd.

Whilst thinking about my life in the suburbs of Birmingham I wanted to know why the houses were there. Why were there three or four types of houses in the same road I came across an article in a newspaper partially explaining why this was so.

It was the arrival of the Railway station on October 1st 1852 it was the first stop out of Birmingham Snow Hill but it only had one or two sheds on the platform. It was followed in 1853 by allowing goods to be transported there. Thus Acocks Green became a Victorian suburb - Although there were some very old houses along Arden Road at this time business men moved out of the smokey city centre into pleasant country district. The rail journey was quick when they returned to work. Retired people also moved to Acocks Green. Much larger Victorian houses were demolished Hyron Hall Brome Hall and Tyseley Farm all had been moated sites Acocks Green House was rebuilt several times and was the last to go when it finally became a Social Club and then eventually was demolished to become flats in Muddy Lane.

In 1872 Warwick Road was a turnpike Road, A large oak tree named the Gospel Oak marked the meeting place of the parishes of Yardley Solihull and Bickenhill <Lyndon> Church wardens walked around the parish boundaries and beat the boundary stones with boughs-: This-was called beating the bounds and occurred on Rogation Day. This Gospel Oak was felled in 1840 and 16 *horses* were required to drag it away. I do recall a huge oak tree in Arden road in the 1950 I used to cycle passed it on the way to school and it was said to be in the centre of the Forest of Arden.

Dolphin Lane and The Dolphin Hotel were named after the Dolphin family who were land owners in Yardley Parish from the middle ages. In 1870 a horse drawn omnibus was pulled from High Street

Birmingham to The Dolphin Hotel on Warwick Road. There were many Inns along the route mainly used as public houses. Later The Great Western Pub was built on Yardley Road next to the station. There were five other inns all along Warwick Road The Britannia The New Inn Red Lion The Spread Eagle and then the Dolphin. They mostly brewed their own beers were social centres for banquets and parties.

The Public Hall was on the corner or Sherborne Road and Dudley Road. It had a fine polished floor for dancing and mum used to attend a tea dance every Wednesday afternoon

The Vineries were names after a nursery and market garden that occupied the site of The Rover factory large quantities of grapes were grown there and I do remember the windmill which used to pump water for the grapes.

By 1890 houses had spread down The Avenue and there were 25 shops in The Green, In 1898 Acocks Green recreation ground was given to the people by Yardley Charity Trustees.

In 1911 they doubled the railway line between Acocks Green and Olton and then Tyseley Station was opened and the North Warwick's line took passengers to Stratford and then Acocks Green station was rebuilt from brick with waiting rooms complete with coal fire places and two covered wooden staircases leading to Yardley Road.

After the first World war the wealthy families moved further afield to Olton and Solihull. The first cinema was opened in 1914 it was A Green Picture Play House and seated 500 people.

1935 brought the Public library to the village and this was the largest branch in Birmingham I spent many happy hours there amongst its all oak interior with shiny brass fittings and a turn style which you clicked through to return your books. It smelled of polish and there was a feeling of grandiose quietness and we always whispered when we talked in there. There were always daily newspapers on wooden stands in the foyer.

All these events in history caused the settlement to alter and eventually residents moved further away out into the country allowing space to be used for council building prior to the Second World War

.

Housing

Embarking on this project for "Living History" I realised how many houses we lived in and what an effect they have had on me.

The first house that I was introduced to was 31 St Mary's Street in Newport; this is where my parents lived in 1946, until we moved to Ireland a few years later. It was a 2-bedroom terrace house in the centre of Newport, pictured below. This picture was taken about 3 years ago and has been considerably modernised

Our second house was on the Derrimore Road, Bessbrook where my sister was born. This too has been extensively modernised, when we moved there it was half the size it is now, they obviously bought up the 2 houses and made into a

very luxurious home. As for having a bathroom I cannot recall but in a previous house were we lived for a short period I remember Mum bathing us in a metal bath by a roaring fire. We called at the house and the people were only too pleased to show us around, and we were pleased to see it was still standing. I don't remember much about the facilities in the house at the time as we soon moved around the corner into a prefab.

The prefab was a little detached house surrounded by fields. There were 3 bedrooms, a largish living room, kitchen and a separate bathroom and toilet, very luxurious compared with our previous homes. My father broke his leg, which meant he lost his job forcing him back to England to find a job. As it took a while for Dad to find a job and housing for the four of us we moved in with my mother's parents in Newport. The house in Ireland had to be cleared so in the meantime I went to school and was very happy living with my grandparents. Thinking back what an undertaking for them to look after 2 young children. I don't ever remember this being a big issue, as this is what families did then.

Several other houses of various friends and relatives have always brought a smile to my face. In particular my great aunt lived in a large house with a telephone, I had never seen one before and I treated it like a toy, it was a 2-piece phone with a separate earpiece what a novelty. My grandmother's next door neighbours had a TV and I was invited in to see Muffin the Mule, this was incredible to me at the time, it had a very small screen and a very fuzzy picture, how times and progress have made this a must have in all homes now with cinema type quality

This is a picture of 19 Ronald Road, Newport that still holds many happy memories for all of us. This is also a very recent picture as it has been extensively modernised. Back then there were 3 bedrooms a bathroom, no toilet, and downstairs a sitting

room, only used for special occasions, main living rooms where we ate and there was always a blazing fire, a scullery and the outside toilet accessed via the back door. The garden was huge with vegetables growing, lilac trees and loganberries growing up the side of the house at the bottom of the garden. I clearly remember the views across Newport as we had quite a hill climb to the house. When we lived there the approach road was completely clear but on a recent visit you couldn't move for cars on each side of the road, rather a disappointment but then that's progress!!!!

After Dad secured a job in Swindon we moved there about 1956 where we lived in furnished rooms in Old Town Swindon. When we were allocated a council house in Penhill in the North of Swindon we moved and I settled into school and lived there until I married in 1970. The first house we lived in was a brand new mid terrace, 3 bedrooms, separate bathroom and toilet, large lounge, kitchen, utility room and a large garden. Dad grew vegetables so we always had fresh produce from the garden; this was not unusual as most of the neighbours did the same. After a few years we swapped houses with our neighbours, they need bigger accommodation so we moved into the house across the pathway. Mum and Dad continued to happily live there until Dad passed away in 1998 and Mum went into a nursing home in Plymouth 3 years later. It was such a friendly community where we knew everyone and all the neighbours helped in the event of illness etc. Penhill is slightly different now; parts of the estate are no-go areas, which is very sad considering how friendly it was.

In the various homes we have lived since I married have been much more luxurious than in my childhood but we have progressed and we were no more deprived than our neighbours.

Housing

I grew up in a 1930s terrace house. Square bay windows, two medium bedrooms and a box room (mine). My parents bought it in, I would think, 1930 and until my father spent his last two years in our village of Prestwood, he lived there all the time, and our children have very fond memories of No 3 Telford Road. Incidentally, my second daughter now lives in an identical house in Cromwell Road, Rugby. Portsmouth was badly bombed and I remember prefabs being built in the late 40s to aid the housing shortage. There was a show house, and I recall people, including my parents, being very scathing of them. After all our house had cost £750 and these makeshift houses were costing £1,000 for what? I thought they were lovely. Modern, compact and light. We are visiting Portsmouth in the spring and I will check up to see if they are still standing. I believe they had a life expectancy of 25 years, but they long outlasted that date and the owners were very fond of and possessive about them.

There is a book called The Tale of a Tub, well we have a personal tale of a bathroom. When David and I were first married he was under 25, and therefore we were not entitled to married quarters. As a bride I came to Bury St. Edmunds to a house where we had the front rooms upstairs and down, and shared the kitchen — and shared a tin bath! How times have changed. Obviously, this was not very satisfactory, it was sharing a kitchen that was the problem. We moved about 10 miles out to a village called Woolpit, Erasmus had passed through it in his day. It was a beautiful village complete with butcher, baker, general store, fish and chip shop where they fried in lard — unbelievably beautiful fish and chips — and we wondered why we were referred to as "that very young couple". We lived in the annex to Evergreen Cottage, which was about 300 years old — it was full of character and ruined me for modern houses for a very long time. It also had large spiders, our very own tin bath and a chemical toilet, which was emptied every now and again by a man called Old Cross. A coordinated man, grey from head to toe.

After returning home to have my firstborn, David had by then been posted to RAF Marham in Norfolk, we lived in an upstairs flat in the vicarage. This was quite spacious and had a covered bath in the kitchen. The house was Victorian, and our stay was very happy, the vicar's wife had her fourth child just before I moved in, and she was a great help to me. Unfortunately, the vicar was moved to Sheringham so we had to look for another home. This time we had the bottom of an older house — Hill House, Wimbotsham near Downham Market. Mr & Mrs Cowan with their 2 adopted children lived on the first floor. We felt that they had come down in the world, but once again we were treated with great kindness and friendship. By the way, we then had a bathroom leading off the kitchen with an outside loo. The house was interesting with flag stones in the kitchen and sitting room, together with an old bread oven. However, the bedrooms were a bit damp, and Christopher had tonsillitis, croup and goodness knows what, and after Caroline was born and David was now 25, we moved into married quarters. There was a system of moving into a prefab, whilst waiting for a brick house to become available. So it seemed a full circle. I remember, the day we moved in — was by then expecting No 3. We had a Raeburn in the kitchen, which one fed with coke and tried to gauge the temperature. The intense heat seemed to sweep right up my already pretty warm, front and engulf me. I felt as if I was back in a cave cooking on an open fire. I was not happy there, apart from the obvious drawbacks — it was dull, the surroundings were bleak and I felt unsettled. However, we had our first conventional bathroom and toilet. After about 4—6 months a brick quarter became available and we then moved Onto a circuit of conventional houses. We moved into 74 Windy Ridge and it was not called that lightly. The washing dried very well. It was a plain standard house, but after the prefab I was well pleased. During our stay there my grandfather died and as his sole relative I inherited £750. By then David was due for another posting, which was RAF Stradishall, not far from Bury St. Edmunds, so with that money we put a deposit on our first house, up till now we had been in furnished accommodation, equipped the house for us and the three children from a second hand shop and we were Set up. It was one of the most profitable decisions we could have taken, as we were on the property market long before most of David's colleagues. We lived in this house three times with postings in between. Our first venture away was to Lincolnshire. David was on a year's course at RAF Manby, during which time we rented a Victorian house about a 100 yards from the sea at Sutton on Sea. The children and I loved it, there were other families in the same situation nearby and we made lasting friendships. The men all suffered together on the SpecN course (specialist navigation — which involved higher maths, including calculus, which was the bane of David's life) we felt the beach was ours, it was sandy. It was a lovely year. After this David was posted back to East Anglia to RAF Mildenhall, which was predominately used by the US Air Force. Once again I was in a prefab — in dire bleak surroundings, after a few months we moved back to our own house in Bury St. Edmunds, which had been let. Home again. This lasted for a few years, when another one year course was necessary. This time we lived at RAF Andover for a year — and David completed Staff College. Housing was a pleasant 4 bedroomed married quarter, nothing worth writing about. Life continued in very acceptable quarters at RAF Honington near Bury St. Edmunds. David was promoted and posted to the Ministry of Defence and we bought a house at Writtle, near Chelmsford Essex. This was a smallish house in The Shrubberies which I was never really happy in but it made a profit during the 16mths we were there. Off we went again, to our one and only overseas tour. RAF Laarbruch, Germany. By then all the children were at boarding school, so David and I plus two cats moved to Europe. Once again you took a quarter that was available, and then moved when one fitting David's rank came free. This was a lovely house. German built, so we had a cellar with several rooms, and may I add bone dry, four bedrooms. Our eldest daughter had the attic which had been built for staff in long days past, and she loved it. This was a good tour. However, at the end we decided to put down roots and I would stay put. On arriving back in the UK David was posted to strike command HQ near High Wycombe in Buckinghamshire, a very expensive place to buy. However, we found a detached thirties house, not what we wanted — but what we could afford. We stayed there four years and then moved next door to a

Victorian house —Anchor Cottage — where we were all very happy and I was at last anchored. It was full of character, very few right angles and a quarter acre of garden. We lived in Prestwood for 26 years and I assumed I'd never move again, until we had yet another phone call from a daughter with problems and here we are. I must say, from the moment we moved in we knew it was the right decision and have been very happy in Rugby.

Sylvia Edwards

Feb. 2011

Housing Through My Life

Life started in a big hospital. The General Hospital, Newcastle upon Tyne. I was then taken back to my parents' house, 8 Kingswood Avenue, High West Jesmond, Newcastle upon Tyne.

I remember this as being a cold and dark house. We had a coke stove in the kitchen and I had a habit of leaning against the cast iron chimney with my hot little hand on the cold metal. Each time I did my Mum would say "Hot!" but I knew it wasn't – until the day, as winter approached and the stove was lit again. I lent on the chimney and there was a searing smell of burning four year old flesh. "I told you it was hot" said Mum. Time to move!

So there we were, I was four years old and we moved next door to my Grandmother. 5 Princes Avenue, Gosforth, Newcastle upon Tyne. (My Grandmother and Grandfather lived in number four). They had one side of the semidetached and we had the other. My Mum was not well (she had TB) so my Grandmother was in charge of bringing me up while Mum convalesced. My Dad got a builder to knock a doorway between the two houses so you could go up one

staircase, through the door, and down the other staircase into Nanny's house. Each house has two bedrooms, one large, one small (mine). The living room was large and there was a small dining room with a miniscule kitchen at the side. Outside there was a garage, a shed, a greenhouse and a coal bunker (detached but brick built with a sloping roof). My grandmother had a huge brick and concrete air-raid shelter, We lived in that house until I left home to join the army at the age of 17. Mum and Dad stayed there until my Mum moved a couple of years after my Dad died. That would make their tenure there about twenty five years.

Life in the army was fun. We got married when I was 19 and we were not allowed a Married Quarter until I was 21. So we set up "house" in a Caravan. We lived here for two years. Pam went home to Newcastle while I went to Aden for a three month tour of "active service".

334

After our two years we finally reached the ancient age of 21 and we were allocated a "Hiring".
This is a private house, rented by the Army, and sublet as a married quarter.   It was located in Alderbury, a village just south of Salisbury and about 15 miles from camp. I was a commuter!.

The house was basically furnished with no fridge or washing machine.   The coal fire in the sitting room was the only form of heating. When our son was born we bought our first household appliance, s spin dryer.

We lived there for a couple of years until our son was born and six months later I was off on active service again.   This time to Salalah in the Oman.   I was there for six months while Pam went back to Newcastle, this time to live with my parents (still at 5 Princes Avenue).

My "House" in Salalah"

My other "House" in Salalah

While I was away we were allocated a Married Quarter on the camp at Larkhill. Again a two bedroom house in a terrace of four. Again there was only basic furnishings; no central heating or fridge and only an electric fire in the sitting room. We bought a paraffin heater to use instead of the electric fire. Electricity was so expensive. We upgraded our spin drier to a twin tub washing machine.

Two years later we moved again into another two bedroom house on camp when our daughter was born. A big improvement as this one had a box-room that was big enough for a cot. Still no fridge or central heating though.

After another couple of years, when we were about 27 years old and the kids were 4 and 6, we moved again. This time it was because I was posted to Stevenage to be a liaison officer with British Aerospace. We were back in a hiring but this time it was one for a commissioned officer. I was a Warrant Officer by this time but they only had Officers Quarters available so we got an upgrade!. Central Heating and a fridge and three full size bedrooms!

Two years later I decided that it was time to leave the army and we had to find somewhere to live. Stevenage is a new town and almost all the houses had been built as "Stevenage Development Corporation

Housing". (Up market council houses) but there was the right to buy so about half of the houses had fallen into private ownership. We bought a three bedroom terrace but now, as well as having to find the mortgage we also had to find the furniture to go into it. A bit of a step change at the age of 30 with two children and changing jobs. Moving from the mollycoddled life and secure employment in the Army to standing on your own feet in a new job.

The next phase of life is even more interesting...........................

Houses I have lived in

JOHN REEVE **23rd**• February 2011

The house that I lived in as a child and on and off until I eventually left it, aged 36 to set up on my own, was typical of, what must be, hundreds of thousands throughout this country.

My parents married in 1938 and moved into their first and only home at 97 Percival Road, Rugby. They were almost literally carried out of it some 61 years later to go into a care home. They never returned.

The house was a typical semi-detached one built on the Ashlawn Estate which was then a new housing development to the south of Rugby during the 1930's. It conformed to the architectural design ideal of the time in homes for working class families. Internally it had two main rooms downstairs, a 'front', and a dining room, a kitchen, a larder, a hallway with stairs leading 'upstairs'. A lobby was attached to the house at the rear and contained a coalhouse and an 'outside' toilet. On top of it was a 'freshwater tank' which caught the water from the roof. Was this early conservation or preparation for the forthcoming war? Anyway we used this for washing our hair. I used to love to climb up the wall and balance myself across the tank and sail a small boat that 1 had. Upstairs were two bedrooms, a 'box room' ,a landing, and a bathroom/toilet. Heating was coal fired with a grate in each of the four main rooms. Gas and electricity were supplied.

An early photograph taken by mother from the window of the rear bedroom illustrates one of the main ideals for working class housing at that time, and that was identical large rectangular sized gardens in which people could enjoy light and fresh air and cultivate their own plots for vegetables. This my parents did, to perfection, including a brilliant flower garden, lawn, fruit trees, greenhouse, cold frame, and chicken run. In front of the house, facing the road was another smaller garden, (also full of splendid flowers and a lawn). The road was also tree lined, with footpaths, but did not have grass verges.

By modern standards the material provision, amenities and comforts of the house were sparse. As I child I vividly remember my parents struggling with coal and wood for the fires, the extreme cold of winters, drying clothes on a freezing washing line and in front of the fire. They did make some modest home improvements, (possibly considered significant for their times), but could never be persuaded, especially as they became old, to install things like central heating, a shower, plastic window frames with double glazing, or to move into sheltered accommodation, which would have made their lives more comfortable and easier. The gardens also became more neglected. This upset my sister and myself despite doing all we could to support our parents. Even now I never drive past the house. I did so once and was very upset at the condition I saw it in. There was white van parked on what was the front garden. Everyone in our neighbourhood took a great pride in their houses and homes, their upkeep and their gardens.

Another building that I vividly remember as a child was the house that my mother's aunt lived in. We visited it regularly. 'Aunt', as my mother always referred to her, lived with her 'no good' husband in a very small 'two up, two down' terrace house in what was Queen Street, Rugby. The site is now the new Asda and Co-operative stores, and library. I remember that 'aunt' was a lapsed member of the Salvation Army, swore like a trouper, had 'bad heads' and took lots of aspirins.

My recollections of the house, and that area, was that it was 'mean' (poor in quality and appearance), and bore no comparison to the nice house and surroundings in which we lived. It had an air of prevailing darkness, gloom and deprivation. The terrace must have been built like so many across the country in the industrial regions, in Victorian times. The street was cobbled and the walls of the houses all seemed greasy, stained and black. The front door and two windows were faded and neglected brown. In contrast my 'aunt' maintained a scrupulously clean and reddened door step and shining brass door knocker. Not that anyone used the front door, which fronted directly onto the pavement. Entrance to the house was down a dark narrow alleyway between the house and the adjoining one.

Inside the house it was also dark and dingy with old, peeling paper on the walls. The house was rented, the landlord being the public house, 'The Shakespeare', two doors down from the house. 'Aunt' complained that they took the rent but never did anything to maintain the property. Furthermore her husband spent more time and money in the pub than he did in his home The backroom' of the house served as kitchen, dining and living area. A door led directly into it from the backyard and there was a tiny window. A large cast iron coal fired range was in one corner. This was the only source of heat in the house but, again, 'aunt' kept it immaculately black-leaded, and polished its fittings. She also did the same with the candle sticks on the mantelpiece. The mantle itself was also kept immaculately clean, white and starched. Lighting as such was by candles or a single gas light, (with its mantle). There was no electricity. Aunt powered her small wireless with large, heavy Exide wet batteries, that were taken to be recharged every so often.

A heavy curtain sealed off the 'front' and 'back' rooms. I only went in the former once, as typically, it was rarely, if ever, used. All I remember was that this also, was dark and gloomy but on the walls were two huge pictures, one of the King George V, and the other, 'the old Queen' Victoria. I never went upstairs.

Outside to the rear of the property was the 'backyard' and a small garden. This was shared with a single neighbour. Down the middle ran a pathway leading to the outside 'privy'. To one side of the yard was the wash house, which, again was shared with the neighbour. In contrast this was lime washed inside and, typically, contained a large wash boiler, tubs and dollies. Washing was also hung in there to dry, although ironing took place in the living room near the range where the irons could be heated. Wash day was always Monday and took up the whole day.

To either side of the narrow garden path were equally small, narrow plots in which aunt and her neighbour struggled to grow a few vegetables. At the bottom of the plot was the 'privy' or outside toilet. This intrigued my sister and I as all we knew were two pull chain lavatories inside our house, and what if you wanted 'to go' in the night, or when it was cold, freezing and snowy. The privy was brick built with a slate roof. It had a rickety door that had a space below and above it. Inside was the wooden plank with its hole in the centre. The privy smelt awful and buzzed with flies but aunt and her neighbour kept it immaculately clean. The plank was scrubbed and the walls and the underside of the tiles were lime washed.

Significantly, directly outside the privy to one side was a mature ash tree. Over the rear brick wall was Parnell's builder's yard.

Sometime in the early 50's the whole area around, and including Queen Street was 'condemned'. Perhaps it was a near as Rugby came to having a slum. The houses were demolished, but as old Rugby residents know, it was not until a few years ago that the whole area received a radical make-over with the development of the new library, the Clock Towers shopping precinct, and lastly the Asda and Co-operative stores. Modern buildings also crept along Corporation Street; itself, at the time, a new road that was pushed through to by-pass the old town centre.

During this long protracted period of development a number of the old roads were left, including Queen Street, Where aunt's house had been was left as derelict waste ground until it became temporary car park. I always knew where aunt's house had been because the ash tree remained and lived on. When parking my own car many years on I always chose the spot next to it. However now Asda has a subterranean car park there I never park my car in that area on the odd occasion that I use it.

Aunt, and her no-good husband were ultimately re-housed in a new pleasant elderly people's bungalow in Lytham Road, . . . near the 'Three Cranes' pub.

HOUSING MEMORIES

All my childhood memories of our house begin in Gosforth, Newcastle upon Tyne. My parents started their married life there. My two elder sisters were born there, when home births were the norm. I was born in Germany while Dad was serving on a Control Commission with the British Army. I returned to England at about six months old.

The flat we lived in was on a small estate in a good area of Gosforth, which was about three miles from the town centre of Newcastle. A super place to grow up. Beautiful open countryside on our doorstep, the unsurpassed beauty of miles and miles of beaches within easy reach, plus the buzz and convenience of all the city amenities.

The flat was probably built in the early 30's. Front and back gardens of medium size, large enough to have a good veg patch at the back. There  was a nice lounge, kitchen and bathroom/toilet. The kitchen was the hub of the house. Always lovely and warm with the coke stove which was used to heat the water. When small, I remember having baths in front of the stove in a tin bath, even though we had a bathroom .It was bitterly cold in the winter as we didn't have central heating. The lounge, when we used it, used to have a coal fire. A coal fire always seemed magical, images of all the flames and embers conjuring up pictures. Years later, probably when we got a TV and the room was in use more,. The coal fire was changed to a gas fire. This was probably when I was about ten years old. Until we had a TV we had all congregated in the kitchen, and were avid radio listeners. Hancock's Half Hour, The Navy Lark, Goons. The Light programme, as it was known, seemed to be some of the favourites I remember being popular with the family, while my sisters and myself loved Children's favourites. Of course, when very young we loved Listen with Mother. The radio was our main source of entertainment and even after we had TV, we still listened mainly - Radio Luxemburg when we got older for the Top Twenty! Dad had a big armchair in the kitchen. The kitchen table and chairs were used by the rest of us. The room of course had the Belfast sink — the work surfaces later had Formica tops (very much the latest luxury). We had a pulley where all the washing was hung when the weather wasn't good enough to peg out. A Gas Boiler which was agitated manually with a ringer attached.

I remember our bedroom being very cold. In winter we could scratch the ice off the windows. We seemed to be warmly dressed for bed in pyjamas/nighties plus an old cardigan and socks. Thick feather eiderdowns and more on the beds to keep warm.- plus a sister to cuddle into as well as a hot water bottle. In my eldest sister's teenage years, her hot water bottle burst as she kicked it down to the bottom of her bed. She had the habit of filling it with boiling water and the rubber perished - it left her with loads of blisters which had to be lanced by the doctor! Needless to say, she learned her lesson!

All in all, it was a great place to live. Lots of children close by and we all got on so well together. Mum hardly saw us on school holidays. Off down the bridle path fishing, playing tracking, etc. After school we used to play skipping, hopscotch and make our own entertainment putting on plays which my sister had written. Always so much to do and so much freedom!!!

I lived in the same place until I left home when I got married and left for new life and home over 200 miles away near Salisbury Plain. So far away from all my family and home, the journey to Newcastle then — before motorways — took about 8 hours!! No running back to Mum and Dad!!

Privies and Early Bathrooms

"Don't sit there all day, John, reading the paper!". This was a comment often made to one of our group. The paper in question was to be found hanging on a nail on the door of the privy. Someone in the family had to cut old newspapers into squares and thread them onto a piece of string to be used for toilet paper. The fore-runner of Andrex! Nearly everyone in the group had this job at sometime. The first purpose made toilet paper was Izal – hard like tracing paper, sometimes in a box and sometimes on a roll.

Early toilets, called "Privies" were situated in the garden, sometimes at the very bottom of the garden. Members recalled going out into the cold with a hurricane lamp, paraffin lamp or candle. One of the group used to have to accompany his sister, as she was frightened of the dark. He said he used to blow the candle out on purpose once they got outside! Another person said that her great auntie's privy was covered in honeysuckle to disguise it and counteract the smell. Not only was it dark, but cold and in winter the privies froze over.

Sometimes there would be a row of neighbours privies and one member said how he remembered hearing all the smokers coughing in the row of three privies at the bottom of his garden.

Russell had looked up the definition of Privy and found that it meant a small private room or special secret knowledge – as in privy counsellor. The privies were not always secret places – some had two seats side by side, often one for an adult and one for a child. The seats were wooden and scrubbed weekly with the soapy water left from the washing.

Under the seat was a bucket to catch the waste. Often ashes from the fire would be used to soak up the sewerage. This would then be collected by "night soil workers". These men came round at night to empty the buckets. Another way of disposing of the waste was to empty it onto a compost heap or manure heap, this was then used to fertilise the soil. Sometimes a trench was dug to contain it and one member said they then grew their kidney beans in the trench! Other times the waste would be collected in a septic tank in the ground. This would then seep into the ground.

Members of the group recalled tin baths, filled with water from kettles and placed in front of the fire. In some homes the water had to be drawn up by pump from a well. The pump might be in the house, or in a yard shared by several houses. The entire family would bath, in turn, in the same water. This usually took place on a Friday night. The water was then scooped out and put onto the garden.

One gentleman was a miner and said that his mum would hear them all singing as they walked home from the pit, covered in coal dust, and would know that she had to get the water warm for their daily bath.

Eventually, around 1937, when the water tower was built, houses in Rugby all got piped water. Many small bedrooms were converted into bathrooms. There would be a wash basin, bath and toilet. The toilet had a tank of water above it, with a chain to pull to make it flush. This chain was often extended with string, so that the children in the family could reach it. How much easier it was then to turn on the taps to fill the bath and then just let the water run away down the plughole.

BILTON HOUSE
Reminiscence Group
Privies and Bathrooms

Privies. Maybe an embarrassing subject but elderly and not so elderly people have clear memories of them. One could not help but having to use them on a daily basis, possibly several times. They were also called by other names; 'ghazis', 'thunder boxes', 'latrines', 'bogs', 'place of ease', and other cruder terms ! The term 'privy' derives from the word private and is used in 'privy counsellor', privy conspiracy, privy purse (a special allowance to the monarch), privy seal, or referring to a private room or a shared secret. Serving the same purposes it would go under other names e.g. the 'heads' in a ship, (this term is still used today in vessels but refers to the old practice of locating them at exposed head of sailing ships, i.e. the bows, where the bow wave or heaving sea would act as a natural flush. They were used by common sailors whilst the captain would use his 'quarter gallery' which was located to one side of the large stern gallery of his quarters).

Privies came in many forms and were used where houses lacked running water, plumbing and sanitation. For obvious reasons they were located away from the main buildings but not too distant from them. Even when lavatories became a feature of more modern homes they were often built 'outside', possibly together with a coalhouse, joining onto the main structure of the house. They could be small separate building in a backyard. To have an 'inside' toilet was considered, at one time, the height of luxury and usually the preserve of the wealthy. Nor did privies always exclusively serve one family. They were often communal and could be designed to accommodate the needs of several or many people at one time. Privies having two, or more, seats were not uncommon. Larger communities e.g. a barracks, a household with many staff, a temporary camp, had even more. There was no 'privacy' in this situation, and possibly it didn't matter at that time and in those circumstances. More permanent privies could be made of wood and/or brick and have distinctive, usually tiled, sloping roof. They were entered by a, usually, wooden planked door with a latch but with a space at the bottom to clear them from the earth or tiled floor. In cold or severe weather they were very cold and uncomfortable places. People of the past were very hardy! During the night time they would use alternative arrangements, utensils, which they would empty when the daylight came.

Schools of the past usually had lavatories/privies for the children which were sited outside the main buildings to one (remote) side of the playground; boys and girls separately. They were remembered with a certain amount of loathing as being smelly and unhygienic places, despite liberal doses of the caretaker's cleaning disinfectant. They were also the subject of 'lavatorial' talk and humour and the scene of pranks, illicit smoking, and other unmentionable behaviour. R. recalled the lighting of newspaper, thrusting it down a pan into a sloping gully which served several cubicles. Good fun if the paper managed to make its way along to one that was occupied !

To maintain the hygienic conditions of the privy was an essential though unpleasant task. In the days before flushing water and sewers, the contents of the receiving receptacle would require frequent emptying. In the countryside this could be onto a manure or compost heap but in towns it was the unsavoury occupation of people who made a living collecting it. Even nowadays in houses or communities that are not served by sewerage systems cess pits or septic tanks receive waste. These are controlled systems which operate on principles of natural decomposition. Temporary privies were/are little more than a hole in the ground which could be filled in after use.

Householders with personal pride, irrespective of their social status, usually maintained their privy in good hygienic condition. The wooden seat and tiled floor was scrubbed and the interior walls lime washed.

Nevertheless one could never escape the inevitable smell, and the buzzing of bluebottle flies in summer. The process of decomposition and more savoury conditions were enhanced with the coming of chemical solutions that could be poured onto the waste. The 'Elsan' toilet is well known.

The slow and irregular coming of mains water supply to homes and houses brought the flushing toilet with its cistern, to carry waste away, either to a sewer or cesspit. The cast iron cistern above the lavatory seat is still well remembered. It was flushed by pulling a chain. Where young children were unable to reach the chain a piece of string was tied to it. Where water cisterns were installed in outside facilities they were prone to freezing up in cold winter conditions. Tanks and pipes could be lagged with straw and sacking to prevent this from happening . Other ingenious methods included the suspension of a small paraffin lamp under the cistern.

Use of the privy included the means of cleaning ones rear end. Fondly remembered was the widespread use of old newspaper. A familiar ritual was cutting up a newspaper into convenient sized pieces, stacking them together, piecing a hole through a top hand corner through which was threaded a piece of string. This was then hung on a hook. Failing this a stack of newspapers could be stored in the privy. Time spent there provided an opportunity to actually read them ! More up-market was a toilet roll, even more a flat pack of individual sheets. Before the coming of 'soft' tissues, these sheets were likened to tough 'tracing paper'. 'Izal' prided itself on its hygienic credentials, instructing its users to 'Now wash your hands'!

Remembered was the sex-discrimination sometimes practiced with lavatories. The 'inside' one was usually the preserve of the females in the household and the 'outside' the males.

Alongside the necessary daily use of the lavatory, in its various forms, was the routine hygienic practice of washing and bathing oneself. Essentially this involved accessing a source of (preferably) clean and warm water, temporarily holding it in a receptacle whilst washing oneself and disposing of it afterwards. These operations were tackled in a wide variety of, often ingenious, ways. Technological development proceeded slowly, erratically and unevenly across many decades, if not centuries, and across social groups. The culture and technology of the Romans with respect to washing and bathing did not become commonplace in this country until recent times.

Living memory includes the pumping of water from wells or a cold water tap serving several families. For general use the water could be stored in tanks or containers of various sorts. Plain cold water was often used for washing oneself, but people have always preferred warm water for either this and especially bathing. The warming of water has been a gradually evolving technology in this country over many decades. Living memory extends back to the kitchen range and the heating of pans, saucepans and kettles of water, or a little boiler that was built into the range itself. The large copper or cast iron boiler in the wash house, with the open fire underneath, heated water for both laundry and bathing. People remembered 'back boilers' behind open fires in living rooms and separate stoves fuelled by coke or 'nuggets'. Although producing clouds of thick (and polluting) smoke the sweepings of coal, called 'slack', was piled onto open fires to build up a good heat.

A common recollection for actually bathing in was the 'tin bath'. This would be brought out and both hot and cold water poured into it. When finished with it could be carried out and the waste water poured down a drain or used to wash the back yard, (or water the plants in times of drought!). Waste water could also be ladled out, and during the war (2), stirrup pumps were sometimes used. More up-market was cast iron baths which were permanent features in a 'bathroom'. Primitive versions could be without plumbed in water supply through taps and no waste water outlet (the 'plughole').

For many households, even up to recent times, washing and particularly bathing was ritualized. Without limitless sources of hot water available at the turn of a tap, or a flick of a switch, bathing was a major family event. Furthermore with many working class families it was costly to heat water. Families would limit themselves to a shallow depth of water in the bath.

Consequently there was a designated 'bath night'. This was usually Friday or Saturday evening at the end of the working week and in preparation for leisure activities, worship or other respectable observances on Sunday. Several bodies in the family e.g. the children and/ or parents would use the same water in a pecking order. One person recalled bathing himself and doing his clothes washing in the bath at the same time!

In winter bathing could be an intensely cold experience, especially in unheated bathrooms. This was before the days of central heating. People used imaginative ways to either avoid or reduce the sensation. The open fire or range would be 'made up' and bathing performed in front of it, (due measures being taken to preserve one's modesty). A hasty exit from a cold bathroom to a warmer living room to rub down and 'get warm' could be made. In an effort to relieve some of the cold small gas or oil heaters could be used.

Many houses in poor working class environments had no access to bathing facilities within the home. Remembered were the local municipal 'slipper baths' where people could go to have a bath. Included in the cost would be soap and a towel. Special sympathy was shown for people whose occupations were physically hard, and demanding such as miners and agricultural labourers. They would return home tired and dirty from their work and have to be scrubbed clean, usually by their wives.

The process of washing and bathing has always been aided by the use of objects and materials; soap and scrubbing brushes being the most popular. Before the introduction of soft and fragrant 'toilet soap', ('Fabulous Pink Camay', an early T.V. commercial), hard washing soaps used for laundry purposes, were used. Popular were 'Fairy' (green), 'Lifebuoy' and Sunlight.

To economize the remaining slivers from the bars were stored in a jar and a little water added. They would then be re-cycled and used in the laundry washing. Scrubbing brushes of all sorts, shapes and toughness were used to remove ingrained dirt,....especially on dirty hands and knees of children.